Organizational Cybernetics and Business Policy

Organizational Cybernetics and Business Policy

System Design for Performance Control

Arthur J. Kuhn

THE PENNSYLVANIA STATE UNIVERSITY PRESS
UNIVERSITY PARK AND LONDON

Library of Congress Cataloging-in-Publication Data

Kuhn, Arthur J.
    Organizational cybernetics and business policy.

    Bibliography: p.
    Includes index.
    1. Organizational effectiveness.   2. Cybernetics.
3. System theory.   4. General Motors Corporation—
Management.   5. Ford Motor Company—Management.
I. Title.
HD58.9.K84   1986   658.4'02   85-31071
ISBN 0-271-00433-9

Copyright ©1986 The Pennsylvania State University

Printed in the United States of America

To Carol Van Steenberg

Contents

Preface

This book presents a planning model to guide designers intent upon building high-performance control systems for complex business organizations. The *system-design-for-performance-control* (SDPC) model outlines a normative design process consisting of seven phases. Throughout the work, the basic theme is that policy decisions taken in the ordinary course of business are simply acts of designing organizations which, if they are to be successful, must follow guidelines of organizational cybernetics and systems theory.

Accordingly, the planning model's theoretical underpinnings are rooted in cybernetics and systems theory: W. Ross Ashby's *An Introduction to Cybernetics* and his *Design for a Brain* and C. West Churchman's *The Design of Inquiring Systems: Basic Concepts of Systems and Organization,* in particular, support the current work. Embedded within the SDPC model, moreover, are other important contributions from system-oriented organizational theorists. To name just a few, Ackoff, Ansoff, Emery, Simon, Stinchcombe, and Williamson have all supplied vital building blocks for the planning model presented here.

The policy-planning model also rests on a strong empirical abutment. It was created, originally, to explain the success of the General Motors Corporation (GM) under Alfred Sloan and the downturn of the Ford Motor Company under Henry Ford between 1918 and 1938. Sloan, along with his principal codesigner, Donaldson Brown, typically followed design suggestions later articulated by cyberneticians and systems theorists like Ashby and Churchman, while Ford pursued a decidedly antiplanning tack that violated such guidelines. I present a more extensive analysis of these early case histories as well as GM's subsequent problems in *GM Passes Ford, 1918-1938: Designing the General Motors Performance-Control System.*

Acknowledgments

I would like to acknowledge and express my appreciation to several individuals and institutions upon whose efforts and resources this work has been built.

Joseph Litterer first stimulated my interest in organization theory at the University of Illinois. At the University of California, Berkeley, John Wheeler, George Strauss, Charles Perrow, Karlene Roberts, Arthur Stinchcombe, Raymond Miles, and especially C. West Churchman helped me strengthen the foundation of organization and systems theory on which this work rests.

Colleagues and students at Duke University also provided significant support. In particular, Richard Burton's continuing comments honed my thinking and sustained my interest. I owe my students the greatest appreciation, for they patiently listened while I developed the system-design-for-performance-control model.

Joseph Litterer, John Wheeler, C. West Churchman, Helmy Baligh, Richard Burton, and Alfred Chandler all read various versions of the manuscript and suggested helpful changes or offered welcome encouragement. Willis L. Parker's "comma chasing" proved invaluable for untangling substantive as well as editorial snags. John M. Pickering and Chris W. Kentera of the Penn State Press offered useful suggestions for tightening my presentation. And, of course, much appreciation goes to those many cyberneticians, system theorists, and organizational writers upon whose work this book has so heavily drawn.

Carol Van Steenberg, throughout this endeavor, earned my deepest gratitude. She listened and responded to formative ideas; she read and edited many draft pages; she asked difficult questions that uncovered inconsistencies or omissions; she initiated discussions that improved conceptual clarity; and she alerted me to many relevant writings.

1

Introducing the Model at the Corporation Level

THE UNDERPINNINGS

Since the mid-1940s interdisciplinary groups of engineers, mathematicians, biologists, and social scientists have been studying control in diverse and complex systems. They hypothesize that all complex control systems operate according to common principles capable of being united within a general theory of communications and control, abstracted from the applied fields but appropriate to them all (Beer, 1964). The general theory of system control has been termed "cybernetics" by Norbert Wiener. Ludwig von Bertalanffy (1968) defines cybernetics as "a theory of control systems based on communication" (p. 21). W. Ross Ashby (1956) summarizes this definition "in a word as the art of *steersmanship*" (p. 1). While Wiener initiated the development of cybernetics, Ashby was responsible for its fuller progress. In extending the cybernetic framework, Ashby (1956, 1966) devoted considerable attention to the control of the very large system. Cybernetics is potentially a unifying theory behind the performance-control design of very complex, multilevel, multivariable systems such as neural mechanisms, national economies, or business firms.

As applied to formal organizations, an introduction to the system-design process begins with the conceptualization of an organization and its environment as a system. According to Ashby, "System . . . means, not a thing, but a list of variables" (1956:40) where "*a variable is a measurable quantity which at every instant has a definite numerical value*" (1966:14). "A system is then defined as *any set of variables* that [an observer or designer] selects from those available on the real 'machine' [organization and environment]. It is thus a list nominated by the observer, and is quite different in nature from the real 'machine'" (1966:16). From the organizational designer's viewpoint, Ashby's set of variables yields "a *system of decisions*" (Ackoff, 1970:2) needed to specify all the variable values. Hence, decisions are the events that occur within a system (Beer, 1964:11).

Thus this work uses the decision as its unit of analysis and treats the human being, albeit the most important decision maker, as only one of several "actors" fixing the organization's and environment's performance-related variables at specific values. Accordingly, the decision variable becomes the elemental building block for the system-design-for-performance-control (SDPC) model.

Using the decision variable as his basic analytical unit, Ashby also postulated a method for measuring size applicable to the organization's set of variables, to its environment's and to its components'. According to Ashby (1956:61), a system's "largeness" refers to the number of distinctions made: either to the number of variables involved or to the number of states, i.e., values, available. Additional variables make possible additional states; and more precise measurement of any variable also results in a larger system, for more states are thereby made distinguishable. Similarly, if the range of values that a given variable or set of variables assumes grows larger, size increases proportionately. Next, an increase in a random variable's variance increases size as a result of the likelihood that a wider range of values is being assumed. The *variety* of variables and the *variety* of states that they are likely to assume thus become the measure of size.

Ashby's variety concept can be extended into the time domain. Given a fixed period of time, system size increases whenever the variables involved fluctuate more rapidly, for more states consequently are assumed. In other words, size expands as the decision frequency increases and diminishes as the pace slackens. When the time period lengthens, system size increases because each variable assumes more values and, more important, apparent constants become variables; i.e., more and more of the low-frequency variables begin to fluctuate.

One can see, then, that the system's "changes occur on a background of constancies" (Ashby, 1966:71). And the system of variables increases with longer time periods, whereas the surrounding milieu of constants decreases. Conversely, the "background of constancies" increases in size with a shorter time, while the system of variables decreases.

So depending on the time period assumed, a given factor may be either a variable or a constant. Mathematically speaking, such an entity is termed a parameter; for though it takes on a series of values over the long run, it remains a constant over the short run.

A more circumscribed system of variables can thus be *defined* by shortening the planning period. From the firm's perspective, a short-time horizon ignores the slowly changing social and political factors but includes within the system of variables the higher-frequency economic variables. Such an initial short-term approach is necessary to avoid information overload. (Eventually, however, one must prepare for shifts in the social and political factors that have been treated as "constants" and thus beyond the system of variables.)

With respect to the system of variables remaining, Ashby's (1956) most important contribution to the design of performance-control systems is his fundamental "law of Requisite Variety" (p. 207). That law—interpreted in light of Simon's (1965) limited-rationality concept—yields this precept: environmental disturbances can be kept from causing performance deviations only when the environment's variety is exceeded (or equaled) by the firm's variety, which, in turn, is exceeded (or equaled) by the management's decision-making capacity, or variety. To block any disruptions caused by the uncontrolled (i.e., the environment's) variables, then, the controlled (i.e., the firm's) variables must encompass sufficient latitude. And to use this controlled-variable variety, management must have adequate capacity for information absorption, storage, retrieval, and processing (Williamson, 1970:20). With sufficient decision capacity and latitude, management can set the controlled variables to buffer disruptions coming from the uncontrolled variables. Hence all *"essential variables"* (Ashby, 1956:197)—like cash balances—hold their desired life-sustaining values.

To see how a firm's internal variety might counter environmental variations, consider a highly simplified example drawn from the automobile industry. From an auto manufacturer's perspective the economy, or environment, can generate roughly three environmental states: depression, normalcy, and boom. A manufacturer of a low-priced car risks doing comparatively poorly during booms, as did Ford in the 1920s with its inexpensive, standardized Model T (and its minuscule Lincoln sales). A manufacturer of high-priced cars risks doing poorly during depressions, as did Packard in the 1930s. A firm that builds a whole range of mass-produced automobiles, however, holds a much safer position, for it possesses the requisite variety to counter the economy's variations. Notably, only GM offered such a variegated product line throughout the 1920s and 1930s.

Another noteworthy example can be found in the case of DuPont before and after World War I. Until the end of hostilities, the firm concentrated almost exclusively on gunpowders and explosives, products that did well during wars but poorly during peacetime. To offset this environmental fluctuation, DuPont executives searched for peacetime products to utilize the firm's excess production capacity. After diversifying into a wide array of nonwar products—paints, varnishes, fabrics, dyestuffs, films, paper stock, rubberized cloth, and the like—the firm possessed considerable internal variety to handle the environment's variety.

But what about the decision-making load placed on the respective managements? Certainly in the cases of the manufacturers of either low-priced or high-priced cars, the chances of swamping the decision makers with excess variety remain slim. Even with the price-diversified auto firm, the likelihood of a management overload remains minimal, since an inexpensive auto is mass-produced and marketed much as are its more expensive substitutes. In DuPont's diversification, however, the probabilities of management overload rise because the firm is moving a fair distance from its original expertise in gunpowder and explosives. DuPont, indeed, began to experience management difficulties and profit losses in spite of the firm's·efforts to concentrate on new products based on the nitrocellulose technology employed in explosive production (Chandler, 1966). A major reorganization eventually alleviated DuPont's management problems and allowed some further expansion.

Still, management's limitations cannot be overlooked. Compared with entering different but well-established industries, moving into new and as yet undeveloped lines adds greater variety to the controlled-variable set. The uncertainties of rapid technological and marketing development demand that a great many decisions be revised frequently.

So as the firm diversifies into different products, technologies, markets, and/or countries, more and more variables demand management's "scarce resource, attention" (Simon, 1973:271). Indeed, many a corporate headquarter's inherent inability to comprehend the intricacies of its dozens of businesses helps explain the recent spate of conglomerate divestitures. In light of Ashby's law of Requisite Variety, then, the ideal firm is *composed* of comparatively few activities that yield inversely correlated performances and utilize narrowly focused skills. While this ideal is rarely attained, it is often easily approximated.

Other approaches are also available for stabilizing performance. Contracts, for instance, can be negotiated to freeze prices and other variables into temporary constants, or parameters, thereby granting the firm some "temporary independence" (Ashby, 1966:158-70) from the environment's full flux.

The size of the regulator, or management, may also be increased until its "capacity is made adequate" (Ashby, 1966:246) to handle the controlled-variable variety. While rarely a possibility in the biological systems studied by Ashby, this technique is an attractive option in organizations. Expanding the corporate offices increases "requisite capacity at the top"; for example, "by creating a team of general executives and providing them with an elite staff" (Williamson, 1970:123). They can enhance the firm's variety or flexibility, say, by preventing divisional inventory accumulations, thereby keeping cash available to mitigate the effects of an economic downturn.

Limits exist, of course, as to how fast (Penrose, 1959:45-46) and how far the top-management level can be expanded. But when the underlying controlled variables can be *decomposed* into subsets that are reducible (Ashby, 1956:60) or at least nearly decomposable (Simon, 1969:105), the decision-making tasks can be separated both vertically in terms of time perspective and horizontally in terms of day-to-day specializations (Simon and Ando, 1961). Numerous lower-level management groups can then set the firm's many high-frequency operating variables.

To heighten the separability of these units, *"walls of constancy"* (Ashby, 1966:165) can hold steady any residual interactions of significance. Establishing standardized parts specifications is one such decoupling effort. "If a high proportion of [such] variables go constant," i.e., become parameters for the decision period involved, the firm's decision problem may be cut into component parts "that are quite independent of one another" (p. 169).

The decision-making limits of the headquarters and subordinate management teams argue for even greater simplicity. Theoretically, maximum simplicity results when the "parts are all identical, mere replicates of one another, and between whose parts the couplings are of zero degree" (Ashby, 1956:65). DuPont's 1920 reorganization, from a functional to a divisional structure after its diversification, provides a classic example of a firm locating a simplified controlled-variable configuration: after the change, all the divisions interacted minimally and resembled each other functionally. When a firm's divisions produce similar products (as a line of automobiles), minimum interdivisional variety results. High-performing units can serve as ideal types for low-performing units; and the headquarters can intervene quickly and frequently as the need arises, since but a single conceptual model (with minor variations) explains all the subordinate components' operations. And when a fair degree of separability and diversity is maintained (as at GM during the 1920s with Sloan's bracketed and variegated price structure), internal complexity is minimized with no loss of requisite variety.

Moreover, when the firm's many components are similar but separate, as at GM in the 1920s, management's capacity can be *amplified* (Ashby, 1956; 1966). One need only train a host of decision makers *en masse* to fill the firm's many comparable managerial positions. An amplification of control results because less communicating and computing capacity is needed to train these decision makers than to handle the entire controlled-variable set directly—in other words, the controlled set of variables is contracted into a much smaller set of training-related variables.

The firm's decision variety can be increased further by periodically reconnecting the segmented managerial units. Such an intermittent communication network ensures that the firm's separate components operate correctly on their own and coordinate their efforts as a whole, time period after time period. In essence, these low-frequency information linkages make *"possible a greater repertoire of* behaviours"—i.e., combinations of variable states—yet minimize the risk of prolonged adaptation time (Ashby, 1966:223). Thus a firm that pools and disseminates the experience of its components via recurring meetings, for instance, can spread the use of successful innovations better than a more fragmented competitor. Similarly, exaggerated or inappropriate local environmental adaptations are avoided by the *recomposed*, or coordinated, firm.

The firm can counter external variety by uncovering constraints in the environment that restrict its range of behaviors (Ashby, 1956:247). Knowledge that consumers demand products with specific characteristics, for instance, reduces the contingencies confronting the firm's decision makers. Once such environmental states are known, the controlled variables can be *synchronized* with them easily.

A firm rarely needs sophisticated research staffs to unearth important environmental information (though there are pitfalls, as will be seen, in this "seat-of-the-pants" approach). An auto maker might simply paint its cars black and see if they continue to sell. Trial and error. No matter how unsophisticated the source, such feedback information reinserts into the firm "the results of its past performance" (Wiener, 1954:61) and reduces the contingencies to be considered. Feedback processes, even better yet, can correct for performance deviations of *unknown* causes. The "cruise control" device now found on many automobiles, for example, maintains the car's velocity simply by gauging or sensing the difference between the desired and actual speeds and adjusting the throttle to compensate. No specific knowledge of the causes for a given speed variation is required. Similar control processes exist within business firms. Corporate-level executives, for instance, often exhort divisional subordinates to increase efforts when performance dips below expectations for unknown reasons.

Unfortunately, though relatively simple and inexpensive, the feedback-correction process actually may prevent timely adaptation to environmental shifts. This lag often can be eliminated by correlating known environmental fluctuations (e.g., the economy's recurring boom-bust cycle) with past performance deviations. Then, by predicting forthcoming environmental variations and by anticipating future performance feedback (i.e., feedforward information), a firm can take corrective action before performance deteriorates (Ashby, 1956:201). Thus, when a decline in consumers' disposable income portends a forthcoming sales slump, inventory levels can be pared to help maintain investment returns. By gaining an increased knowledge of the environment's movements, a firm can literally import the variety needed to counter or exploit forthcoming environmental variations.

Finally, the system (i.e., the firm and its variable environment) ideally must be *evaluated* as a whole. Intersystem information must be exchanged to compare respective performances. Pursuant to such comparison, high-performing companies receive additional resource allocations for the next operating period and low-performing ones are cut back. More important, the system of variables must be evaluated in the context of the larger societal/political milieu; that is, the "background of constancies." If the system's low performance in the economic arena threatens long-term public interests, political parameters must be shifted to improve its forthcoming performances. Under these circumstances, a firm might lobby successfully for extended relief, say through tax credits, loan guarantees, and import quotas. If, on the other hand, a system's high performance in the economic arena undermines important public interests, shifts in society's long-term parameters must correct the imbalance. New restrictive legislation was passed, for instance, when American automobile manufacturers produced and their customers purchased too many unsafe, polluting, gas-guzzling cars. What had been business as usual for more than fifty years was suddenly and dramatically altered.

Though such shifts in the "background of constancies" are rare, their profound impact on the way business is conducted makes their prediction vital for long-term survival. Had the American automobile firms anticipated the cataclysmic societal/political shift that began with the safety, pollution, and energy legislation of the 1960s and 1970s, for instance, they could have developed the requisite technological and marketing variety. But they were unprepared: when the system of variables suddenly grew larger, they sustained monumental losses in the early 1980s.

In the final analysis, then, the firm should be prepared for shifts beyond the original system of variables; for, as more and more time passes, even long-term constants shift values. While the fast-acting (i.e., business-as-usual) feedback-feedforward processes should provide stability against the frequent minor disturbances from the economic arena, the slow-acting feedback-feedforward processes should provide stability against the infrequent major shifts in the societal/political realm. The longer-term feedback and feedforward linkages, "working intermittently and at a much slower order of speed," ought to provide the final defense and make the system "ultrastable" (Ashby, 1966:98).

In sum, the above methods in principle reduce the variety impinging on the essential variables. Ideally, "the limit of this reduction is the regulation that holds the outcome [i.e., essential variables] rigorously constant" (Ashby, 1956:215). Viewed in terms of a single summarizing performance measure M, the perfect SDPC would be one that held at zero the difference between the system's desired state M_c and the system's actual state M_s; i.e., the error $E = M_c - M_s$. That is, the ideal system *"blocks the flow of variety from disturbances to essential variables"* (p. 201). Besides buffering unwanted environmental fluctuations, the perfect SDPC also transmits variations in M_c immediately to M_s so that E remains close to zero. A perfect SDPC, in summary, connects the system-performance measure to the desired state and disconnects it from the environment so that the error variable becomes a constant with a value of zero.

Churchman's system work helps relate these cybernetic concepts to the problems of organizational design. Of particular importance are Churchman's conditions that something S be conceived as a system: the teleological S serves a client, who sets the standard for a measure of performance coproduced by an environment and teleological components; the latter, in turn, are changed via the resources of a decision maker influenced by a designer with the realizable intent of maximizing S's value to the client (Churchman, 1971:43). Thus Churchman introduces the policy planner to the major players and props in the SDPC story: clients, designers, and decision makers; system, components, and environment; system and component performance measures; and resources.

While these players and props receive much detailed attention subsequently, a brief example here helps to focus the scene. Consider GM in its formative system-design days under the guidance of Alfred Sloan and Donaldson Brown; figure 1-1 lists the GM counterparts for Churchman's story characters and stage props.

As Churchman concentrates on broad philosophical issues rather than on detailed steps of the design process, he does not concern himself with presenting an explicit planning process to guide designers. Thus the task remains to mesh the cybernetic concepts and the system characters and props into an SDPC model capable of guiding the actions of organizational planners.

CHURCHMAN	GM
Clients	Stockholders
Designers	Board of directors
Decision makers	Corporate and divisional managers
System	Firm, government, competitors, labor, suppliers, customers, and public
Components	Corporate headquarters and divisions
Environment	Government, competitors, labor, suppliers, customers and public
Performance measure	Return on invested capital
Resources	Capital, labor, materials

Figure 1-1. The early GM characters and props.

THE MODEL: AN OVERVIEW

The SDPC model consists of seven phases:

1. Identifying the goal: *Defining* the variables and parameters; i.e., setting the boundaries or limits (chapter 2).
2. Formulating the strategy: *Composing* the controlled and uncontrolled variables; i.e., selecting the activities to be included in the controlled-variable set (chapter 3).
3. Organizing the structure: *Decomposing* the dependent and independent controlled variables; i.e., separating or factoring the controlled variables into simpler components (chapter 4).
4. Training the decision makers: *Amplifying* regulatory capacity over the dependent and independent controlled variables (chapter 5).
5. Coordinating the firm: *Recomposing* the dependent and independent controlled variables; i.e., linking the decomposed components (chapter 6).
6. Monitoring the environment: *Synchronizing* the controlled and uncontrolled variables (chapter 7).
7. Valuing the performance: *Evaluating* the variables and parameters (chapter 8).

Figure 1-2 depicts the seven phases of a single system-design cycle. Those phases on the left—*definition, composition,* and *decomposition*—deal with the creation of boundaries, or partitions, around and within the system. The segments on the right—*recomposition, synchronization,* and *evaluation*—focus on the establishment of communication channels across the (previously) drawn limits.

Thus separation and connection become the principal counterpoints of the SDPC model. During the separation-oriented phases of *definition, composition,* and *decomposition,* planners locate boundaries among variable (or parameter) sets along cleavage lines that create relatively independent clusters of decision variables. Across these boundaries, variables interact either infrequently or minimally (i.e., cause little change) and thus transmit minimal variety among the separated decision centers. Since complete separation is always impossible in a real system, communication is necessary to handle residual interactions. So during the connection-oriented phases of *recomposition, synchronization,* and *evaluation,* planners must span the boundaries among variable (or parameter) sets with communication lines that coordinate dependent groups of decision variables. In sum, boundary separations are drawn to achieve independence, and communication connections are strung to coordinate dependence.

Definite limits exist as to how far any single planning team can carry its

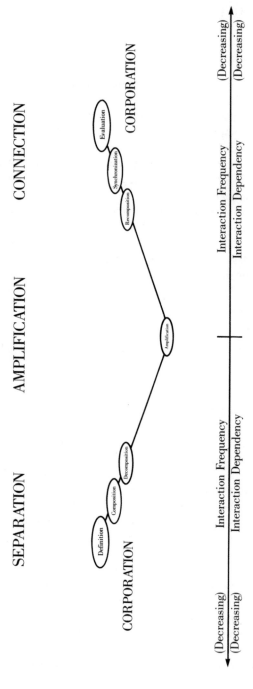

Figure 1-2. The seven-stage SDPC model at the corporation level.

separation and connection activities. So *amplification*, the central phase of the SDPC model, involves neither further factorization nor coordination. Instead, the remaining variables are treated as an inseparable whole, an impenetrable black box.

Note in figure 1-2 that the *definition* and *evaluation* phases are parallel; similarly, *composition* and *synchronization*, *decomposition* and *recomposition*. This "level pairing" reflects a sharing of the same parameter and/or variable sets. Thus, at each level, variety, or size, is equal—as is shown by the oval areas in figure 1-2.

The decrease in size that occurs from the *definition* and *evaluation* phases to the *composition* and *synchronization* phases reflects the shift in focus from variables and parameters to variables alone. In the *decomposition* and *recomposition* phases the focus narrows from both the controlled and uncontrolled variables to only the controlled variables. In the *amplification* phase, instead of all the controlled variables, only a much reduced set of training variables is pertinent. Training a series of proxy planners, or decision makers, to design and operate the firm's many components both amplifies control and alleviates the need for further subdivision and recombination by system-level planners.

As shown in figure 1-2, expanding the scope from *amplification* to *decomposition* and *recomposition*, then to *composition* and *synchronization*, and finally to *definition* and *evaluation* decreases the interaction dependency and interaction frequency among the decision clusters. Interaction dependency must decrease as size increases; otherwise, the number of variables or parameters requiring simultaneous attention would explode exponentially. Common sense suggests, too, that large entities are more independent of their surroundings than smaller groupings. Interaction frequency must also decrease as size increases because bigger decision-making units take longer to coordinate their responses to external changes. Furthermore, if large clusters of variables interacted frequently, turmoil would be without end and equilibrium impossible.

More concretely, a division's departments will interact more strongly and frequently than the firm's divisions. In turn, the divisions will interact more strongly and frequently than the economy's firms, which in their turn interact more strongly and frequently than the society's economic, religious, educational, and political systems.

Accordingly, from the *definition* phase to the *amplification* phase, each successive boundary the planners draw must sever variable connections of higher dependency and frequency. And, from *evaluation* to *amplification*, the corresponding communication lines need to be more copious and free-flowing. In fact, at the amplification phase, the intensity of interaction dependencies and frequencies makes further separation and connection by the system planners impossible: only a new team of detail-oriented, faster-acting, shorter-term planners (i.e. lower-level decision makers) can complete the design work.

Given the progressive binary subdivision and recombination inherent in the SDPC model, interset dependencies and frequencies are lower than corresponding intraset relationships. Within the controlled variable set, for instance, the interaction dependencies and frequencies are more intense than those between the sets of controlled and uncontrolled variables.

An interset-intraset difference in time perspective also exists. The low-frequency interset activity occurs over a relatively long term and high-frequency intraset activity over a comparatively short term. And since the interaction frequencies among and within sets rise when size decreases, the time perspective shortens as the planners move from *definition* and *evaluation* to *amplification*. Similarly, dichotomies such as low frequency/high frequency and long term/short term are relative. Thus the same interaction between variables seems, in the *definition* and *evaluation* phases, to be high-frequency and short-run in character and, in the *composition* and *synchronization* phases, low-frequency and long-term if it spans the uncontrolled and controlled variable sets. And a comparatively high-frequency short-term interaction within the controlled variable set appears as a low-frequency/long-term interaction when it occurs between independent sets during the *decomposition* and *recomposition* phases.

To handle these multiple breadth and time perspectives, the organizational planners, too, separate themselves into specialized committees and then reconnect into a coordinated team. As outlined in the next chapter, the arrangement of these subgroups is hierarchical.

Finally, the SDPC model treats organizational planning as an ongoing cyclical—rather than a finite linear—process, with no strict beginning or ending. Hence an underlying assumption throughout the next seven chapters is that the planning team repeats the design process many times, with increasing expertise. In reality, design work in the seven planning phases proceeds simultaneously. But, for expository purposes, description of the design process starts with goal definition and ends with performance evaluation.

2

Identifying the Goal:
Defining the Variables and Parameters

Logically, one of the first planning tasks is to establish the system's outermost boundary. Concomitant to finding a goal or deciding whom the system benefits is operationalizing that goal by discovering a performance measure that summarizes the state of all the variables within the system's bounds.

DRAWING THE BOUNDARY

Defining the system/nonsystem boundary "means dividing the variables of the universe into two classes: those within the system and those without" (Ashby, 1966:71). (Immutable constants are ignored in this analysis, since, by definition, they cannot cause performance variations.) "Systems can be isolated as separate entities only if they maintain some constancies in the face of environmental change, that is, if they maintain some boundaries vis-à-vis the environment. If every event within a system were a direct consequence of some event outside the system, it would be impossible to draw a boundary for the system; it would, in effect, be [an indistinguishable or inseparable] unit in a larger complex" (Mayhew, 1968:583).

Variables within the system boundary must satisfy two conditions: (1) they must vary during the planning cycle; (2) they must be addressed by the designers on behalf of the clients. Conversely, nonsystem variables either hold steady throughout the design cycle or exert no influence on the planners' concerns regardless of their values.

Variables and Parameters

Ashby (1966) treats as parameters all nonsystem variables, since they impose an *unvarying impact* on the system's variables throughout a given observation period or planning cycle. Parameters can be either "effective" or "ineffective"; effective parameters are those that influence the system variables. That is, effective "parameters are determinants that are known or suspected" ultimately to affect the system's performance measure, "but in the investigation at hand, are made or assumed not to vary" (Smelser, 1968b:16). In this context, the values of effective parameters and their influences on the system's variable values, i.e., behavior, can change only from cycle to cycle, not within a given cycle as the system variables do. Thus effective parameters must be considered initially in setting the system's variables. Then they can be forgotten until subsequent planning cycles, when they might assume different values. In contrast, the system's variables are conditions known or suspected to influence the performance measure (p. 16) that must be reconsidered periodically, since their states vary during the planning cycle under study.

Cycle-Length Relevance

Whether something that influences the planners' concerns is treated as a variable or as a parameter is a function of the planners' time perspective. Hence the length of the planning cycle must be specified to define the variable/parameter boundary. As the planning cycle lengthens (and the planning horizon recedes), the variable or system set grows and the parameter or nonsystem set shrinks. Simply put, the longer the run, the more changes occur; fewer nonsystem variables remain constant. Accordingly, in the truly long run the system becomes immense. On the other hand, with a short planning cycle the system's variable set stays relatively small because more variables hold constant values, i.e., become parameters. Thus a system can be shrunk or have its variety reduced by analyzing it over a shorter time period. These relationships between system size and planning-cycle length are shown in figure 2-1.

In the first design cycle, a short time perspective is necessary so as not to overwhelm the planners with variety. However, with successive planning cycles, previously considered variables will require less time to set, so longer time cycles, along with their broader variable sets, become manageable. An extended perspective also becomes necessary; otherwise, certain conditions assumed to be constant will be ignored when indeed they are changing as time passes. With a longer time perspective, the planners will be less likely to be caught unprepared for serious long-term environmental shifts; a greater variety of courses of action can be explored.

Client Relevance

The second criterion a variable must meet to be included within the planners' system is that it influence their clients' well-being. Ashby (1970) terms such a test of relevance the "primary generating question" (p. 104) from which the system's variable list derives. To answer this question, the planners must ask their clients, or sponsors, what they want to achieve with the resources at their disposal. In short, what is their goal? Once this objective is articulated for a given clientele, the planners can identify the variables that influence it.

Not surprisingly, complications quickly arise. The designers soon find that variables which affect their clients' well-being influence other potential sponsoring groups as well. Thus a series of secondary generating questions emerges. In particular, what influences the welfare of these derivative clienteles? The problem the planners now must face is whether to admit the secondary clienteles' concerns to the system's variable space or to exclude them as parameters.

From a given client's perspective, the system's planners should concentrate exclusively on that client's narrow concerns. Design capacity thereby will be

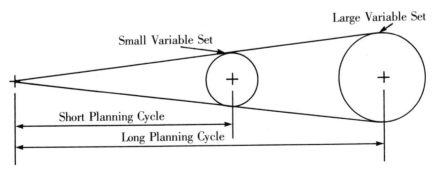

Figure 2-1. The relationship between system size and planning-cycle length.

neither overloaded nor diluted. For example, family members owning a privately controlled business often resist "going public." To them, improved capital availability and general visibility do not offset the loss of concentration on the family's concerns that occurs when outside shareholders become involved. Similarly, stockholders in public corporations want management to focus primarily on short-run profits, not on the long-run concerns of workers, consumers, or the like; concurrently, workers desire their union leadership to emphasize labor concerns to the exclusion of capital, consumer, and public interests. Thus serving a single homogeneous clientele that is at most only *loosely and infrequently tied* to surrounding client groups presents the neatest design situation. Multiple client groups make the designers' task harder, for they introduce many new variables into the system.

However, from a true systems, or long-run, perspective, the planners ideally should concern themselves with improving the well-being of all potential clienteles (Churchman, 1968a). In practice, a design team cannot long restrict itself to a single clientele, completely excluding all others. The concerns of secondary clients cannot be overlooked, for they quickly grow restive against such neglect.

In a given planning cycle the primary client's welfare may partially depend on the secondary clients' variable settings also. In other cases, such partial interdependencies may surface only over several planning cycles. That is, a secondary client group may tolerate exclusion temporarily, then shift its behavior abruptly after a particularly bad cycle. The secondary clientele then thrusts itself into the primary clients' system domain by changing constants to variables: what once was a nonsystem parameter now becomes a system variable. For instance, labor can assault the variable space of stockholders by changing a nonstrike attitude to one where a strike is a serious option. Such a change not only increases the variable spaces for both design teams (the stockholders' as well as labor's) but also presents them with a series of potentially unfavorable variable settings.

Given that a few partial dependencies will usually exist among client groups, designers must assume a broad perspective so as not to overlook other groups' more serious concerns. Yet planners cannot go too far, in light of their limited capacity. How should they proceed?

In the initial planning cycles, the designers, of necessity, will focus narrowly on the variables affecting their primary beneficiaries and treat the secondary clients' concerns as nonsystem parameters. Other design groups more in tune with the latter clienteles' objectives can be expected to accept them as their principal beneficiaries and, in contrast, treat the first clientele's concerns as nonsystem parameters rather than system variables.

Ideally, as more and more planning cycles are completed, growing experience allows each design group to extend its planning horizon, that is, the length of each planning cycle. With the lengthened time perspective, each system's variable space grows; increasingly the spaces overlap and become more nearly coterminous. In other words, the client groups' partial dependencies increase in the long run, less can be gained by one group at another's expense, and the groups' coincident interests must be addressed simultaneously.

Partial Dependencies

As time elapses, the various planning groups face situations where their clients' interests partially overlap with others'. Within such intersects, common decision variables, or *"points of dependence"* (Galbraith, 1977:202), simultaneously influence the well-being of two or more clienteles. The partial dependencies remain in the variable sets of all affected clienteles.

Unfortunately, these shared variables can transmit disturbances endlessly among the systems. And they can impose excessive variety loads on the planners during each design cycle.

For particularly high-dependency interactions, the various planning groups may want to cooperate in reducing the variety flowing among their systems. A degree of "temporary independence" (Ashby, 1966:158-70) can be achieved by holding these critical overlapped variables constant throughout the planning cycle; "for a variable, so long as it stays constant, cannot . . . have an affect on another; neither can it be affected by another" (1956:66). So "if some of the variables . . . are constant for a time, then during that time the connexions through them are reduced functionally to zero, and the effect is as if the connexions had been severed in some material way during that time" (1966:169).

Thus the more vital partially dependent variables are made parameters to the interacting systems and removed from each unit's variable set. Since parameters shrink the overlapped set at these critical junctures, they serve to separate the systems. This isolation, in turn, lets each design group proceed with its respective tasks, unconcerned about significant disruptions arriving from surrounding systems. The setting of long-term contract terms by labor and management negotiators exemplifies such system-separation activity.

Of course, the parameters we are discussing will be effective and cannot be overlooked completely. But they need be considered only initially, not continuously as fluctuating variables must. Hence the variety load impinging on each of the cooperating design groups drops.

Low-dependency interactions, however, can be left safely in the partially dependent or overlapped variable spaces of the several groups and negotiated during the planning cycle by lower-level designers, i.e., decision makers. How, then, do the designers distinguish between the important variables to be fixed as parameters and the less critical to be left as variables on the outermost peripheries of the interacting systems?

In general, a variable's importance or "essentialness" to a particular group of planners depends on how much its variation changes their clients' level of satisfaction. Implicit in assessing how sensitive the clients' welfare is to a variable is the factor's own inherent variability. Variables possessing little variety themselves, for example, pass on little variation to the clients' state of well-being. Conversely, interdependent variables that fluctuate widely or oscillate rapidly should be stabilized as low-frequency parameters if the clients' satisfaction is at all sensitive to their movements.

Priority rankings among a system's variables (whether or not shared with other systems) are discovered by using either theoretical or experiential approaches. The theoretical method requires the planners to build a model that relates the variables to an overall goal measure. A sensitivity analysis can then be conducted by mathematically changing the system's variable values and measuring the resultant fluctuations transmitted to the goal value.

The same knowledge can be gained experientially through observing fluctuations of the system's variables during normal operations. Because many variables shift simultaneously in a given planning cycle, tracing their impact through to the final goal measure may require numerous design periods to isolate each cause's effect. The empirical approach to priority ranking is further complicated by the fact that as more design cycles pass more changes can occur—including parametric shifts.

For example, consider the American automobile industry. Before the 1920s engineering and production decisions occupied center stage as auto manufacturers strove to raise product reliability and manufacturing efficiency. During the 1920s and into the 1930s styling and marketing variables ascended to prominence as the market first became saturated and then severely contracted. Midway through the 1930s, labor-related issues gained importance when strikes stopped profit generation completely. Throughout the 1940s production swung back into the spotlight to meet war needs and then pent-up postwar demand. In the 1950s and early 1960s marketing-oriented variables regained their stature as the market again became saturated; during the late 1960s and into the 1970s government-related decisions grew in importance with the government's growing involvement in the industry. Most recently, foreign competition has assumed top priority.

Once armed with their respective priority rankings for the partially dependent variables, the design groups can begin to bargain for the settings most advantageous to their clients' well-being. When no conflict emerges, the shared variables need only be set at mutually satisfactory values.

More likely, however, conflict erupts. Then a given group of planners tries to fix the parameters at values that optimize its primary patron's goal while satisfying—simultaneously—the minimum performance standards demanded by the other interacting clienteles. For example, owner-oriented designers seek to maximize stockholders' profit yet minimally meet management's salary requests, labor's wage claims, suppliers' price requirements, customers' quality expectations, and the community's pollution laws. Design teams with workers as their principal beneficiaries strive to benefit labor maximally while minimally meeting stockholders' profit hopes. This perspective makes apparent how labor's goal imposes a limit on the stockholders' benefits and vice versa: "One man's goal may be another man's constraint" (Simon, 1964:8).

Once negotiated, the parameters tend to hold constant throughout the period: the interacting systems seek to maintain their own equilibria. That is, all the planning groups have a mutual stake in keeping a large number of high-dependency interaction variables as interim constants, thereby temporarily severing their respective systems into more easily managed segments. Moreover, little new information will be available upon which to reopen the negotiation process.

While maintained at steady states throughout any given period, these temporary constants can shift abruptly—as stepwise functions—at the period's end. At this juncture, each client group evaluates its well-being in comparison to other surrounding groups, in particular as it has been influenced by the partially dependent variables. Unless all client groups are minimally satisfied with the comparative results, these postcontrol evaluations will lead to precontrol changes. Then the parametric conditions facing all systems in the next planning cycle will be altered.

For example, the rank and file of labor demand that their union leadership negotiate aggressively when employers have earned high returns while paying comparatively low wages. The representatives of capital, on the other hand, demand considerable concessions from labor after employers report poor results due in part to excessively high wage payments. Similarly, when the government observes that neglected safety and pollution concerns have generated record profits, it may well impose stringent and costly regulations. But when the economy does poorly, political pressure shifts abruptly and the regulated firms can lobby more effectively to have the standards eased for future periods.

Regardless of how dependent a client group may be on a particular parameter's (or variable's) setting, there is no guarantee it will be able to negotiate a favorable value. Another dimension of the bargaining process becomes germane: a given clientele's success in improving its position in future periods ultimately depends on its power.

From a cybernetics viewpoint, power can be seen as the "causal effectiveness" of a given unit's decisions—be that unit a person, an organization, or a nation. In other words, "a decision unit's power is the *amount of information* [variety] *added* about what is going to happen [to a parameter's or variable's setting] by knowing the decision of that unit" (Stinchcombe, 1968:164).

That significant power differences exist in the society is obvious. The decision of a single consumer, for example, means little in relation to the decision of a large corporation. If left unprotected, the unorganized mass of consumers would be almost unilaterally dependent upon—and wholly dominated by—large businesses. This disparate bargaining power could diminish seriously the well-being of certain clienteles simply because they lack the effectiveness to improve their condition.

The Government Buffer

To correct power inequities, society intervenes. As businesses have coalesced into larger and larger units, government involvement has kept pace. In Downs's (1967:148) words, *"Any attempt to control one large organization tends to generate another."*

Government agencies more and more set the parameters linking society's various systems. Boulding (1973:179) named such bodies "intersects." "The term 'intersect' is particularly appropriate for organizations of this kind, because they do in fact occupy the intersection of two sets, i.e., they belong in some sense to two groups or organizations, or fill odd-shaped spaces between the organizations" (p. 181). More specifically, "intersect organizations serve as 'buffers,' . . . to separate two organizations that otherwise might be in unbearable conflict [and] to negotiate and mediate, connect and interpret, between two or more other organizations" (p. 181).

When management representing the stockholders' interests and union representatives championing workers' concerns cannot agree, for instance, the National Labor Relations Board steps in to facilitate a contractual agreement. To protect various nonstockholding clienteles, government bureaus impose strict policy guidelines (i.e., parameters) on the economy's corporations. Consequently, businesses cannot legally use certain kinds of inputs (like poisonous chemicals), whereas they must employ others (like minority workers). Manufacturing techniques endangering workers or causing pollution hazards are eliminated from consideration, and certain products or product characteristics dangerous to consumers are outlawed: thus some drugs cannot be sold legally, and automobiles must meet strict safety, mileage, and pollution requirements.

Several government agencies exist to protect stockholders themselves from unscrupulous designers and decision makers. The Securities and Exchange Commission (SEC), for instance, owes its existence to the widespread stock frauds and management failures unearthed during the 1930s depression. Similarly, the Federal Trade Commission (FTC) and the Antitrust Division of the Justice

Department—along with protecting consumers against monopolistic prices by ensuring a degree of *control diversity* within the economy's various industries— safeguard stockholders of one firm from the predatory practices of another.

By filling the interstices among systems and converting high-dependency interacting variables into long-term constants, the government (representing the broad public interest) serves to stabilize intrasocietal relationships, as well as to steady the general social-political-economic environment. Not only does such government activity separate the interacting systems in a given planning cycle, but the accumulation of judicial precedents, legislative acts, and administrative rulings over many periods presents the corporation's planners with the very basis for their design work. *Organizational design, in fact, begins from this vast cumulative foundation of long-term societal constancies (or parameters) set by the government in conjunction with society's various political interest groups.*

Naturally, the more parameters encompass a system, the more initial conditions the designers must consider. Even so, parameters are preferred to high-dependency interacting variables in terms of the variety loads imposed on all the design teams. For this very reason it behooves government to hold a steady course throughout the planning cycle. Otherwise, the various constituency groups will be locked in continuous high-frequency contact, thereby overwhelming their planners with variety. But avoiding frequent reversals in societal policy is a dictum somewhat hard to follow in democratic societies, where changes in administration occur regularly and make themselves felt in the short- and long-run business environments.

From a purely cybernetic viewpoint, extreme policy shifts like the alterations enacted in labor law during the 1930s and in consumer and environmental law during the 1970s are more troublesome than incremental steps. Small stepwise shifts are preferred since they present a *constant* rate of change from period to period.

Akin to cataclysmic policy shifts, in terms of the problems they create for business planners, are the imposition of excessive and—even worse—conflicting societal constraints. Given business's focal position in a society with a capitalistic economy, such situations can easily develop. Numerous government agencies charged with protecting various clienteles often work in isolation from one another, increasing the likelihood of too many or contradictory constraints being imposed. Moreover, when cumbersome or discordant social policies combine with highly restrictive union contracts and tradition-bound managements, as is the case with many American railroads, survival for the firm becomes particularly problematic. In sum, government—like corporate headquarters with respect to their divisions—must carefully balance the amount and quality of centralized control against the corporate responsiveness needed for a dynamic economy.

The Societal Parameters and the Economic Variables

To this point, the discussion has considered organizations in general. Now the focus narrows to a particular type of organization: the large American corporation. From here on, the society that surrounds the economy constitutes the corporation's long-term parametric environment, whereas the more immediate economy constitutes its short-term variable environment. In other words, the low-variability societal constraints imposed on the economy and on its component firms *define* the set of parameters for the corporate planners, while the high-variability production and distribution decisions taken within the economy *define* the system of variables for the corporate planners.

In this framework, then, *"economic processes are always conditioned by . . . the parametric characteristics of the non-economic [systems] of the society"* (Parsons and Smelser, 1956:307). But while noneconomic systems (e.g., political, legal, educational, religious, and cultural) will influence the economic system over the long run, it is assumed that such comparatively stable factors will hold constant throughout any given corporate planning cycle and thus will not modify the economic system's operations (Smelser, 1968a:500). It is further assumed that at the end of each corporate planning cycle the state of the long-term societal or parametric environment may shift abruptly, only to hold steady again throughout the ensuing cycle. Though this assumed correspondence between society's long-term shifts and the corporation's planning cycles might seem unlikely at first, it should be remembered that the society will be most apt to tighten or loosen its constraints when the final evaluative results of the corporate planning cycle become available. Moreover, the corporation will be most likely to begin a new planning cycle just after the society adjusts its constraints on the economy's businesses.

It should also be reiterated that many of the long-term parameters fixed by the larger society were once economic decision variables set principally by the business community. Product standards and pollution tolerances, for instance, are now decided beyond the bounds of the economic system to safeguard consumers and the public interest. And to some extent, labor has removed the setting of wage rates and working conditions from the economic arena. In the 1930s labor organized itself politically so that its clientele would no longer feel the full vagaries of the economic system.

The business community's failure to widen voluntarily its planning perspective beyond the narrow interests of its stockholders largely accounts for the diminution of economic decision making. Had American corporations taken a longer-run view and encompassed consumer, worker, and public concerns more fully, it is quite unlikely that the larger society would have constrained the prerogatives of its economic decision makers.

Despite this imposition of societal constraints, the American economy still operates as a comparatively independent system within the larger society. The economy by and large retains most of its *free*-enterprise characteristics. So when deciding how scarce resources are allocated to produce, distribute, and exchange goods and services for consumption, American corporations possess a remarkably free hand. This independence becomes even more apparent given how slowly society's constraints change compared with the high-frequency fluctuations found throughout the economy and especially within the corporation. (The American economy's independence from the society's other systems will be discussed more fully in chapter 9.)

Client Representatives: The Board of Directors

Since the American economy remains essentially a free-enterprise capitalistic system, where capital interests take precedence, the stockholders are treated as the corporation's primary clientele and nonstockholding groups such as management, labor, consumers, and the public are treated as secondary. So whenever these latter groups are not protected by long-term societal constraints, their interests will tend to be subordinated to those of the stockholders. And the shorter the planners' time horizon, the more they will concentrate on stockholders' well-being to the exclusion of nonstockholding interests.

Given this setting, who represents the stockholders, i.e., who functions as the designers? The board of directors serves as the shareholders' principal representative and, through its committees, guides and monitors the firm's decision makers (i.e., management).

The board should be dominated by outside members. Otherwise, "the more a corporation moves to a preponderance of 'inside' directors, the more the 'internal' management affairs are under no scrutiny but that of the management itself" (Stone, 1976:127). When the board of directors consists primarily of outside (i.e., nonmanagement) members, it exists as a metacontrol instrument for the stockholders and perhaps even for the wider society, if the composition is broad enough.

To maximize its impact upon management, the board must focus on specifying critical long-run policy variables. (These plans, in turn, guide the firm's decision makers as they deal with less important, shorter-run operating variables.) Should the clients' minimum performance standards not be met, for example, the directors may decide to modify the firm's lobbying efforts, alter its diversification strategy, change its organizational structure, or adjust its personnel policies.

To best concentrate its attention, the overall board should be broken into a series of committees. First and foremost, there should be a *nominating committee* composed exclusively of outside members to select board replacements and make committee assignments. Next in importance there will be an *external-relations committee* and an *audit committee*, each again consisting exclusively of outside directors. Specifically, the external-relations group should look toward the long-term societal environment. To this group falls the responsibility of assessing the likelihood of shifts in the surrounding society's parameter settings that will require corresponding changes in the firm's policies. The audit committee will endeavor to ensure that the full board, the stockholders, and the secondary clients receive reliable performance data for judging the firm's accomplishments and shortcomings. Particularly important will be securing the external auditors to verify the firm's performance-measurement apparatus. Together, then, the nominating, external-relations, and audit committees will concentrate primarily on the definition and evaluation stages of the planning process.

A fourth subunit of the board, generally called a *finance committee,* should focus on strategy-oriented economic matters associated with the composition and synchronization phases of the planning process. While this committee should also be dominated by outside directors, it will need some inside directors who manage the various activities included within the firm's controlled decision space. The specific policy concerns of the finance group include: (a) the allocation of resources to the firm (via the approval of stock issues and loan requests); (b) the return of benefits, i.e., dividends, to the stockholders (simply another dimension of the original allocation decision); and (c) the allocation of resources to activities within the firm.

A fifth board group, the *executive committee,* should focus less on the external matters associated with the firm's societal and economic environments and more on the firm's internal decision-making arrangements. That is, this group must develop during the decomposition and recomposition design phases the organizational structure necessary to decide the many technical matters associated with the firm's operation. Accordingly, even more inside directors would be on the executive committee than on the finance committee.

The final subunit of the board should be the most internally oriented—the *bonus-and-salary committee,* which concentrates primarily on establishing personnel policies. As the committee with the greatest preponderance of inside directors, it provides for the motivation, education, and selection of the firm's decision makers. In other words, its concerns are those of the amplification phase of the design process.

In descending the board's hierarchy of committees, therefore, the proportion of outside directors can and must decrease. Three factors explain this shift in committee composition. First, since the lower-level committees play less of an external oversight role, the presence of insiders will not result in self-serving judgments. Second, lower-level committees focus less on external affairs and more on internal matters. For instance, the higher finance committee needs more outsiders with their knowledge of general economic conditions, whereas the lower executive committee needs more insiders with their heightened awareness of the firm's internal workings. Third, since the board's lower-level committees concentrate less on low-frequency, low-dependency external relationships and more on high-frequency, high-dependency internal connections (see fig. 1-2), their work demands more of their members' attention, including the attendance of frequent meetings. Accordingly, their membership must be drawn primarily from insiders who can afford to devote full time to company operations.

Even with committees concentrating attention on specific policy areas, the board of directors requires considerable staff support. The board's most vital advisory unit is the *financial staff*. This unit is so critical, in fact, that it should report directly to the board (via the audit and finance committees) rather than to the corporate executives, as would less vital staff units. The financial staff's importance stems from its role in providing reliable financial-performance information—data absolutely essential to setting the firm's policies.

OPERATIONALIZING THE GOAL

The financial staff, then, has the charge of designing and operating the firm's performance-measurement apparatus. Central to this task is defining an overall performance criterion to evaluate explicitly and efficiently how the system variables and nonsystem parameters influence the primary clients' well-being. In other words, "the measure of performance of the system is a score . . . that tells us how well the system is doing. The higher the score, the better the performance" (Churchman, 1968b:31).

Accordingly, the domain of values for all system variables and nonsystem parameters must be mapped onto the variable values of a single performance scale. The conversion function, $M = F(S_k, P_l)$, connects the system's variables S_k and the nonsystem's parameters P_l to the ordered values of the scalar performance measure M. Eventually, when evaluating performance, it should be remembered that a change in value of any parameter in P_l shifts the range, or subset, of values generated on the M scale by the domain of values for the variables in S_k.

Undoubtedly, one of the finest examples of a performance indicator designed to summarize a system's overall state of well-being is Donaldson Brown's identification of the return-on-investment (ROI) measure. Just prior to joining

Sloan at GM in 1921, Brown finished the now-famous and widely adopted DuPont performance-control system, culminating in the DuPont Company's chart room. There "statistical data pertaining to each segment of the company's operations were displayed [in relation] to the end-result of return on invested capital" (Brown, 1957:27). Brown, like Sloan and the duPonts, thought the ROI variable was the final and fundamental measure of industrial efficiency in terms of management's primary responsibility: the stockholders' interests.

The basis of Brown's model for evaluating financial performance was a relatively straightforward rate-of-return formula: $ROI = T \times P$, where ROI means return on invested capital, T refers to turnover of invested capital, and P stands for percentage of profit on sales (Brown, 1957:26). Both turnover of invested capital and the percentage of profit on sales were disaggregated further (Sloan, 1964:142). The invested capital in T was broken into fixed-capital components (such as plant and equipment) and working-capital items (such as cash balances, in-process and finished inventory, and accounts receivable). These essential variables then were reported in terms of a ratio to sales, the reciprocal of which represented the rate of turnover T. Cost variables were factored into significant categories, then deducted from and divided by sales to obtain the percentage of profit on sales P. Moving toward the final ROI measure rather than away from it resulted in an aggregation or summarization process.

Practically speaking, Brown's analytical model yielded "a specific disclosure of causes and effects for the return on investment. . . . Effective control, or lack of it, for any item [in either term, T or P] of the equation could be identified, thus making possible efforts to improve conditions" (Brown, 1957:27). In addition, the model established a trade-off principle (Churchman, 1971:47) that told how much one subgoal would be relinquished to increase another; for example, the level of lost sales that could be tolerated when inventories were pared to reduce capital investment.

Despite its widespread use by business practitioners, the ROI measure is sharply criticized. Some academics, for instance, advocate multiple measures because "return on investment, when used alone, can lead businessmen to postpone needed product research or the modernization of facilities" (Andrews, 1980:136). (In the final analysis, however, comparison and choice require a single scale, even if implicit.) To minimize such problems, the designers can emphasize—as Sloan and Brown did at GM—an average rate of return earned over the long run. With such a measure, the delayed effects of ill-advised exigencies become unmistakable.

Not only do designers desire a single performance scale for the system, but they also want a measure that can be used to *compare* a wide variety of investment possibilities. Clients desire externally commensurable performance data—that is, standardized data that are comparable on a common scale—to allocate their resources optimally among alternative firms. A portfolio of corporate investments guarantees that no one group of planners exerts undue influence. Similarly, if internal projects, activities, units, and the like are judged against a standard scale, the planners and their decision makers can achieve an optimum internal resource allocation.

To generate such commensurability in a whole series of organizational performance measures, the designers and their colleagues in adjoining firms must agree on a valuation scheme applicable to each organization as well as to its many internal investment opportunities. In capitalist economies, the network of market prices coupled with generally accepted accounting practices furnishes the valuation scheme needed.

Moreover, to arrive at a standardized performance scale, designers must reference the benefits generated in the clients' behalf to the resources used to create them. That is, how well a corporation or a division within a corporation converts stockholder resources into stockholder benefits must be gauged in terms of alternative external or internal resource-allocation possibilities. The return-on-investment (ROI) measure facilitates such comparisons by dividing dollar profits by the dollar value of the investment—working capital, plant, equipment—used to generate these profits. Thus, the ROI indicator can measure the commercial success of enterprises of different size, in different times, or in different countries dealing in different currencies. When rate of return is used as the performance measure, the commercial success of compared enterprises becomes *commensurable*. The comparison of company with company, division with division, or company in 1985 with company in 1975 is meaningful and valid—assuming, of course, such factors as inflation hold or are made constant analytically. (In contrast, an unreferenced performance indicator like net profit fails to allow for the different amounts of capital employed across investments and over time.) Intercomponent and intertemporal performance comparisons thus become possible through the use of the ROI indicator.

Finally, strict comparability across corporations (or divisions) requires using exactly the same accounting techniques in each case. If any variations exist from firm to firm (or within a firm), their impact must be discounted to generate a valid performance comparison. Similarly, to achieve commensurability over time, the designers must hold constant the accounting practices used to measure the benefits and costs across planning periods. In other words, measurement artifacts or variations must be stabilized. In sum, the measurement apparatus must be kept in the parametric set rather than in the variable set.

At the very least, performance measurement must not vary within a given planning cycle. Otherwise, the board of directors, stockholders, and other clienteles will not be able to compare their initial goals or expectations with the final results achieved at the design cycle's close. But much strategic, structural, and personnel planning needs to be done before any such final comparison can even be considered.

So at this point attention switches from goal definition to strategy formulation. In this next phase of the SDPC model, the finance committee, while trying not to overload the firm's decision makers, should extend its boundaries to the cleavages where the environmental variables either hold essentially steady or transmit little variety to the firm's performance measure.

Exactly where this boundary location falls will depend on where the finance committee decides to place the firm's long-term capital investments. And once set, of course, these low-frequency decision variables will tend to maintain fairly constant values over long periods. However, as soon as the firm's strategic investments start to generate cash flows, other investment possibilities (and economic fronts) can be tried in the event that the performance appears unsatisfactory, based on preliminary feedback. The more mature enterprise, possessing a spectrum of long-term investments at various stages in their life cycles, will possess sufficient reallocation flexibility to test several variations of its basic strategy before the final results will be evaluated.

3

Formulating the Strategy: Composing the Controlled and Uncontrolled Variables

The designers thus confront their second boundary-definition problem: partitioning the uncontrolled or environmental variables from the controlled variables managed directly by the firm. When composing or selecting the variables to include within the controlled variable domain, the designers want to encompass sufficient internal decision variety to counter exogenous disturbances without overloading management's capacity.

In business-policy terminology, composing the controlled set simply means formulating the firm's strategy via *channel* integration and *product* diversification. Strategy formulation is synonymous with creating the *"concept of the firm's business"* (Ansoff, 1965:103), and it "involves 'portfolio' decisions regarding what business the firm is in or should be in" (Hrebiniak and Joyce, 1984:56).

In organizational-cybernetics terminology, the designers seek "to model the organization's behavior in the form of an equation in which the measure of performance is equated to some function of those aspects of the system . . . subject to management's control (C_i) and . . . to those uncontrolled aspects of the system (U_j) which also affect the outcome" (Ackoff, 1969:125). The organization model thus takes the form:

$$M = F(C_i, U_j)$$

where

C_i = the controlled variables (the firm)
U_j = the uncontrolled variables (the environment)
$C_i \cup U_j = S_k$
$C_i \cap U_j \neq \emptyset$.

Figure 3-1 illustrates the second boundary-definition problem: partitioning the system S_k into uncontrollable and controllable variables.

The shaded area in figure 3-1 indicates that the intersection statement, $C_i \cap U_j$, is not equal to the null or empty set $\emptyset$. The real-world significance of this statement is particularly important, for it implies some overlap between the uncontrolled and controlled variables. But what can be simultaneously uncontrolled and controlled? A *partially* controlled variable is influenced by two or more separate parties—say, management and labor—neither of which possesses exclusive direction. As with the longer-run parameters in the intersect areas discussed in chapter 2, bargaining assumes prominence here as each of the intertwined parties seeks a favorable settlement that is also minimally satisfactory to the other(s).

Designers cannot move the boundary between C_i and U_j at will to incorporate just any variable within their controlled system. Both management's limited decision capacity and, more important here, other organizations' strategy decisions limit them. In short, any given firm—regardless of its size—faces a somewhat restricted strategy field even before its designers begin their composition work.

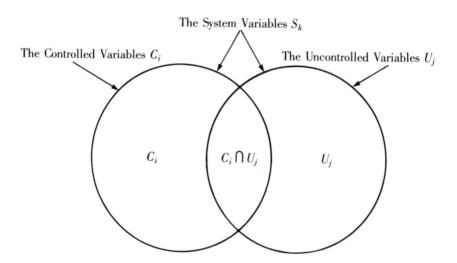

Figure 3-1. Partitions between the controlled and uncontrolled variables.

Vertically, more powerful or dominant organizations such as government bureaus will have set parameters to exclude firms from particular variable spaces. Antitrust laws and rulings, for example, prevent large firms from forcing their smaller competitors out of business. Such constraints provide additional options to smaller firms: (a) by lessening the large firm's internal variety and performance prospects and (b) by reducing simultaneously the variety of the external environment faced by the small firm. Horizontally, parallel organizations like labor and competitors may have established exclusive rights or garnered a comparative advantage in particular decision areas. When such barriers prove permanently impermeable, the decisions under question remain forever in the firm's environmental or uncontrolled space, potentially capable of damaging its performance.

In spite of these limitations, the firm retains considerable latitude in creating its particular environmental niche (Miles and Snow, 1978:5). That is, significant technology, product, and market choices remain to be made.

Usually the board of directors' finance committee (see chapter 2) guides the enterprise's strategic policy choices for several reasons. First, and foremost, the firm's long-term internal resource-allocation decisions, i.e., its capital budgeting, are "areas of strategic decision-making" because "the results continue over an extended period" (Weston and Brigham, 1969:170). Until the enterprise can *reconvert or recycle* these fixed assets into more liquid resources available for reinvestment, it surrenders considerable flexibility, or internal variety. In other words, the firm, once committed to a particular portfolio of long-term assets, becomes "a hostage of future events" (p. 171). Second, the client representatives can exert a vast influence on overall performance without being overloaded, since only a comparatively few aggregated investment decisions are involved. Third, setting these capital-investment variables in turn determines which variables the firm's management ultimately decides; i.e., which activities are circumscribed within the decision makers' controllable set. When the board defers these critical investment choices to the decision makers, the business, or composition, strategy may go awry. Stone (1976) cites a classic example, the Pennsylvania–New York Central: "A tragic panorama of ineptness, deceit, and self-dealing had been going on under the directors' noses from almost the moment the Pennsylvania and the New York Central merged. . . . Instead of giving its fullest attention to the floundering rail operations [which were] in dire need of cash to replenish rolling stock," management toyed "with an ill-conceived empire" (pp. 128–129). This strange realm included a hockey team, real-estate ventures, an airline subsidiary of questionable legality, and management's own "private" investment trust. Hence management's decision makers cannot be left to make their own strategy selections; rather, the full board, on recommendation of its finance committee, must decide what business ventures management controls.

The board's finance committee dominates these strategic decisions, since external and internal resource allocations interact inextricably. For instance, external capital costs must be weighed against internal rates of return in establishing the firm's expansion limits. Of course, significant decision-making input must come from internal directors who, as the firm's uppermost managers, must operate the board-determined investments. Because of the infrequency and brevity of normal board meetings, additional contact points may become necessary to achieve adequate communication between the finance committee members and the top operating officers. To start, the firm's president should be seated on the finance committee and several outside directors should involve themselves in internal operations. Throughout much of its history GM used its Executive Committee to involve outside directors. Composed primarily of inside directors, GM's Executive Committee operated as the top policy body of the firm's internal management. Outside directors and Finance Committee members, like Pierre duPont and his close associate John Raskob, sat on this Executive Committee to acquaint themselves with the operating management's control needs and capacity limitations.

Where should a finance committee draw the boundary between what the firm manages and what others control? That is, which activities, along with their concomitant variables, are to be included within the controlled set C_i and which are to be left with uncontrolled environment units U_j?

Ideally, the designers would locate the boundary between the controlled variables and the environment so: (a) the variety in the controlled variables equals (or exceeds) the variety in the system's uncontrolled environment, and (b) the variety of the decision makers equals (or exceeds) the variety in the controlled variables. To the extent that the designers fail in these connected balancing acts, a proportional amount of environmental variety filters through to M and thereby disturbs the clients.

The influences on overall system performance of the investment activities selected by the board and managed by the decision makers can be determined via the equation:

$$M = [x_1 m_1 + x_2 m_2 + \ldots + x_l m_l + \ldots + x_n m_n] + x_{n+1}[m_{n+1} + m_{n+2} + \ldots + m_{n+p}]$$

where

m_l = scalar performance indicator, which measures how well the lth activity converts resources into benefits

x_l = percentage of the system's resources allocated to the lth activity

x_{n+1} = 0, which indicates that zero resources have been allocated to the m_{n+1} through m_{n+p} activities.

The first line of this equation, then, represents the firm's actual investment portfolio. In this single term, the performance of the whole corporation is expressed as "an explicit function of only a few key variables" (Mesarović, Macko, and Takahara, 1970:62): the performances of the individual investments and their respective proportions of the total capital pool. (The performance-measurement experts on the financial staff, of course, will standardize [i.e., establish uniform] cost/benefit and resource accounts across activities m_1 through m_n so each is commensurable with the others as well as with M.) The second term of the above equation represents the firm's many noninvestments; that is, the lost opportunities (or implicit costs) of not investing in activities m_{n+1} through m_{n+p}.

In guiding the finance committee's initial investment decisions, the designers want to establish the firm in an area where its management holds greater expertise than its competitors. Given this comparative advantage, the firm's management will be able to make the finest distinctions, or choices. Not only will this heightened decision-making capacity provide the maximum protection against environmental fluctuations, but it will also allow the firm to impose the maximum variety loads on its competitors.

To safeguard such a high performance potential, the firm's planners will endeavor to exclude other businesses from their favored territory. Since "the mere presence of an experience curve" cannot keep aggressive or imitative competitors from gaining ground, a competitive advantage based on experience alone offers a somewhat "ethereal entry barrier" (Porter, 1980:16). More formidable exclusionary strategies would include erecting entry barriers based (a) on economies of scale and (b) on patent-law sanctions enforced by the larger society.

Once other firms gain access to the area of specialization, pressure is on the focal firm to diversify, for the designers often can improve performance by increasing the number of activities controlled by the firm. Samuels and Smyth's (1968) work with British firms confirmed Alexander's (1949) observation that small firms' variations in rate of return exceeded those for larger businesses. Even large-volume single-line firms can improve performance by diversification. Alexander (1949) hypothesized that "the average large corporation may gain stability of earnings from the fact that its operations are the sum of individual independent operations. Thus the rate of profit of a large corporation might be regarded as the mean of the rates of profit of a number of smaller enterprises into which it could be decomposed" (p. 233). With n the number in a sample, the standard deviation of the sample's mean is approximately $1/\sqrt{n}$ of the original population's standard deviation (p. 233). Thus designers could expect a large corporation composed of n activities to show profit-dispersion rates smaller by a factor of $1/\sqrt{n}$ than a corporation composed of a similar single activity.

Alexander explains the discrepancy between his theoretical and his empirical findings by the extent to which activities correlate with one another and with the economy in general. And since roughly 35 to 40 percent of many firms' annual earnings fluctuations may stem from the economy's perturbations and a further 10 to 15 percent from industry variations (Brown and Ball, 1967:65), diversification offers only limited risk reduction in practice. Accordingly, the planners can reduce but not eliminate risk for their clients.

The floor under which risk cannot be lowered via a "naive" diversification strategy—i.e., by simply adding activities without considering how their performances covary—is labeled by stock-market theorists "the level of systematic risk." It is a measure of the inherent variability contained in the economy as a whole. For a firm, the systematic risk can be defined as the amount of its ROI variability correlated with the economy's fluctuations. This performance instability cannot be eliminated from a composition portfolio encompassing *many* ventures, regardless of the selection strategy used by the planners. Thus the "ultimate diversified company," involved in all economic sectors, has "by definition . . . an average return" and bears "the risk associated with major economic cycles" (Rumelt, 1974:81).

Only a modest expansion of the activity portfolio is necessary to drop the firm's risk value close to the systematic level. So, "from a practical point of view, it is important to note that [in light of the factor $1/\sqrt{n}$] substantial reduction in the dispersion of portfolio return can be achieved with a relatively small amount of diversification" (Fama and Miller, 1972:254). As discussed later, a still more circumspect or sophisticated diversification strategy may attain risk values below the level of systematic risk.

But it is the possibility of an overexpansion lowering the expected return rates of the individual ventures, rather than the limits of risk reduction, that caps the number of activities a firm may pursue. As the second constraint of Ashby's law of Requisite Variety warns, the addition of each new variable reduces the time available for those variables already under control and, at some critical point, weakens overall performance-control ability.

Decision-capacity overloads can be mitigated somewhat by expanding into areas where the firm can continue to exploit its comparative advantage. The "search for strategic options," accordingly, "will be driven by distinctive competence and a desire to maintain the competitive advantage it denotes" (Hrebiniak and Joyce, 1984:44). Besides reducing management's variety load, this expansion strategy lets the firm transfer technological developments rapidly via a cross-fertilization process.

In the face of limited control capability, whether the designers include or exclude an activity (i.e., a variable set) in the controlled set of variables hinges on: (a) how essential the endeavor is to the performance of other controlled components, or (b) how well its performance offsets periodic poor performances by other components. Usually, the first condition relates to channel integration and the latter to product diversification. (The terms "*channel* integration" and "*product* diversification" have been substituted for the often-used expressions "*vertical* integration" and "*horizontal* diversification" because throughout this work the terms *vertical* and *horizontal* are used only when referring to hierarchical authority relationships.)

CHANNEL INTEGRATION

Channel integration typically is the means of including variables within the firm that are essential to the performance of its other activities and in turn to M. On a firm's input side, for example, "to have control of supply—to rely not on the market but on its own sources of supply—is an elementary safeguard" (Galbraith, 1967:28) against being dependent on an oligopolistic or, worse, on a monopolistic environmental sector. From the firm's perspective, inclusion of the supply source in the controlled set of activities "converts an external negotiation and hence a partially or wholly uncontrollable decision to a matter for purely internal decision" (p. 28).

In channel integration (whether toward suppliers or consumers), however, the planners must always weigh the firm's possible improvement in control over its essential variables against the additional demands placed on the management. If the prospective addition is very similar to an already controlled decision set, little extra variety results, as when large-scale automobile manufacturers make their own transmission components or body parts. If an activity diverges widely from prior experience, on the other hand, overall control deteriorates as the new variables siphon off too much capacity from other decisions.

Via channel integration, then, the designers attempt to *cluster* within the controlled-set boundary (i.e., to internalize) variables that exert considerable influence on performance, fluctuate rapidly or widely, and thrust little new variety onto the decision makers. That is, the planners expand C_i's boundaries to separate the organization from its surrounding environment without overloading their decision makers. Variables that are only loosely coupled to performance or that hold essentially constant can be left safely in the control of other enterprises, just as variables requiring much additional decision capacity must be left to the control of external enterprises.

An important limitation to the channel-integration strategy "occurs when the activities which precede or follow a major mission *fan out* rapidly" (Thompson, 1967:41) into widely different products and markets. Here, then, continued integration "introduces new technologies" beyond management's experience and lowers the production and marketing "relatedness within the organization" (Porter, 1980:83). To avoid this debilitating possibility, further integration moves must be highly selective, concentrating on those support activities that could become crucial environmental contingencies (Thompson, 1967:41–42).

To improve their knowledge of costs and leverage in negotiations, some enterprises like GM and Ford practice *"tapered integration,"* combining some in-house production of a needed item with purchases from outside suppliers (Porter, 1980:25). This practice husbands capital resources and executive talent for more lucrative endeavors, yet it provides a readily expandable supply should outside sources fail.

In some industries, channel integration not only can improve performance by providing control over essential variables but also can be used to offset periodic poor performances of the various integrated activities. In automobile production during a recession economy, for example, poor finished-auto revenues can be countered by good parts profits, since the sales of replacement parts—which are substitutes for finished autos—usually increase.

Whenever designers include a supplying or receiving activity within the controlled set, they should establish transfer prices to value interactivity transactions. Since these prices influence both the revenues generated by the supplying units as well as the costs incurred by the buying units, determining them is serious business. In fact, a fistfight between the refining and marketing division managers once settled a major oil company's intracompany transaction policy (Dean, 1955:65).

External market prices, wherever available, offer the best solution, inexpensively evaluating transfers in the same manner as outside purchases and sales. Each activity has input and output connections with the environment that also evaluate the overall system, and m_1 through m_n are easily commensurable with M. Furthermore, the external-market *valuation of interactions* makes the subsequent evaluation process more objective and less subject to internal bargaining and power manipulation.

Market-based transfer prices also provide a gauge for assessing the feasibility of further channel integration. When a firm's internal selling units can no longer compete with external suppliers, the enterprise may have expanded too far; i.e., beyond its capacity to control this activity at par with other, more specialized firms.

Transfer-pricing techniques, in fact, could assume such importance that designers might even foster the creation of competitive markets to embed into their intracompany activities. For example, the parts or services transferred between divisions may be standardized, the specifications published, and some share of production then purchased from several environmental suppliers.

Beyond the availability of transfer prices, firms can accrue additional benefits when an entire industry adopts common standards. By promulgating standardized material specifications, for instance, trade associations and professional societies "can simplify environments and shrink variety" (Weick, 1979:193). While such "interorganizational networks" are often dominated by their larger corporate members, even small enterprises benefit from the simplified environmental setting. That is, each cooperating firm is now surrounded by a simplified marketing environment, for standardization reduces "the infinite number of things in the world, potential and actual [,] to a moderate number of well-defined varieties" (March and Simon, 1958:159). In short, the standardized specifications serve as parameters separating the firms.

When competitive, external markets also provide several supply sources or outlets and thus a *diversity of control* over critical variables. They ensure continuity of operations when, for example, fires, floods, or other natural disasters stop production (even) in internally controlled facilities. More important, by scattering its dependence among multiple external and internal alternatives, the firm reduces the environment's oligopoly and oligopsony power over it. Hence the variety loads that noncooperative units can thrust upon the enterprise are significantly reduced. Increased communication costs, however, limit the extent to which this dependency-dispersion strategy can be pursued.

Along with transfer prices goes the need for transfer payments. While designers want external price setting, they do not wish to turn over to external systems expensive resources better employed internally. Using intrafirm script or computer accounting rather than cash payments minimizes this problem, thereby freeing liquid capital resources for other uses.

Finally, where critical variables must remain in the domain of external enterprises because of the variety they would otherwise introduce, designers nevertheless can cushion their impact on performance. How? First, some decision variables can be moved toward or into the partially controlled domain. Other firms may be induced to set the variables they control at values favorable to the designers' firm. Better yet, the firm can enter interorganizational agreements that grant some "temporary independence" (Ashby, 1966:158–170) from the full environmental vagaries. Most notably, contracts—backed by common law and commercial codes—can freeze key variables into parameters, or temporary constants. Once negotiated and fixed, material prices, product specifications, and delivery dates help separate the internal fluctuations of one firm from those of another. "*Walls of constancy*" (Ashby, 1966:165) are thus interposed at the two firms' boundary surfaces. System complexity and environmental variety drop (for both) because such "*constancies,*" as Ashby explains, "*can cut a system to pieces*" (p. 169).

Second, designers can separate their firm from particular environmental fluctuations by pursuing a diversification policy with respect to external enterprises. Under such circumstances, no one environmental unit becomes tightly coupled to the designers' firm. Multiple sources of critical steel supply, for example, may be used by an auto manufacturer so that a strike, an explosion, or the like affecting one supplier will not endanger production.

PRODUCTION DIVERSIFICATION

Product diversification usually is the means of including activities within the firm to offset expected poor performances of other endeavors. Like the designers' channel-integration work, their product-diversification effort increases internal variety—and survivability—by establishing the firm in multiple activities.

At a minimum, the several activities ensure that no one endeavor becomes too tightly coupled to M; the others dampen or diversify away its influence. Designers can weaken environmental dependencies further by including within the controlled set product-diversified activities exhibiting out-of-phase performances. (Occasionally, product additions can even improve existing endeavors; for example, when a full line is required to serve customers' needs.)

Most product-diversification strategies, in fact, start as attempts to find alternative uses for the resources idled in a poorly performing venture. Thus a common policy response to poor performance resulting from excess capacity has been the firm's redesign by diversification; i.e., the development of new products or services (Thompson, 1967:46-47).

When a business combines two activities, the long-run average performance of each must be satisfactory (unless, of course, the new activity has been added to eventually replace the old). In the short run, however, this requirement need not be met; for given that the short-run results of each activity fluctuate between good and bad, the designers hope to stagger the variations for maximum shock-absorbing capacity, or risk diversification. In the extreme— hypothetical—case where profits lost by one activity are perfectly negatively correlated with profits gained by another activity, the profit variance, i.e. risk, of the combined activities is exactly zero. Under these ideal circumstances no fluctuations in component performances filter through to damage overall survival prospects.

In attempting to achieve such stability, the designers will need to consider increasing degrees of product and market diversification. For instance, the firm could produce essentially the same product for the same price class but under several different nameplates or brands, offer the same product in several price classes (basically only a price-differentiated strategy), enter a few different yet still closely related product markets, or move into wholly different technologies, markets, or economies.

Mild diversification, such as minimal price differentiation in a single product line directed toward a single consumer group, is advantageous where great uncertainty (high variety) exists about the product characteristics that will succeed; for example, in industries where consumer desires fluctuate or technological states progress. Under these high-variety environmental conditions, the clients' interests are best protected by risk pooling; i.e., by offering several competitive products in the hope that at least one will succeed and generate resources for the others until they succeed in their turn. This strategy often involves staggering product life cycles. Consider the case of R.J. Reynolds in the mid-1970s: when its unfiltered Camel cigarettes declined in popularity and its Winston and Salem brands matured, the success of the firm's new offering, Vantage, helped offset the declines.

While usually administratively untaxing, because all the various nameplates are likely to be relatively similar technologically as well as directed toward the same market, mild nameplate diversification aids little in filtering general economic fluctuations from M. Indeed, the competing brands may amplify damage to M as internal competition forces resources to be underutilized. Even the administrative advantages may vanish as the decision makers face a tightly coupled controlled set of variables requiring extensive and frequent coordination.

With price-class diversification within a single product line, designers attempt to stabilize overall performance by moving the organization into performance-generating activities that covary negatively with each other and/or with the economy. As was shown in chapter 1, producing automobiles over a *wide variety* of prices, for instance, provides some protection against fluctuations in the economy. This diversification adds little variety to the decision makers' controllable set C_i because the products possess the same technologies and basically the same market. Furthermore, the price differentiation segments the market, reducing the intensity of interactions between the controlled activities.

However, since all models remain linked to industry-wide demand, to consumer-durable demand, and to general economic fluctuations, the achievable amount of negative correlation or sophisticated diversification is limited. As Markowitz (1972) puts it when considering a stockholder's investments: "A portfolio with sixty different railway securities, for example, would not be as well diversified as the same size portfolio with some railroad, some public utility, mining, various sorts of manufacturing, etc. The reason is that it is generally more likely for firms within the same industry to do poorly at the same time than for firms in dissimilar industries" (p. 417).

Diversifying into a number of closely related products and/or markets, while still not introducing massive variety loads, can further diminish the firm's performance fluctuations. Ansoff (1965) calls this strategy one of increasing the organization's "defensive flexibility," whereas "the single-customer defense industry firm, or a 'captive' supplier to Sears are examples of firms with the least flexibility" (p. 56). Hence, when the number and activity of investors diminished in the mid-1970s, brokerage houses expanded customer services beyond their traditional stock and bond operations to include all phases of financial planning. Armco Steel's performance in 1977, a generally disastrous year for the steel industry, shows the earnings stability generated by diversification. Armco, which had moved 33 percent of its business outside basic steel production, enjoyed a 3.4 percent return on sales compared to stiff losses suffered by other large steel companies.

Unfortunately, finding out-of-phase manageable alternatives is difficult at best. Two opposing problems underlie this difficulty. First, the environment—in spite of its vastness—presents decidedly few investment opportunities that exhibit negatively correlated performances. Consequently, planners must search widely to discover worthy avenues. But their expansive environmental exploration quickly encounters a second obstacle: to maintain the firm's comparative managerial advantage, they cannot stray too far from the enterprise's specialized expertise.

Planners seeking a sophisticated diversification should lean slightly toward a broad search, for most managers quite naturally concentrate on what they already know well. Such nearsighted entrepreneurial behavior spotlights only a few options, obscures many others, and blocks out still more possibilities completely (Cyert and March, 1963:101-13).

Severe diversification across markets and industries, while placing yet more strain on the enterprise's control structure, is commonly desired because firms in different industries supposedly exhibit still greater internal flexibility. "Thus a firm which sells refrigerators in the United States, the Common Market, and Japan has a higher flexibility than a solely domestic supplier" (Ansoff, 1965:56). Similarly, "a firm in electronics, biochemistry, and molecular optics would have a high degree of flexibility." Combined, the diversified activities should show a reduction of dispersion, i.e. risk, around the desired value of M.

However, remember that excessive or superfluous diversification captures less than the optimum risk reduction available. While the diversification may dampen the impact of any one venture's faltering (by offsetting management's random errors against its successes), the economy's "systematic" variability still remains to buffet the firm. At best, the naively diversified conglomerate's performance variability exactly matches the economy's fluctuations, and it will exhibit the same risk characteristics. At worst, the overdiversified conglomerate may find itself doing more poorly than the overall economy, having squandered its comparative advantage. Corporate-headquarters decision makers may well be overwhelmed, in spite of the loose interactivity connection, by the new industry and market variety and be unable to set the controllable variables at values that ensure satisfactory performance. Additional risks arise then from "management's inability to run" unrelated businesses and to correct the weaknesses of new acquisitions (Hrebiniak and Joyce, 1984:45). Moreover, the divisional managements are not likely to provide the requisite decision-making capacity, for they will have lost the necessary autonomy they once had as freestanding enterprises. Hence the overlarge conglomerate will not be able to buffer either the economy's longer-run fluctuations or the many higher-frequency shocks buffeting its individual businesses. Performance will be substandard. A study of 246 companies listed on the *Fortune* 500, for instance, revealed that for the period between 1949 and 1969 unrelated diversification failed "to reduce the variability of the firm's earning stream" (Rumelt, 1974:103). In addition, conglomerates with "aggressive programs for the acquisition of new unrelated businesses" (p. 32) had to assume added risk and use borrowed funds "to boost a below average return on capital to an above average return on equity" (p. 151).

On the other hand, sophisticated (countercyclical) diversification provides a firm with more variety than its environment has and enables it to experience less riskiness (i.e. variability) in its performance than the large conglomerate experiences. Under these fortunate circumstances, not only are management errors reduced or canceled, but, in addition, some of the economy's fluctuations are absorbed. While this ideal is difficult to achieve, it may be approached when carefully focused firms pursue "concentric diversification" (Hrebiniak and Joyce, 1984:45) with new but related products. As such firms enter "only those businesses that build on, draw strength from, and enlarge some central . . . competence" (Rumelt, 1974:103–4), their competitive advantages are exploited and management overloads are avoided. Though often developing new products and entering new businesses, these companies "are loath to invest in areas . . . unfamiliar to management" (p. 104). Hence, "a central strength or skill spans all of their activities." These enterprises, "neither totally dependent upon a single business nor true multi-industry firms," are "unquestionably the best overall performers" (p. 150). They follow the dictum of Mark Twain's character Pudd'nhead Wilson not to "scatter your money and attention."

It is not surprising, then, to see more diversified enterprises reverse their diversification policies and contract their controlled domains. In the mid-to-late 1970s, firms as different as Bell and Howell, Gillette, and Playboy Enterprises all pruned sideline ventures to concentrate on their respective core enterprises (applied photography, low-cost repeat-purchase products, and magazine publishing). During the early 1980s, an era of billion-dollar mergers, spin-offs continued as well. Conglomerates assembled in the corporate-building days of the 1960s were uncoupled as their executives failed to master the expertise needed for dozens of disparate businesses. Disgruntled investors also shunned the conglomerate stocks because of their below-average returns. Ironically, by the mid-1980s many conglomerates were worth more as separate enterprises than as a single unit.

But why do some firms maintain their conglomerate strategies? While one may attribute this behavior to a mindless competition for sales volume, the conglomerate in fact may use its huge cash flows to excise critical decisions from the open political arena. Accordingly, performance improvements expected from heightened political influence might explain some expansions.

At present, there is little justification for allowing conglomerates to grow unchecked. Certainly the economy as a whole gains little in the way of improved managerial efficiency from these disparate and unintegrable mergers. Even the often-claimed improvement in the capital allocation process (over the stock market's delayed and distant regulation) becomes questionable when one reads of a corporate controller complaining of information overload and experiencing "difficulties in controlling the more than 120 profit centers of his company" (Hamermesh, 1977:125). Access to inside information offers only minor advantages when the detailed data cannot be analyzed properly because there are hundreds of divisional performance reports vying for the corporate officers' limited attention.

In addition, the continued diversification of a firm's investment portfolio forces significant changes in organizational structure. Movement from a single-industry enterprise to a multi-industry conglomerate necessitates a shift from a centralized (headquarters-dominated) structure to a more decentralized (division-controlled) framework. Such alterations may not appeal to cautious planners.

At this point, strategy issues and structural considerations begin to intertwine. So while structure follows strategy here as in Chandler's *Strategy and Structure*, the SDPC model goes further. Specifically, it shows why several structures may be tried for each strategy and how structure may influence strategy.

Briefly: In choosing the firm's strategy—i.e., in composing its controlled set of variables—the finance committee would strive to leave only low-frequency, low-dependency relationships spanning the firm/environment interface and would attempt to internalize within the firm the comparatively high-frequency, high-dependency relationships. Next, the executive committee would take these internally controlled variables and try to create the firm's organizational structure or decomposition scheme. Like the finance committee, the executive committee will endeavor to locate the firm's internal boundaries along the lowest-frequency, lowest-dependency cleavages available to it. But since the variable relationships spanning the internal boundaries generally fluctuate at higher frequencies than the corresponding relationships at firm/environment interface (see fig. 1-2), the executive committee can work faster than the finance committee. Simply put, the executive committee will get its feedback more quickly than the finance committee. Moreover, internally controlled structural arrangements are more easily revised than external strategic relationships, which must be negotiated with or sanctioned by external decision makers. Thus the executive committee will have sufficient time and control to try several structures for each finance-committee strategy.

And should a compatible structure still not be found after the several trials, structure must start to influence strategy. That is, the executive committee must petition the finance committee to alter its forthcoming strategic choices so that a viable structure may be developed. So just as structure follows strategy, strategy follows structure—albeit less frequently.

Once the finance committee shifts strategies, the executive committee would renew its search for the optimal structure. (This search for a compatible strategy/structure combination would proceed much as if a workable strategy/structure combination had been discarded for low performance.) Thus structure and strategy intertwine in a circular design process.

4

Organizing the Structure: Decomposing the Dependent and Independent Controlled Variables

While activities are being accumulated during the composition phase, the designers must develop a means for setting the associated controlled variables at their optimum values. Since C_i is generally far beyond any single group's cognitive capacity, the designers need to decompose, or separate, the controlled set of variables by assigning relatively independent subsets of these variables to particular decision centers.

Here, again, Ashby's law of Requisite Variety provides the designers with an important structuring criterion. In bounding any particular component, whether in the vertical or horizontal direction, designers must balance the control capacity of the unit's management team against that required by its decision variables. Although each decision center needs sufficient variety to counter both environmental disturbances and endogenous perturbations (emanating from inside the controlled set), the more variables its managers attempt to control with their fixed channel capacity, the less successfully they can control them. The designers must therefore strive to develop a decomposition scheme that simplifies the choices to be made by reducing the variety faced by any single unit.

In business policy terms, decomposing or factoring the controlled-variable set creates an *organizational structure* for the firm. "*Structure* can be defined as the design of organization through which the enterprise is administered" (Chandler, 1966:16); i.e., through which the decision variables are set at their optimum values.

Ideally, each group of decision makers nestled within the organization's structure would behave optimally with respect to the entire controlled-variable set as they manage their small portion of C_i's total variety. While this Churchman (1968a:1-16) ideal is unobtainable, an overall perspective can be approximated with a simplified decision-making structure.

Simplicity is achieved primarily by adopting a "nearly decomposable" (Simon and Ando, 1961) organizational structure. With such component decomposability, the highest-frequency, highest-dependency interactions are clustered within separated decision centers, leaving only low-frequency, low-dependency interactions connecting these segregated decision units. By isolating within components the most varying and tightest connections, the disruptions and disturbances ricocheting through the firm are minimized. Localizing turbulence, in turn, minimizes the variety that each unit must counter.

Concomitantly, over the short run, near decomposability allows each subordinate component to operate independently of its neighbors (Simon and Ando, 1961:132) and of the superior unit. With near decomposability, interunit connections are either approximately constant compared to the interactions within the components or, if variable, have relatively insignificant consequences. That is, interunit connections may be treated as parameters. And within the framework, or background, of these parameters, short-term decision making can proceed independently.

Over the long run, interunit dependencies may be adjusted by the superior unit without reference to each subordinate component's tightly coupled internal connections. These internal interactions may be ignored safely (Simon and Ando, 1961:122) because the long run provides sufficient time (decision cycles) for them to be in constant relationship, i.e. equilibrium. And with intraunit relationships in essentially a steady state, the superior unit need consider only a handful of slowly changing aggregate variables connecting the components. (From the short-run perspective, these variables are the previously mentioned parameters.)

With component decomposability, then, organizational functions can be separated both vertically in terms of time perspective and horizontally in terms of day-to-day specializations. Thus the central headquarters can focus on the firm's long-term interunit variables without concern for the short-term intraunit variables controlled by the host of subordinate components. Since the variables within each lower-level unit "move roughly proportionately," they "can be aggregated into indexes" (Simon and Ando, 1961:132). In turn, the superior unit can adjust the firm's long-term performance simply by using these (comparatively few) aggregate performance indicators as guidelines for varying the parametric (i.e., policy) relationships between it and each of the subordinate units as well as the long-term relationships and resource allocations among the subordinate units. The headquarters unit, for instance, can make successive budget allocations among the subordinate components without being concerned about their short-run, high-frequency internal fluctuations during the interim periods. What transpires within the subordinate units between the (low-frequency) periodic reallocations means little or nothing because their separability allows all to stabilize long before any operating budget cycle ends. All that matters to the central unit is each subordinate component's steady-state performance, given a particular resource allocation, and the interunit resource balance that will produce a satisfactory composite performance for the firm over a given operating cycle.

Each subordinate component, in turn, proceeds independently over the short run within the longer-range parameters imposed to satisfy the leading unit as well as its fellow operating components. Thus the subordinate units can concentrate on their particular subsets of day-to-day concerns, safely ignoring their neighbors' high-frequency decisions; many small management teams can be arrayed in parallel to handle the firm's repetitive, routine operating decisions.

Near decomposability among components also limits the variety load imposed on each management team. Although the central headquarters takes the long-run view, over which many variables may change, it need handle only the low-frequency variations. And although each subordinate component deals with the high-frequency fluctuations, it does so over the short-run when many variables remain constant. Overloads and errors thus become less likely. More important, a multilevel, multicomponent structure results—one capable of controlling numerous variables of diverse frequencies and interdependencies.

Because the headquarters unit not only must handle interunit connections but sometimes correct or even take over aspects of a subordinate component's decision making as well, even greater simplicity is desirable. Similarities among the subordinate components in performance measurement and causation, for instance, enable the central headquarters to improve their long-term performances because high-performing units serve as "ideal types" for low-performing units. Moreover, such similarities enable the central unit to set the subordinate components' more critical decision variables, since only a single conceptual model (with a few minor variations) is needed to understand all their operations.

Indeed, if the subordinate components are extremely similar (and admittedly somewhat less separable), as GM's auto divisions, considerable centralization becomes possible. Facing only minimal interdivisional variety, the headquarters unit has the opportunity to ensure that all the divisions perform well over the long run. Although the divisions continue to handle most short-term matters, they do so within tighter constraints. Hence, their long-term performances are more dependent on headquarters' decisions. Obviously, then, a corporate error could be catastrophic.

Who decides how centralized the firm should be? Ultimately, the executive committee. In fact, this group is charged with designing the firm's entire organizational structure; for, as mentioned in chapters 2 and 3, the executive committee typically acts as the pinnacle policy-planning group for the operating management.

As in composing the board of directors, the nominating committee must carefully select the members of the executive committee. One or two influential outside directors establish the committee's authority over the president, who, as the principal operating officer, chairs the body. The other inside members should come from the group executive and corporate staff positions. Choosing all these representatives from the major line and staff positions ensures that corporate policy is coordinated wisely so as not to overconstrain the divisions' decision makers, who generally are excluded from executive-committee membership.

Second-level managers should be prevented from dominating this committee for the same reason that inside directors should not dominate the corporate board: divisional managers cannot be trusted to act effectively as their own metacontrollers. Donaldson Brown, for instance, when at DuPont and later at GM, vehemently opposed the inclusion of division managers on the executive committee. Sloan (1964) likewise observed that divisional-management dominance here produced a horse-trading approach to the control of critical variables. In exceptional cases, however, one or two division managers from the most critical or best-performing units might be included for centralization or information purposes.

CREATING THE SUPERIOR COMPONENT

Centralization versus Decentralization

To the rationalist designer, "whose basic ontology is monism, the question as to whether [the organization] should be managed centrally or decentrally is trivial: centralization in principle is always required" (Churchman, 1978:61). Not surprisingly, then, many top-level executives only grudgingly delegate control to subordinate decision makers. ITT's Harold Geneen asserted, "If I had enough arms, legs, and time, I'd do it all myself" (Burns, 1974:19).

Variables assigned to the subordinate components become uncontrolled, or environmental, variables for the superior component that provides overall control. Therefore, it is possible for these variables to be set at detrimental values that generate too much variety for the central unit to counter successfully. Under these circumstances, the central unit becomes too *dependent* on its subordinate units over the long run.

But centralizing many variables within the superior component reduces the diversity of control and makes the firm more dependent on the single control unit. That is, the headquarters becomes too dependent upon itself. Should the central unit falter, the damage, rather than being isolated, would be disseminated throughout the controlled set. More important, Ashby's law instructs the designers that overloading variables onto the central headquarters (regardless of its close proximity to the clients and designers and its heightened corporate perspective) may damage performance even more. The proponents of decentralization would add that when a subordinate unit *constantly* performs to expectation it buffers the superior unit from many trivial short-run concerns.

Though a balance must obviously be struck between decentralization and centralization, the latter is the alternative preferred here. Still, assuming that the superior component's decision capacity is small relative to the controlled set of variables, the designers assign only the most important (i.e., long-term interactive, essential, and corrective) variables to it. Identification of these most essential variables (as noted in chapter 2) may be done *a priori* via the sensitivity analysis of the functional model $M = F(C_i, U_j)$, or it may be done empirically over multiple operating periods. The latter approach is likely to be politically advantageous to the designers, for it may be easier to remove variables from the subordinate components' jurisdictions after they have been shown to be inadequate controllers. Of course, should the capacity of the headquarters increase relative to the controlled set of variables, it will then expropriate more of the subordinate components' decision variables.

Methods of Centralization

Decision variety (and dependency) may be removed from the lower levels and placed with the central headquarters by having the latter set long-term policy parameters for the subordinate components. For example, acceptable ranges can be placed on a given variable: divisions of a firm can be given strict limitations on capital expenditure, inventory levels, or the like. In this situation, the corporate headquarters appropriates a portion of the variable's variety from the divisions and restricts the divisions' decisions to those areas having only short-range effects. The divisions now have fewer states (less variety) from which to choose in setting a variable, and the designers have diminished potentially damaging performance variations resulting from previously uncontrolled internal variety.

The designers also may remove the entire variable from the divisions, rather than just a portion of it. Divisions may no longer be permitted to select their own raw-material and supply sources; for instance, when significant economies of scale or improved purchasing practices can be had via centrally negotiated long-term contracts.

Another method of setting parameters is for the designers to grant *powers of control* (Ashby, 1956:214) such as goal specification and policy determination to the central headquarters and *powers of regulation* such as goal achievement and policy implementation to the divisions. With its power of control over a variable, the central headquarters specifies the value it is to assume, while the division regulates the variable so that it indeed assumes this value. In short, the corporate headquarters *premolds* the choices of lower-level managers via its "standing guides to . . . decisions: that is, policies" (Litterer, 1963:383). This arrangement makes the central unit less dependent on divisional mistakes; moreover, when the divisions operate within such long-term policy parameters, they may conduct their daily business affairs without corporate interference, i.e., with relative independence over the short run.

Designers also can expropriate whole vectors of variables from subordinate units. A legal department, a styling staff, or an engineering group, along with the multiple variables they control, may be removed from the divisions and placed in the central headquarters. At ITT, for instance, "the staffs had taken over some functions to the point of completely emasculating division management. Financial management and long-range planning were securely in staff hands. They also controlled the operations research, project management, and the market research" (Burns, 1974:62).

Further, the central headquarters may buffer itself from internal variety by setting variables that in turn fix many subsequent variable decisions. Ashby (1956:128) notes that many vectors (or sets) of variables exhibit dependency or constraint; that is, once the *dominant* (often aggregate) variables are fixed in value, many of the other variable settings are dictated or at least are highly limited. For example, if the corporate headquarters controls the cash resources of all its divisions, many divisional decisions will be restricted, for without cash it is impossible to stockpile inventory, hire personnel, build plants, or purchase machinery, except within the most narrow limits. Similarly, "if one set of decisions is made . . . about aggregate work force, production rate, and inventories, then these decisions can be used as constraints in making detailed decisions at subsidiary levels about the inventory or production of particular items" (Simon, 1964:18). Extending this analysis even further: By controlling a variable such as the aggregated production rate of the *final* division of a channel-integrated firm, the corporate headquarters may greatly constrain the decision variables of all the firm's divisions, since the final-product division interacts with all the variables.

Variety reductions, in conclusion, are achieved by constraint imposition.

Designers, by carefully selecting the variables to be constrained, can restrict many others indirectly through interactions that are, of course, constraints themselves.

Degrees of Centralization

The tightness of a vertical—or horizontal—couple can be measured *over the long run* in terms of the number and importance of the variables that are decided by one unit but that influence another's long-term performance. Thus a subordinate unit is said to be tightly coupled to, or dependent on, a superior unit that controls many variables which influence the subordinate unit's performance m_k. The unit is loosely coupled to, or relatively independent of, a superior unit that controls few of these variables. Similarly, the superior unit is said to be tightly coupled to a subordinate unit when the overall performance M is influenced greatly by the variables that are controlled by the subordinate unit; but it is loosely coupled to, or relatively independent of, a subordinate unit that controls few variables that significantly affect M.

In a given firm, the subordinate component that is most tightly coupled to the superior component is the one over which the superior component exerts the most influence. Similarly, the subordinate component to which the superior component is most tightly coupled is the one that controls the variables to which the aggregate performance M is most sensitive.

Designers should vary the tightness of the subordinate-to-superior unit coupling as a function of the tightness of the superior-to-subordinate unit coupling. More important contributors to the firm's performance should be more centrally directed or tightly coupled. (There is, however, a trade-off: the more intertwined components become, the more difficult it is to fix performance responsibility.) Less important subordinate units, on the other hand, should be permitted to operate relatively independently of the central headquarters unit to conserve decision capacity for the more important units.

To visualize these varying vertical connections, imagine an organizational chart where the spatial distance between the superior and each subordinate component illustrates the particular coupling's relative tightness or looseness. At GM, then, one would expect to find the Chevrolet Division tucked more closely under the corporate headquarters while the much less critical Delco-Remy Division dangled loosely at an appreciable distance.

Interfirm comparisons are also possible. Designers who pursue conservative strategies toward channel integration and product diversification can impose comparatively tight vertical couplings, while designers who follow expansive strategies specify, by necessity, loose vertical couplings for their structures. Controlled sets with much variety (many variables and/or variable states) must have looser vertical couplings than smaller businesses; they must be more decentralized than the smaller firms. Downs (1967) stated this in his law of Diminishing Control: *"The larger any organization becomes, the weaker is the control over its actions exercised by those at the top"* (p. 143). The top level may still control the same number of variables as before, but it now controls a relatively smaller proportion of the controlled-set variables. As firms grow, then, the long-term vertical couplings in both directions weaken. Subordinate-component performances become progressively decentralized from the superior component's intervention, and, since more of the subordinate components are contributing to the firm's performance, the superior component becomes relatively independent of any one subordinate component. Conglomerates, composed of many divisions each controlling numerous variables, survive because the corporate headquarters, relatively independent of each of its divisions' performances, need not attempt to control them intensely. At some point, ties weaken so much that the single firm fractures into many components that possess only the loosest affiliations, such as pooled dependencies stemming from the need to allocate such scarce common resources as managerial talent and investment dollars.

So in comparing the overall tightness between corporate headquarters and divisions at GM, DuPont, ITT, and Textron, for example, one could hypothesize that GM, with its limited product line, would exhibit more centralization than DuPont, given the latter's greater diversity of product and market. Still, DuPont's planners could centralize more than ITT's designers, since the conglomerate's myriad holdings enforced considerable decentralization on its corporate headquarters. Last, a conglomerate like Textron, with almost no corporate staff compared to ITT's, would be the most decentralized.

In turn, firms with structures that promote flexibility tend "also to pursue strategies relying on these management attributes"; whereas firms with structures that promote "tight control and production efficiency" tend to pursue "corresponding strategies" (Pfeffer, 1982:139). So designers wanting to avoid decentralized structures should build large corporate offices and eschew expansive diversification strategies as GM did in the 1920s and 1930s. Structure thus constrains strategy (Miles and Snow, 1978:7).

But even in the GM case one should expect the divisions to be relatively loosely coupled to the corporate headquarters compared with the subordinate units of a much smaller firm. This comparative long-term divisional independence stems from the large number of units found in the bigger corporation.

A phenomenon observable in the ongoing design of many organizations with fixed numbers of variables and states is a control transfer to the top of the organization: a centralization of decision making in the superior unit. First, such progressive centralization occurs because with increasing experience the top level learns to fix its controlled variables at their optimum values more quickly and continually switches the released channel capacity to controlling and/or regulating new variables previously attended to at lower levels. Second, once the designers begin to build it, the corporate headquarters tends to expand on its own. Corporate-staff executives, for instance, usually advocate greater control over the operating divisions "because they wish to perform their function better and because [greater control] increases their significance" (Downs, 1967:150). GM, not surprisingly then, had a minuscule corporate headquarters when Sloan assumed command in the early 1920s, but by 1964 this unit had absorbed almost "1 percent of the corporation's net sales" (Sloan, 1964:431).

The Subunits of the Superior Component

To handle the centrally controlled variables, specific decision-making groups and positions must be created in the central headquarters; namely, the president's office, the group executive positions, the corporate staffs, and the interdivisional committees. Figure 4-1 portrays the prototypical arrangement of these corporate-headquarters subunits for a nonconglomerate enterprise much like GM in the 1920s and 1930s.

The first corporate-level decision subunit created by the executive committee, naturally, would be the office of the president. This pinnacle subunit of the managerial hierarchy provides the executive committee with a supplemental source of decision-making capacity for handling more immediate matters. Hence the full executive committee, meeting relatively infrequently and taking longer to deliberate (given its broad membership), focuses on longer-term, lower-frequency policy decisions and presidential reviews. The president's office, in contrast, deals with those issues too minor and too pressing to warrant the delays associated with a full executive-committee meeting; i.e., shorter-term, higher-frequency problems requiring less consultation and fast solution.

But even when the president has a fairly large staff of immediate assistants, his or her channel capacity remains seriously inadequate, especially if the firm continues to expand its activity set. To overcome this problem, the president's staff itself needs to become hierarchical in structure. For example, similar operating divisions can be clustered and assigned to a group executive. "The capacity to supply requisite control at the top" is maintained by having these group executives, rather than the larger number of operating divisions, report directly to the president (Williamson, 1970:160). Ralph Cordiner (1952), a key General Electric (GE) designer, considered his group executives as "an extension of the mind and arms of the President, working closely with him, familiar with his aims, plans and organization concepts; and able to speak for him . . . to

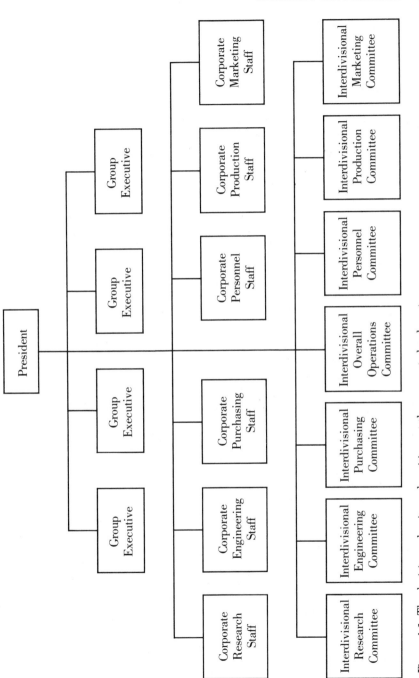

Figure 4-1. The decision subunits and positions at the corporate headquarters.

the Divisional or Departmental Operating Managers within their respective Groups" (p. 13).

The group-executive level in the hierarchy increases the distance from the president to the divisions, and lines of communication within the firm are extended, with predictable consequent losses of control (Williamson, 1970:160). Sloan of GM seems to have solved this problem early in his presidency by not filling the group-executive position designed to oversee GM's critical auto divisions; these vital units he kept directly under his own scrutiny. Thus GM's early group executives controlled only the less important parts and accessories divisions as well as the relatively minor foreign auto investments, thereby freeing more of Sloan's time for the key auto units.

A corporate president plus a handful of group executives alone cannot furnish adequate decision capacity for the variety load of the corporate headquarters. Consequently, "attachment of an elite staff to the general office is a vital adjunct in supplying the . . . requisite capacity" (Williamson, 1970:124). Typically, such a staff consists of subunits comparable to the division's functional subunits; for example, research, engineering, purchasing, personnel, production, and marketing. Not only does this corporate staff *advise* the line managers, but it also referees and *decides* many long-term intercomponent matters, since lower-level managers often feel obliged to accept the "advice" of elite staffs closely associated with the executive committee. Further enhancing this staff decision-making authority (as is shown more fully in chapter 6) is the fact that the corporate staff gathers information on and conducts audits of divisional operations. The corporate staff, in this regard, plays the exact same role for the executive committee and president that the financial staff plays for the finance committee (see chapters 2 and 3).

Finally, between the headquarters and subordinate levels the executive committee usually must establish intermediate decision subunits to set the (ideally few) variables that overlap subordinate-component boundaries. That is, groups of decision makers drawn from the concerned units must set those variables that jointly influence multiple subordinate components—the variables that make them dependent on one another over the long run.

Should a divisional decomposition scheme be adopted in a firm that produces a series of similar products, for instance, it likely will be necessary to use interdivisional committees, or coordination groups, to recoup any economies of scale that might get lost in research, engineering, purchasing, and the like because the divisional structure does not enable these low-frequency, loosely coupled connections to be made naturally.

One of the earliest examples of the successful design of such a *matrix* structure was Sloan's development in the early 1920s of GM's Interdivisional Committees. Eventually, these "intersect subunits" included committees for the functional areas of engineering, production, sales, advertising, and maintenance.

When DuPont still used a functional structure (after World War I), it discovered the need to employ a series of "product steering committees" to coordinate the *many* high-frequency, tightly coupled overlaps between its functional departments of purchasing, manufacturing, and sales (Chandler, 1966). Since these product-line intersect bodies proved far easier to manage than the functional departments themselves (because high-frequency, high-dependency interactions were kept within unit boundaries), they became the nuclei around which the DuPont planners built the firm's new product divisions.

In addition to GM's interdivisional functional subunits, Sloan instituted an Operations Committee, consisting of GM's Executive Committee members plus the general managers of the more critical auto, body, and parts divisions; this subunit coordinated and evaluated the divisions as a whole. Generally, such a corporate committee plays a vital role for the highly integrated or conservatively diversified firm in that it establishes a forum in which overlapped variables may be set at mutually satisfactory parametric values, thereby separating the divisions' high-frequency decision making.

The selection of participants for these intercomponent decision groups also affects the firm's centralization, for through such groups, headquarters decision makers can extend still further their influence over the subordinate components. If the intercomponent decision bodies are composed primarily of corporate executives, the joint variables tend to be controlled centrally. Furthermore, should the participants exhibit major power and status differences, central control again increases; subordinate-component participants are unlikely to exert much influence in the shadow of prominent headquarters officials. And the central headquarters gains added sway when corporate line and staff executives hold key chair and secretary positions, since they then handle the committee's higher-frequency decisions between meetings. Thus the hand of centralized control is likely to penetrate into the subordinate units via the intercomponent decision groups.

SEPARATING THE SUBORDINATE COMPONENTS

Boundaries among the firm's subordinate units should be drawn so as to create subordinate-component decision sets that promote: (a) control diversity, (b) performance commensurability, (c) causal comparability, and, of course, (d) component decomposability. In organizations where these simplifying characteristics are achieved, the designers reduce to a minimum the internal variety they and their decision makers must face.

Control Diversity

Control diversity—spreading the controlled variables among numerous decision centers—is advantageous for three reasons. First, to protect the firm's overall performance, designers do not want any subordinate component to dominate the corporate fate. Should such a component's decision makers err, the damage to M would be substantial. Hence, by diversifying control internally, the planners decouple the superior component from a particular subordinate component's mistakes. Second, with a small number of variables under the control of a single component, the probability of error decreases, given the reduced potential for overloaded decision capacity. And third, should an error occur, the central headquarters can intervene quickly when the unit is small and easily understood.

To allow a heightened concentration on operations and to improve the promise of increased returns, for instance, the SCM Corporation in 1976 split its Glidden-Durkee Division into four geographically dispersed units: coatings and resins, food, chemical-metallurgical, and organic chemicals. Similarly, in the late 1970s, when IBM carved the sizable unit making its medium- and large-size computers into two separate divisions, the firm stressed that the split would provide additional management focus.

Any design team faces, however, a definite upper limit on the amount of control diversification obtainable. First, breaking the controlled set into many components significantly increases the communication linkages required (in later design stages). Worse yet, insurmountable communication difficulties can result from subdividing highly dependent variable sets. Second, when the controlled set of variables is broken into too many components, the central headquarters must spend more time in switching its attention among units than in improving their performances. Under such circumstances, the scarce attention capacity of the central headquarters (Simon, 1973:270) will be squandered needlessly.

Ideally, the designers would assign each of the n activities included in the controlled set during composition to an individual and unique subordinate component that, along with the superior component, is responsible for its performance.

The n activities usually set the upper bound for the number of subordinate units but not always for the lower. Economies of scale often tempt designers to group more than one activity within a subordinate component. Whenever this is done, the economies obtained must outweigh the potential damage arising from reduced control diversity.

Finally, it is easier to achieve control diversity with divisional structures than with functional forms, especially where there are many product or service activities. With the divisional structure, each activity can be assigned its unique product division. Simply put, the divisionally organized firm is amenable to a *finer subdivision* than is the functionally structured business.

Performance Commensurability

In separating the controlled set into subordinate components, designers must employ decomposition schemes that maintain performance commensurability (see chapter 3). By providing a single performance measure for both the firm and the components, the designers greatly reduce the variety with which they and the headquarters decision makers must deal. The single performance indicator enables many decisions across numerous components to be normalized and *summarized* simply, and it permits easy comparisons among units for purposes of identifying future performance-improvement possibilities.

Not all horizontal decomposition schemes cluster variables so as to be coincident with such commensurability efforts. In business firms, functional structures do not yield commensurable performances, while divisional structures do (Williamson, 1970:132). For instance, divisional factorizations permit easy mapping of resource benefits and costs onto a particular component via its product: each product division thus becomes a "profit center" and—as was noted by an early GM designer, Albert Bradley (1927:424)—an "*investment center.*" The combination, of course, yields a series of highly commensurable ROI focal points. Functional structures, in contrast, confuse the picture. Should a given revenue or expenditure item be allocated to manufacturing or marketing? More important, how can the cost-incurring capital-intensive production department be compared to the revenue-generating low-investment sales unit? Or even within the manufacturing component alone, how can the designers be expected to separate capital investments for the various products (Chandler, 1966:121)?

Furthermore, functional specialization makes it difficult to evaluate contributions to component performance, inasmuch as markets rarely exist between the functionally decomposed units. In contrast, product divisions of firms are readily treated as profit centers. The output market for the product sold by the division can be used to evaluate the revenue contributed by the division's activity, and the input markets can be used to evaluate the cost to the client of the division's activity. Since all the economy's (input and output) markets are interconnected, divisional activities are judged against a single externally referenced performance scale. The product-line decomposition, then, generates a set of components with readily and objectively commensurable performances.

Causal Comparability

Designers, in attempting to achieve performance commensurability, are concerned primarily with *output* comparability. In contrast, when they direct their attention to causal similarity, their concern is with performance *inputs*. That is, planners want to achieve comparability in the *ways* the various subordinate components achieve their performances. They attain such input similarity: (a) by composing each component with a similar subset of controllable c_i (and uncontrollable u_j) vector(s) of variables, as well as the same function f_k for converting these inputs into the performance output m_k; and (b) by measuring the states of these variables via uniform accounts and procedures.

What advantages accrue from the designers' attempt to establish causally similar subordinate units? There are several. The first advantage is that if the *cognitive* span of control is only one, designers can enforce tighter vertical couplings throughout the firm because the actual variety across the component units is extremely low. After all, the planners and superior-unit decision makers need only understand a *single model* for all their subordinate units. Stated more formally, variety is low across a series of causally similar components because they all take on identical variable states; thus potential interunit differences become unvarying parameters for the superior component. And since repetitiveness among units is high and variety low, the head has the capacity to set a large proportion of the controlled set of variables, assuring that many longer-range decisions are made from a corporate-wide perspective with the clients' well-being intimately in mind. Hence high causal similarity permits increased centralized control should it be desired. At GM, for instance, the extremely strong similarity among its principal auto-producing units—Chevrolet, Pontiac, Buick, Oldsmobile, and Cadillac—enabled the Sloan-Brown team to direct centrally a large number of decisions, which in a more diverse organization would have been left of necessity to the divisions.

At lower levels of priority where comparatively unimportant decisions are typically decentralized, high causal similarity still permits easy corporate-office intervention should long-term divisional performances go awry. In other words, since each component operates much like its neighbors, corporate management can switch attention among units swiftly to correct unwanted deviations. Even the large number of components required for control diversity are easily managed, given that only a single conceptual model, with minor variations, explains all their behavior. Thus top management's scarce attention capacity is conserved.

Causal comparability also eases the work of the subordinate-component decision makers. From their poor vantage point below the superior unit, executives for the respective subordinate components (i.e., division managers) have difficulty in assuming the corporation-wide perspective. But the work is easier when all other components look similar to theirs. When the other units are *mirror images* of their own (that is, what is controllable to them is uncontrollable to the others and what is uncontrollable to them is controllable to another), they can readily visualize how their variable settings aid or hinder other components' long-term performances.

Similarity among the subordinate components also means that managers can be moved easily among units. This increased flexibility lessens personnel and training problems (see chapter 5) and facilitates internal communication (see chapter 6).

A final advantage of high causal similarity is that long-term performance-improvement information may be discovered and tested through comparisons among components that serve as control and experimental units for each other. As variable-by-variable comparisons among units uncover mostly interunit constancies or parameters, the influence of one or a few intercomponent variations may be readily isolated and analyzed (Smelser, 1976:154). Thus if "similarities" between pairs—or better yet, among whole sets—of components exist "when solving certain problems concerning one . . . , the other . . . of the pair can be used, and vice versa. In such cases one . . . is said to be a model of the other" (Klir, 1965:37). The variable states observed in the *exceptionally good* units can be replicated in the *exceptionally bad* components.

Designers and central-office decision makers may construct *planned experiments* by instituting designed variations among components, or they may discover *serendipity findings* by permitting natural variations (not instituted by designers or central decision makers) to determine the variable states that yield the highest subordinate-component performances. Although organizational planners cannot achieve the isolation that classical scientists demand for their experiments, quasi-experimental comparisons may be advantageous where designers encounter much uncertainty and have no *a priori* model to optimize the components' performances.

One of the DuPont Company's early designers, Hamilton Barksdale, consciously employed this *"comparative analysis"* (Dale and Meloy, 1962:145) in setting corporate policies. For instance, on encountering a problem, Barksdale frequently compared the experience of the different plants, studied them for relevance, culled them for comparability, and then adapted them as necessary to solve the current problem. Later, he or his staff summarized these comparisons to distill guideposts for solving future problems and setting policy guidelines.

In light of these component-similarity advantages, it becomes natural to ask: What decomposition schemes promote high causal comparability? Divisional structures yield higher causal comparability than functional structures. Arrays of divisions are highly similar, for each division—composed of subunits such as engineering, purchasing, production, and marketing departments—looks much like every other division. The causal similarity can grow startlingly strong when the divisions all produce closely comparable products, such as lines of automobiles. Functional structures, on the other hand, yield poor causal comparability among components because engineering is very different from marketing, and so on.

While divisional structures engender high intercomponent similarity, they yield poor intracomponent comparability, since each division circumscribes subsets of highly dissimilar variables. More concretely, a given division within a firm typically will be composed of such disparate subunits as engineering, purchasing, production, and marketing departments. Conversely, functional factorizations result in high intracomponent comparability; each subunit within a given component bears a close resemblance to its immediate neighbors. Engineering for Product One, for example, is likely to be very similar to engineering for Product Two, especially where the products are highly comparable themselves. (Once products begin to differ, however, even a functional structure generates only limited intracomponent similarity.)

Hence, with a divisional decomposition, comparability gained across the product divisions must be traded for similarity lost among the functional departments composing each division. With a functional factorization, on the other hand, comparability achieved within the functions must be bought via similarity relinquished among them. In the large multiproduct firm, designers typically choose the divisional structure. The early DuPont designers, one of the first planning teams to encounter this intercomponent-versus-intracomponent-simplicity trade-off, recognized that rather than joining similar functional activities within a component, they often had to combine related but dissimilar efforts. For example, "while the production of dyes is quite unlike the sale of dyes, nevertheless the union between them is so close that union is *more economical* than segregation" (Dale, 1957:49).

In sum, designers desire their simplicity *across* components rather than within components because the variety-reduction advantages at the corporate level greatly outweigh the advantages at the component level. *In short, intercomponent simplicity is preferred to intracomponent simplicity.*

Component Decomposability

Underlying the above analysis, of course, is the assumption that the components are "nearly decomposable" (Simon, 1969:105). Once again, component separability *greatly* simplifies the work of the designers and their superior- and subordinate-component decision makers.

With the presence of high-frequency, high-dependency interactions, on the other hand, complexity, confusion, and chaos abound. Though organization charts with myriad dots, dashes, and other graphic variations may be used to describe the relationships, every decision made ramifies almost endlessly and unknowably throughout the organization (Emery, 1969:23). Not surprisingly, then, it becomes difficult to distinguish the superior performance of a component from aggressive suboptimization. "Moreover, even when superior performance can be recognized, assigning quantitative importance to it in terms of profit may be virtually impossible" (Williamson, 1970:151).

But with nearly decomposable sets of variables the designers and their decision makers can readily determine the effect of a change in a component and its effect on the performance of the whole. "A system S is [completely] *separable* with respect to some part if the measure of effectiveness of the part is independent of the states of the other parts. This means that whatever happens to the other parts, this part's contribution remains invariant" (Churchman, 1971:53). So the more the components are separable with respect to their individual measures m_k, the more straightforward becomes the relationship between their summarizing performance measures, $m_1 \ldots m_k \ldots m_n$, and the overall M. The optimum value of M, therefore, can be obtained by simply optimizing the individual measures without worry about raising m_1 at the expense of m_2. A minimal number of cross-connections exist.

The design group, then, wishes to create a series of relatively "self-contained" components, each with its own "socially meaningful goal" (Simon, Smithburg, and Thompson, 1950:268). Such loosely coupled components are termed *"unitary organizations."*

To achieve a loosely coupled horizontal decomposition, the planning team "assigns to a single branch of the hierarchy all the tasks, and only those tasks, connected with an independent objective. This provides a high degree of independence, and thus reduces the amount of coordination required" (Emery, 1969:23). Consequently, intracomponent linkages are generally stronger than intercomponent linkages (Simon, 1969:109).

Viewed in terms of variable interaction frequencies, the planners should find the least-frequently interacting linkages among the firm's possible decision sets and draw the internal administrative boundaries through these cleavages. Hence, after decomposition—as with composition where high-frequency interactions were kept largely within the firm and only low-frequency connections were allowed to transgress the environmental boundary—the highest-frequency interconnections will be lodged mostly within the separate components, and only the low-frequency interactions will traverse the components' perimeters. Thus the firm's resultant structure will contain tight pockets of high-frequency interactions connected by comparatively weak strands of low-frequency interactions.

Divisional structures usually approximate these conditions; the tightly coupled functional subunits within each division demand and receive a frequently coordinated, simultaneous decision-set solution, while the loosely coupled product divisions create few overlapped or interconnected decision clusters. Functional structures for multiproduct firms, in contrast, do not have loose intercomponent couplings.

But finding the desired cleavages in the controlled-variable set is not always easy, as DuPont executives learned around 1920, when they tried running a multiproduct firm with a functional structure. Indeed, DuPont's 1920 shift from the functional to the divisional form hinged on its decision makers' inability to coordinate the high-frequency, high-dependency interactions. As the firm diversified after World War I, interdepartmental coordination worsened. The production and sales staffs grew distant and failed to coordinate product development. Of a more immediate nature, DuPont's purchasing, manufacturing, and sales departments made estimates and set schedules independently (Chandler, 1966:111). Once adopted, the divisional structure quickly alleviated these managerial problems and replaced losses with significant profits.

The multidivision organizational form easily has become the most widely adopted decomposition scheme among large multiproduct American corporations. Clearly, the divisional structure allows the firm's components to operate on their own for the longest time interval.

Nevertheless, the divisional structure alone does not ensure a loosely coupled factorization. Still other separating steps must be taken. For instance, market-referenced transfer pricing may be required to clarify interdivisional boundaries: control of the critical price variables is transferred to the markets (i.e., shifted toward or into the uncontrollable set) so as to improve boundary definition around the divisions. In this way, a large organization can be made nearly equivalent to a large number of separate activities whose connections are substantially as weak as those of unrelated firms (Arrow, 1964). Perfectly competitive markets, of course, separate divisional bargaining interactions most completely, but even then the transfer price still influences all concerned units. Thus market mechanisms cannot separate divisions completely in the long run, but they can clarify their controllable/uncontrollable boundaries over the short run. And in terms of the quantities transferred between units, markets can help absorb any *momentary* (i.e., short-term) production overages for the supplying units and can help fill any temporary supply shortages for the consuming units. Here, again, the market serves as a short-term decoupling mechanism.

All couplings among components, then, need not be internal to the firm. "For example, one product department of a decentralized company may engage in practices that harm the reputation of the entire company, affecting the sales of all other departments" (Emery, 1969:22-23).

Several boundary-location strategies are available to reduce such external interactions. All of them attempt to position the components in separated or loosely connected environments. Designers can locate divisions in different geographical areas so they do not interact through such input markets as labor and transportation. In extremely diversified firms the output markets are usually separated; their interconnections, for the most part, are weak and are related to the general economy. Less diversified firms' output markets are often relatively tightly coupled, tightest where all products dump into a single market. Yet even here designers can reduce interactions through placing the similar products in different price classes, or market segments, so customers come to view them separately.

Note that designers here must trade comparability for decomposability. Comparability requires that components have similar controllable and uncontrollable variables influencing their performances. In short, they should all exist in exactly the same environments. Unfortunately, that placement tightly couples them. Accordingly, one could expect GM's strikingly similar auto divisions to be highly comparable but less separable, while DuPont's somewhat dissimilar divisions should be less comparable but more completely separable.

While certain horizontal decompositions (e.g. the divisional) and certain boundary-clarification techniques (e.g. market segmentation) result in relatively loose couplings across component boundaries, some connections always remain. These leftover linkages the designers will want to weaken, or *decouple*. Decoupling simply means reducing the impact of interactions remaining after the internal decomposition—or external definition and composition—boundaries have been drawn. It is achieved by converting the interacting variables into long-term parameters.

Emery (1969) describes such a decoupling effort as the "standardization of interfaces" (p. 26). Two common examples of this effort are the adoption of common data formats throughout a firm and the creation of standardized parts specifications for materials being transferred between channel-integrated divisions. In the latter case, for instance, the supplying unit insulates the rest of the organization from its own internal variations by always holding its delivered product to specifications. Accordingly, such temporary constants lengthen the time period between component interactions (p. 26). Standardization, in general then, erects "walls of constancy" around the firm's components and keeps the high-frequency interactions isolated within the relatively independent components. And should a high proportion of such overlapped variables "go constant," the whole firm can be temporarily equivalent to a set of unconnected components (Ashby, 1966:169).

One should note that while standardized interfaces reduce the horizontal couplings among components, they usually tie these subordinate components more closely to the superior unit. To induce several interacting divisions to adopt standardized parts, for instance, the corporate headquarters often must fix the specifications initially or, at a minimum, occasionally oversee the negotiations. Hence looser horizontal couplings achieved through standardized interfaces generally induce slightly tighter vertical linkages; i.e., greater centralization.

Finally, to diminish the sensitivity of any dependencies remaining among serially or circularly connected components, designers can use component *slack*—namely, flexibility, or the lack of constraint—in certain critical variables under the component's control (Galbraith, 1973:24). Buffer inventories, for example, cushion high-frequency or short-term differences between a unit's input and output rates, negating the need for external coordination so long as the deviations fall within the prescribed limits (Emery, 1969:26). Similarly, high-variety flexible resources such as multipurpose machinery provide for a further desensitization. Whereas specialized machines might operate more cheaply on a given job, general-purpose equipment readily handles a variety of jobs received from either the internal or external environments. Moreover, increased fixed-capital investment for a division can make excess productive capacity available for periods of high demand. And when the production-level variable does range over a broad band of values, such increased adaptability, or variety, within each component allows it "to absorb minor random disturbances so that they are not propagated very far from their source" (p. 27).

However, when variables *within* a component approach the limits of their ranges or just "freeze up, danger results because they are then unavailable to absorb changes occasioned by normal fluctuations" (Weick, 1979:78). This absence of slack reduces the component's "capacity to absorb some of the buffeting from the environment." And without such flexibility, each component "is likely to be extremely sensitive to random shocks, and a slight deviation from plans may cascade into larger and larger deviations" (Emery, 1969:27), which are disseminated throughout the firm's many components.

In sum, slack decouples components by ensuring that all units have sufficient variety to counter any internal or external disruptions. And since all units should exhibit improved performance stability, they in turn will impose minimal variety loads on their neighbors. Slack then severs the firm's internal decision-making structure into a series of easily managed independent components.

This analysis assumes, of course, that the components' managers use their decision-making latitude to contain rather than create performance-deviation problems for neighboring units. To avoid the latter possibility and, more important, to ensure their adequacy for the task at hand, the decision makers must be properly oriented, educated, and selected.

Accordingly, the executive committee now yields to the subordinate bonus and salary committee that fills the various roles or positions specified in the firm's structure. Since individual executives can be shifted more rapidly than structural arrangements, the bonus and salary committee will have several chances to find the right managerial group for any particular structure devised by the executive committee. If after these successive trials the bonus and salary group cannot discover or develop the requisite talent, the executive committee then must reorganize the firm's structure so it demands less from the managers available. Should the executive committee, after several attempts, not uncover a simplified structure appropriate to the firm's talent, the finance committee must formulate a less ambitious strategy. So while the large enterprise must avoid the hopelessly complex task of designing its structure or strategy around individual executives, their common limitations cannot be ignored.

But before resorting to structural or strategic modifications, the firm will first want to increase management's capabilities so that it is most able to handle the structure's demands and, in turn, the environment's variety. To accomplish these ends, the comparatively small bonus and salary committee must greatly amplify its decision-making power.

5

Training the Decision Makers: Amplifying Regulatory Capacity over the Dependent and Independent Controlled Variables

When designers decompose their controlled set of variables into a series of loosely coupled and similar components, they greatly simplify the performance-control problem. Since each component is relatively small and independent, the decision makers can quickly master its short-term operation. The similarity among components further helps the central-headquarters and subordinate-unit managers deal with the longer-run dependencies among their units, since all can quickly comprehend how they might improve (or impair) the long-term performances of neighboring units and thereby the firm as a whole. More important, the designers can treat the relatively independent yet comparable components *en masse*. Since the components are separate but quite similar, mass orientation and education schemes can provide the proper value and factual premises for both corporate and divisional decision makers. With mass orientation and education programs the clients and designers can deal with far fewer variables—i.e., have their control vectors shrunk—yet still achieve detailed and continuous performance control; their control is amplified. Careful selection of corporate and divisional decision makers who either possess the desired value and factual premises or attain them quickly further amplifies performance control.

Why do policy planners want to amplify their regulatory powers? "After all, what any one individual can accomplish is not great, but through the power of organization the effect of a few may be multiplied almost indefinitely, especially if the few have the capacity for real leadership" (Sloan, 1941:155). Shortly after taking over as GM's president, Sloan (1924) wrote: "My office force is very small. That means that we do not do much routine work with details. They never get up to us. I work fairly hard, but it is on exceptions [less-repetitive policy issues] or construction [long-term organizational design], not on routine or petty details" (p. 195). Hence Sloan needed to amplify his decision-making power by training a host of lower-level decision makers to handle GM's many high-frequency decisions in his stead.

Ashby (1956) has shown that when performance regulation is achieved in hierarchical stages—that is, when a group of designers act so as to create a series of lower decision makers—the possibility arises that the decision makers may be of a regulatory capacity greater than the designers alone. Thus an amplification of regulation is achieved. *"The provision of a small regulator at the first stage may lead to the final establishment of a much bigger regulator"* (Ashby, 1956:268).

Regulatory amplification results from removing the designers from the primary high-frequency control cycles, where their channel capacity is inadequate to handle the large controlled set's variety, to a level where they need infrequently design, monitor, and redesign (if necessary) the component decision makers. In any amplification of regulation, of course, the designers are really achieving only a supplementation of their capabilities by "robbing" some easily available and abundant source of decision capacity (Ashby, 1956:267). For an example of the control-amplification concept, consider the modern digital computer, now a mainstay of practically all large organizations. This device solves many complex problems quicker than people can, and it can grind out the solutions for repetitive decisions without tiring. Even more to the point, its myriad binary decision circuits quickly handle computational and storage tasks that once were humanly intractable. Thus the electronic computer, like the properly motivated and thoroughly trained executive, increases the variety of choices open to the organization; it amplifies decision capacity.

Since the act of designing the components' regulators (whether electronic or human) is essentially an act of communication from the designers to the decision makers, "and the principles of communication theory apply to it" (Ashby, 1956:253), the designers' channel capacity must be considered. Designers achieve an amplification of control only when it requires less of their communicating and computing capacity to design, monitor, and redesign component decision makers than to design and control their components directly; that is, *when there is a contraction of the controlled set of variables into a much smaller set of training-related variables.*

For example, assume the designers construct a controlled set of variables, consisting of twenty-five similar components, numbered 1 through 25. Each component encompasses c_i variables that must be fixed at their optimum values. Leaving nothing to chance, the designers begin by gathering all pertinent data concerning the decisions necessary to regulate component 1's variable set c_i. Then they fix each of the c_i variables at the predicted optimum value. Now, if components 2 through 25 differed from component 1, the planners would need to repeat this expensive process until all $24c_i$ remaining variables were fixed. However, since the first matches the successive once the designers determine the optimal values of the variables of 1, they have also found the optimal settings for all $24c_i$ variables of the other units. All the designers need do now is to ensure via decision-maker orientation, education, and selection that the other 24 components do, in fact, take on the same variable settings.

Decomposability, or in Ashby's terms, "reducibility," of the controlled set is critical here. Ashby (1956) draws "the conclusion that if a responsible entity [the planning group] is to design (i.e. select) a machine to act as regulator to a very large system, so that the regulator itself is somewhat large, the achieving of the necessary selection within a reasonably short time is likely to depend much on whether the regulator can be made in reducible form" (p. 262). The information-handling and decision-computing capacity necessary for the individual component decision makers, in a nearly decomposable controlled set, is much smaller than the capacity needed to handle the controlled set in its entirety. Moreover, many small, easily designed decision units can be compounded readily to create one large composite control unit.

With a tightly coupled controlled set, on the other hand, small control units cannot be created for the components, nor can they be accumulated simply into a single unified controller because of their many interactions. Building such a controller would require as much design attention from the designers as would regulating the controlled set directly. Therefore, no amplification of control results.

Not only should the controlled set be decomposable, but, in addition, the component decision processes must be repetitive. When decision processes are repetitive, designers can create a series of regulators that "once built, . . . will carry out a regulation of indefinite length" with only infrequent design intervention (Ashby, 1956:251).

Regulation processes can be repetitive along two dimensions: over time and across components. Obviously, if the regulation is temporarily repetitive a great amplification results: a single design effort produces an extended period of regulation. Amplification also results if the design and regulation processes can be extended across repetitive or similar components. If regulation processes are extended both over time and across components, a single design process can be repeated to create hundreds of similar performance regulators operating over many future cycles.

Still greater amplification of the designers' control powers occurs when all component regulators are designed and built simultaneously; that is, during a single *mass* communication process. Examples of such situations include the college classroom, the managerial-trainee program, or on-the-job training of decision makers via committee meetings.

In these and similar group educational settings, the participants learn *standardized* decision rules or processes. Once mastered, such generally applicable methods are usable time and again in unit after unit at an extremely high frequency.

Not only can organizational decision-making roles be repetitive across components within a particular firm, but they can also be similar across numerous businesses. Consequently, "employees find that their training is applicable in many organizations and that they can go from one to another" (Simon, Smithburg, and Thompson, 1950:369). Given this interorganizational similarity, still other organizations, like universities, can specialize in training and selecting society's decision makers. Thus "general knowledge is acquired chiefly by pre-entry training in the schools. Organizations hire people already trained in economics, engineering, medicine, law, or biology; they do not create them by post-entry training" (p. 372).

The United States Forest Service, for instance, like most modern technically oriented organizations, relies almost exclusively on the country's colleges and universities to train its Ranger recruits. Graduate foresters' common technical tools, lore, and body of knowledge in a sense build into them appropriate behaviors. "Their receptivity to agency directives is thus produced not only by the constraints upon them, but also by the education and training which results in their wanting to do of their own volition what they are formally required to do" (Kaufman, 1960:166).

Designers of specific organizations, fortunately then, can avail themselves of the training and selection processes that go on within the larger society. And by hiring externally trained engineers, economists, statisticians, accountants, managers, and the like, business firms *import* much of the decision variety needed to regulate successfully their internally controlled variables. Accordingly, society's vast educational establishment supplies a wellspring of choice capacity from which properly designed enterprises amplify, or supplement, their principal designers' and top decision makers' regulatory capacity.

But society's educational institutions cannot possibly tailor their necessarily general products to the exact needs of a given organization. So attention now is turned to the designers' postentry creation of the firm's decision makers: in particular, their value orientation, factual education, and selection. These design activities ensure that the decision makers possess the appropriate internal constraints. That is, the "internalization" of influence "injects into the very nervous systems of the organization members the criteria of decision that the organization wishes to employ. The organization member acquires knowledge, skill, and identifications or loyalties that enable him to make decisions, by himself, as the organization would like him to decide" (Simon, 1965:103). As Simon points out, the designers must infuse their managers with both value and factual premises. While the distinction between the two sometimes blurs, because value and factual premises cascade in means-ends—i.e., hierarchical—chains, basically value premises instill managers with objectives, or decision rules (Ansoff, 1965:38), which fix attention on particular concerns to the exclusion of other values. Accordingly, value premises restrict the decision makers' vision by focusing their attention on one value framework. Similarly, factual premises require the decision makers to make *preformed* decisions (Kaufman, 1960:91). Hence factual premises exclude certain variable settings from the decision makers' freedom of action (Ansoff, 1965:38).

The firm's personnel plans for decision makers and managers lie in the domain of the board of directors' bonus and salary committee. Besides setting the enterprise's policy regarding stock bonuses and options, the bonus and salary group should oversee the firm's salary structure, especially as it applies to the uppermost managerial positions. Unless board members *closely* associated with the investors set these salaries, management might displace the firm's primary beneficiaries. The bonus and salary group will also want to supervise the firm's investment in educating its decision makers about the correct factual premises for their choices, since the annual training budget can be a multimillion dollar investment. Such outlays support a host of instructional endeavors, beginning with entry-level training sessions and ending with executive-development programs from which a few senior corporate officers eventually emerge. The last charge of the bonus and salary committee is to select the organization's chief leaders. As with regulating the firm's motivational and educational schemes, "choosing and removing top leadership is a way of controlling indirectly all delegated decisions: decisions on policies and on choice of other leaders who are appointed by top leaders" (Lindblom, 1977:148).

VALUE ORIENTATION

First and most important, the personal value structures of the firm's decision makers must be oriented to the clients' value premises. In essence, the designers must induce every decision maker to decide as the owner would if placed in the same position, with the same information. So "if the decision maker's intentions are not 'good,' . . . the designer's role will be to try to change the decision maker, i.e., to change his value structure" (Churchman, 1971:48).

"The organization's objective [M] is the central value that members must accept if the organization is to succeed (Simon, Smithburg, and Thompson, 1950:371). Why must subordinate decision makers be oriented not only to their own component's performance measure but also to the firm's overall performance measure? "The necessity for indoctrinating those at lower levels with general purposes" stems from the desire to keep all decision makers "cohesive and able to make the ultimate detailed decisions coherent" (Barnard, 1966:233). More specifically, since it is always impossible to separate or decouple completely the components of a formal organization in the long run, decision makers must come to realize that their actions, even though they may increase the performance of their particular units, are inappropriate unless they increase the overall M. For an example of this suboptimization problem, consider the case of U.S. Steel shortly after its formation in 1901: "The management of each constituent company troubled itself solely about the success of its own particular unit and took no interest in the success of the other subsidiaries or of the corporation as a whole" (Cotter, 1916:36). Within U.S. Steel in its early days, then, competition dominated cooperation wherever units interacted.

Moreover, in firms with similar components innovative decision makers must be willing to share with participants outside their immediate unit any variable settings capable of improving the long-term performances of other components and, in turn, M. At the newly formed U.S. Steel, as was to be expected, "secrets of economy . . . discovered by those in charge of a furnace or mill were rigidly guarded as giving an advantage over [internal] competitors; all of which did not contribute to a general high average of efficiency and economy" (p. 41).

Thus the designers must motivate the principal subordinate-component decision makers, like the superior-component decision makers, to assume—as much as possible—a corporate perspective in their decision making. One way to encourage a long-term view of the clients' interest is to make the decision makers "surrogate clients" (Churchman, 1978:63). Creating an identity of interest between clients and managers acknowledges that to have managers function well in their area of decision making they must be rewarded appropriately.

As a consequence, when pursuing their own interests, they will be pursuing the larger clientele's also, and they will be less concerned with narrow, parochial views. Where a corporation's client is envisioned as the stockholder, key decision makers can be tied closely to the clients' interests by making them stockholders also, via stock-option bonus plans.

The principal designer of GM's and DuPont's early motivational schemes, John Raskob (1927:130), attributed to Andrew Carnegie the idea of making a firm's principal executives partners with the owners. With Carnegie's business as its main subsidiary, U.S. Steel, too, adopted Carnegie's "owner-manager" approach: "to make the interests of the corporation, the controlled company and the individual worker identical." The scheme, known as the Stock Subscription and Profit Sharing Plan, was designed "to interest employees in the Steel Corporation as a whole," not just in their own subsidiary; "to give them an incentive . . . to reduce expenses and correspondingly increase profits"; and "to offer them an inducement to stay with the corporation and identify themselves with it" (Cotter, 1916:37–38).

To ensure that the stockholder clients remain the primary beneficiaries of the firm, certain safeguards must be designed into stock-option bonus plans. First, the individual performance contributions must be ferreted out—a feasible task in an organization exhibiting diversity, commensurability, similarity, and decomposability. Without these properties, particularly the latter, determining individual contributions is exceedingly difficult. Early in U.S. Steel's history, for example, "often the entire operating expense of steel making, from mining to . . . the finished product, had been 'lumped' at the end of the year, and there was no means of arriving at the knowledge of just where profits, if there were any, were made" (Cotter, 1916:41).

Second, all individual performances should be judged in terms of a firm-wide optimum, wherever interactions exist, to avoid rewarding aggressive short-term suboptimization, which lowers global long-term performance. Hence the designers must very carefully balance component competition for high individual achievement against corporate cooperation for high overall performance.

Third, to safeguard the owners' interest further, benefits must be paid first to stockholders and only afterwards to decision makers. Participating executives, for instance, should benefit from a stock-bonus plan only after they have earned a satisfactory minimum return for stockholders; their benefits, in addition, should increase proportionately as they raise the return-on-investment figure above the specified floor level.

A fourth client-oriented safeguard prevents decision makers from diversifying away their risk; the decision makers should remain wholly dependent on their own performance. In the stock-bonus example, they should be prohibited—to the extent feasible within the law—from converting the stock into a portfolio of investments that minimizes their personal risk and thereby reduces their motivation to perform well for the particular firm employing them.

In general, high variety is the most important safeguard the designers can establish in their motivational scheme. High variety in the motivational scheme is necessary to counter the variety introduced into the clients' and designers' environment by the decision makers.

> The degree of discrimination in the reward system itself—that is, the amount of information in the flow of rewards for behavior— . . . increases power. . . . Thus

fine-grained [high-variety] control of behavior depends on fine divisibility of rewards and punishments. Those men who control fine-grained punishment and rewards are likely to have more power. . . . This is one reason why most complex administrative systems use monetary controls, for a money payment can carry a great deal of information along with the reward. (Stinchcombe, 1968:167)

Hence an individual decision maker's reward should move both up and down in rather fine increments depending on a particular period's performance. Bonuses, because of their inherent variability, are more important than salaries, which have a tendency to establish *fixed* floors on compensation.

Just as reward variability is sought for the individual decision maker, variability in motivational plans used across classes of decision makers is also desirable. Low-level decision makers need not receive the same high motivational rewards as high-level managers, who work within looser constraints and exert greater performance influence. As the designers descend in the firm's hierarchy, a worker's identification with the central, long-term objective assumes less importance, for the participants possess reduced freedom and decide less essential matters. Hence a multiplicity of graduated reward schemes is desired, ranging from significant multiyear stock bonuses at the top to common hourly piece-rate premiums at the bottom.

Monetary incentives are not the only motivators available. Status inducements encourage executives by holding out substantial ego gratification. Moreover, the educational apparatus—whether the firm's or the society's—imbues managers with necessary value premises. Not surprisingly, then, "the importance attached by the Army to West Point training or by the Navy to Annapolis training refers more to the attitudes and values that are supposed to be inculcated by these institutions than to the training they provide in military skills" (Simon, Smithburg, and Thompson, 1950:371).

FACTUAL EDUCATION

Even if the decision makers eagerly accept the clients' goal structure as theirs, they actually may behave, through ignorance, in a way that jeopardizes the clients' well-being. Consequently, "they need the knowledge, the factual premises of decision, to select those means or actions that will best accomplish the goal within the value framework supplied them by the organization" (Simon, Smithburg, and Thompson, 1950:370). Specifically, the objectives of organizational education are: (a) to focus the decision makers' attention on the variables under their control—out of the infinite set they might consider—that influence the clients' satisfaction, and (b) to show them how the variables under their control influence their own component's performance as well as the firm's performance.

General knowledge and generally approved or successful solutions to the kinds of decisions frequently encountered, as was noted before, can be provided for the organization by external agencies. Even with higher-level decision makers, the designers may occasionally engage outside educators. Thus a few top-level administrators with the Forest Service "are selected for specialized training in the Intern Management Program sponsored by the Civil Service Commission in Washington, D.C." (Kaufman, 1960:174). Similarly, private enterprises send promising upper-middle managers to training schools like Harvard Business School's Advanced Management Program.

External training institutions, of course, only begin or supplement the decision makers' factual education. The organization designers themselves must continue the process by training new recruits and by retraining seasoned employees. Training new recruits might range from a brief on-the-job orientation session to a multiyear job-rotation scheme designed to heighten the novice manager's corporate-wide perspective. Ringling Bros. and Barnum & Bailey's Clown College presents a particularly colorful example of an entry-level training program. In Venice, Florida, for eight weeks starting every September, fifty aspiring clowns under the guidance of sixteen instructors study movement, mime, acrobatics, clowning, gags, and makeup.

Periodic meetings of employees performing similar functions in different units can be used to provide continuing education for seasoned employees. When jobs are quite causally comparable, employees can educate each other regarding performance-improvement techniques newly discovered in their respective units.

As with the motivational schemes, a wide variety of educational programs should be employed by the designers to handle decision-maker variety. Specifically, as decision makers ascend the corporate hierarchy, their training should focus less on intraunit short-term operations and concentrate more on interunit long-term dependencies. For one example, consider the diversity of postentry training methods offered by the Forest Service: Group orientation to the service's history, mission, and place in the federal government, the basics of federal employment, and the nature and importance of the job is provided to new junior foresters in the regional offices. Subsequently, conferences, schools, and training camps offer refresher courses, introduce new policies and procedures, and provide instruction in handling special problems and applying new scientific discoveries. To supplement these comparatively infrequent activities, "training bulletins, film strips, motion pictures, and other materials are provided by personnel officers in Washington and the regions." And on still a more frequent basis, "every supervisory officer is continually urged, consciously and deliberately, to train his subordinates. On-the-job training is unquestionably the largest single element in the Service training armory" (Kaufman, 1960:171). Moreover, at higher organizational levels Forest Service administrators are expected to participate in short university courses on public administration and in group conferences on managerial skills, as well as to study the better writings on administrative management. In sum, then, "post-entry training in the Forest Service expands the abilities needed to conform to preformed agency decisions [and in addition] tends to reinforce dedication to the agency and its objectives" (p. 175).

SELECTION

Designers also can attempt to select individuals with the desired value orientation and/or factual education, or at least with the ability to acquire these traits rapidly. As Kaufman (1960) notes, an eager employee without technical knowledge and practical skills cannot carry out the preformed decisions of his superiors, and a knowledgeable, trained employee who opposes the decisions to be executed is also likely to cause problems. "It takes both the will and the capacity to conform for a member of an agency to do his job as the leaders of the agency want it done" (p. 161). Accordingly, "Forest officers are selected in a fashion that winnows out many of the men who probably lack the inherent predisposition to conform to the preformed decisions of the Forest Service" (p. 198).

In selecting new recruits to fill decision-making roles within its organization, the firm's policy planners want particularly to engage candidates who are both sensitive and adaptive toward their new environment, for new managers possessing these traits synchronize themselves quickly with the organization's internal environment. The sensitive and adaptive recruit, in short, presents a fertile field for the designers' value-orientation and factual-educational plantings.

Selecting receptive managers is particularly crucial during the early history of an organization's operation, when extensive indoctrination and instruction time is not available to the designers. Yet even ongoing organizations benefit from choosing impressionable managers, since a continuing flow of management talent is required throughout the organization's life. For instance, once a business has operated over several cycles, if orientation, education, and the initial selection prove insufficient to secure adequate performance control, it may be necessary to select new decision makers. It may also be necessary for the designers to replace decision makers who leave because of dissatisfaction or retirement. Finally, vacancies may be created purposefully as an extension of the organization's factual training programs. Planned managerial rotation schemes exist almost universally among large American firms as well as among many public organizations like the military. In this vein, the Forest Service shifts personnel via "a vast game of musical chairs, . . . in preparation for advancement to positions that require a broader understanding of national forest administration" (Kaufman, 1960:176).

As is to be expected, the organization possessing similar subordinate components has a role-interchangeability advantage if decision-maker reselection or rotation is necessary. Relatively unimportant subordinate units offer a training ground for the more critical units, and consistently high-performing subordinate decision makers eventually can be selected for the headquarters unit as educators for poorer-performing decision makers.

Not only do continual interunit transfers broaden a manager's factual understanding of the organization, but these shifts also break down his or her parochial affiliations—and the tendency to make short-term suboptimal decisions; there is too little time to build local identifications. Similarly, but of more questionable long-term usefulness, these rotational schemes weaken the decision maker's community associations. The forest ranger, for instance, "barely becomes familiar with an area before he is moved again. Only one thing gives any continuity, any structure, to his otherwise fluid world: the Service" (Kaufman, 1960:178).

When combined with careful preentry orientation, education, and selection, along with extensive postentry indoctrination and training, these rotational selection programs "practically merge the individual's identity with the identity of the organization; the organization is as much a part of the members as they are of it" (p. 197). Under these circumstances, then, one can easily envision that the designers can leave their decision makers safely to regulate many of the controlled variables. Only relatively infrequent management-by-exception interventions should be needed to maintain course. Thus the designers have amplified their own as well as their clienteles' limited decision-making and information-handling capacity.

Throughout this chapter the basic theme has been a rationalistic one of fitting people to organizational roles rather than of adapting the *structure of positions* to individual differences. To the rationalistic designer, "the critical concept is management, not manager. He sees management as the process of turning the appropriate knobs of the component variables, and he usually does not include in the image the characteristics of some individual manager" (Churchman, 1978:60).

Serious dangers exist, on the other hand, in not taking cognizance of individual preferences as well as in forcing people into standardized, interchangeable roles. "The freedom of individuals to make choices based on their own wills and perspectives is a freedom that has a value of its own within the system and should be permitted to occur" (Churchman, 1968a:14). Norbert Wiener in his book *The Human Use of Human Beings: Cybernetics and Society* (1954) similarly emphasized that

> variety and possibility are inherent in the human sensorium—and are indeed the key to man's most noble flights—because variety and possibility belong to the very structure of the human organism. . . .
>
> Those who would organize us according to permanent individual functions and permanent individual restrictions condemn the human race to move at much less than half-steam. They throw away nearly all our human possibilities and by limiting the modes in which we may adapt ourselves to future contingencies, they reduce our chances for a reasonably long existence on this earth. (p. 52)

6

Coordinating the Firm: Recomposing the Dependent and Independent Controlled Variables

Along with designing the firm's orientation, education, and selection schemes, the planners must oversee the design process that ties the decision makers together. In other words, the board's executive committee needs to recompose, or reconnect, the previously decomposed controlled set of variables by superimposing on the underlying organizational structure an internal communication network that furnishes necessary "information to the various decision nodes within the organization" (Emery, 1969:34). Ideally, this hookup will link the various components into a unified corporate body capable of coordinated decision making, where needed.

With this chapter, then, the theme switches from *separation*—the focus of chapters 2, 3, and especially 4—and *amplification*—the focus of chapter 5—to *connection*. Thus the designers' search for short-term or temporary independence among decision clusters gives way to their creation of communication channels to handle the long-term dependencies remaining among decision centers. (Communication for coordination is also the theme of chapters 7 and 8.)

To connect the decision makers of the decomposed components, designers must "provide each 'operative' employee with an environment of decision" (Simon, 1965:243), i.e., information. Creating this environment of information requires that the planners (a) build, or encourage the fashioning of, communication channels and (b) develop the information that flows through these lines of communication (Chandler, 1966:16).

But why is information needed from other parts of the firm in addition to data contained within the decision makers' own unit? When the designers decompose the controlled set of variables, a particular unit (whether superior or subordinate) may not receive control of all the factors upon which its performance depends—especially over the long run. "In the face of ever-present interaction, the 'optimal' behavior of any given [unit] depends on the activities of other [units]. Communication channels are therefore required to provide information about such activities" (Emery, 1969:11).

Each component must receive "information that describes its own required actions as well as the anticipated actions of other [components]. This information is designed to induce each [component] to behave in a way that is consistent with the global objectives of the organization and with the activities of other parts of the organization" (Emery, 1969:28). Obviously, such intra-organization communication entails a two-way process, including transmittal "of orders, information, and advice" *to* a decision center "and the transmittal of the decisions reached *from* this center to other parts of the organization. [The] process takes place upward, downward, and laterally throughout the organization" (Simon, 1965:155). So after recomposition, "the functionally distinct [components] (parts of the [firm]) can respond to each other's behavior through observation, or communication" (Ackoff, 1971:670). Or, as Norbert Wiener puts it: "Communication is the cement that makes *organizations*. Communication alone enables a group to think together, to see together, and to act together" (Deutsch, 1966:77).

The symphony orchestra exemplifies this need to coordinate interdependent decision makers. While beating time for all the orchestra with the baton in his right hand, the conductor must also guide players of cellos, woodwinds, violins, horns, and other instruments through succeeding passages. The movements of his left hand and the rest of his body—a flutter of fingers, a sweeping gesture with his left arm, a scowl, a glare—lead the individual players through their virtuoso and concerted performances. Above all, they must be together.

While the coordination problem facing the symphony conductor is certainly difficult, it is by no means as complex as managing a firm with thousands of employees spread across the nation or even across the world. Not surprisingly, then, in large corporations "a formal and orderly conception of the whole is rarely present, perhaps rarely possible, except to a few men of executive genius, or a few executive organizations the personnel of which is comprehensively sensitive and well integrated" (Barnard, 1966:239). Luckily for GM throughout its formative days, the firm possessed such an executive genius in Sloan, who, in turn, built a particularly well-integrated organization. "Here, then, in briefest outline, [was] a pattern of bigness that work[ed]. [GM] escaped the fate of those many families of vertebrates whose bodies grew constantly larger while their brain[s] grew relatively smaller, until the species became extinct. It . . . escaped because Mr. Sloan . . . contrived to provide it with a composite brain commensurate with its size. His achievement may be summed up as one of intercommunication, getting all the facts before all the people concerned" ("Alfred P. Sloan, Jr.: Chairman," *Fortune*, 1938:114).

Organizational planners desire *extensive* information interchanges among the components of the controlled set because *"they make possible a greater repertoire of behaviours"* (Ashby, 1966:223) than is attainable with a sparsely connected decision structure. Considerable decision capacity (minds and computers) can be mobilized, thereby enabling subtle distinctions to be made and broad views to be taken in the solution of problems. Hence an organization possessing a far-reaching internal communication network can evoke a wide variety of responses (i.e., coordinated decision solutions) to counter its environmental variety.

The performance improvements achieved through a richly connected communication apparatus, however, are bounded. First, and most obviously, communications lines are expensive, so costs must be weighed against benefits. Second, "increased connexions between the reacting parts . . . bring in . . . the disadvantage of lengthening, perhaps to a very great degree, the time required for adaptation" (Ashby, 1966:223). Time delays arise from transmission bottlenecks, processing lags, instability problems, and, more important, from information overloads—the last of which can be handled only by having each component queue incoming data until they can eventually be processed (Miller, 1969:317).

Since the *"richness of connexion between the parts . . . has both advantages and disadvantages"* (Ashby, 1966:224), a minor planning dilemma emerges. Happily, farsighted designers through their decomposition efforts will have already laid the groundwork for solving this problem satisfactorily, for they previously instituted a loosely coupled organizational structure requiring a minimum of high-frequency communication linkages. Given such an information-saving factorization, the requisite low-frequency connections can be fashioned at the residual interaction points without creating excessive costs or breeding dangerous delays.

In passing, one should note that a controlled set's internal connections are likely to be quite sparse during its early life since development time has been brief. But with time, added intercomponent linkages should take root. Thus, an organization as it matures can address less critical interactions that previously had been ignored of necessity. With the passage of still more time, however, the information-overload problem surfaces, and a growing number of interconnections may inhibit the organization's ability to decide matters quickly. In short, too much bureaucracy, with its attendant paper shuffling to and fro, may develop. With this caution for older organizations in mind, we now resume attention to the design problems of younger enterprises.

Hindering the designers in their attempt to connect the firm's decision makers are three significant communication impediments: (1) the technical problem, (2) the semantic problem, and (3) the effectiveness problem (Shannon and Weaver, 1949:96). The technical problem deals with accurate information transfer among the firm's managers. Truly great progress has been made in eliminating transmission impediments within the last 100 years—witness the telegraph, telephone, automobile, airplane, computer, and satellite. In fact, these communication inventions have permitted designers to assemble extremely large national and international business firms. "It is perhaps no accident that the Age of Organization is also the Age of the Telephone. Organizations as large as General Motors, or the United Automobile Workers, or the Farm Bureau, or the Department of Agriculture—even the present-day United States itself— would have been almost unthinkable in 1850; the sheer difficulties of hand-written communication would have bogged them down" (Boulding, 1968:207). Unfortunately, the clock of progress may have turned full circle: organizational planners are no longer encountering problems of information scarcity but, instead, those of information overload. (See, for example, Simon's article "Designing Organizations for an Information-Rich World.") Hence technical breakthroughs like photo-optical signal transmission may have little beneficial impact on noncommunication businesses.

The semantic issue centers on "how precisely do the transmitted symbols convey the desired meaning?" (Shannon and Weaver, 1949:96). Some limited progress has been made on this front too. Practically all large firms possess their own specialized jargon, which can be quite "cryptic, relying on a highly developed and precise common technical language understood by both sender and recipient" (March and Simon, 1958:3). *Once assimilated* by the decision makers, such specialized internal languages, or codes (Arrow, 1974:42), greatly improve understanding as well as comprehension speed.

The final problem is effectiveness, or "how effectively does the received meaning affect conduct in the desired way?" (Shannon and Weaver, 1949:96). Less progress has been made here than with the semantic problem. Feedback control, or review, remains about the only device available to address this communication difficulty. By checking on colleagues' or subordinates' actions after receipt of an instruction, one can hope to elicit the desired behavior. Thus control over others' decisions can be strengthened through feedback mechanisms.

But what about the specifics of designing the organization's internal communication network? As with the previous decomposition discussion, the detailed consideration of the firm's information linkages is separated into two parts: horizontal and vertical recomposition, or, in the more applications-oriented language, horizontal and vertical coordination. Horizontal recomposition focuses on linking the subordinate components to each other, and vertical recomposition focuses on linking these subordinate components to the superior unit. The horizontal dimension is discussed before the vertical—the reverse of the decomposition sequence—since the movement back up the decision-making hierarchy has now begun (see fig. 1-2).

CONNECTING THE SUBORDINATE COMPONENTS

Designers must provide horizontal communication linkages, then, so that a subordinate component: (a) receives the data from parallel units needed *to control* its own variables and long-term performance and (b) provides the necessary data about its variable settings to other components in order *to coordinate* all subordinate-component behavior over the long run. Designers, of course, must prevent an overload in communication volume, where volume is simply the amount of information a decision center must receive to set its variables and the amount it must send to meet the other units' requirements. If the subordinate-component decision makers have insufficient time to control their units' variables because of the time spent in communicating with their neighbors, they cannot achieve an amplification of control for the designers. Performance will deteriorate.

How the controlled set is decomposed affects its recomposition. A loose horizontal decomposition scheme supplemented with much parameter decoupling requires little or no contact among the subordinate components; separation reduces the need for communication and allows the components to communicate mostly on an infrequent-exception basis. Only if the unit begins to operate beyond certain limits do the other units with which it interfaces need to be informed (Davis, 1974:94). Therefore, the designers need to build few high-frequency communication channels and the decision makers need to devote little short-term attention to neighboring information sources. Indeed, the loose horizontal couplings sought during the decomposition phase are designed not only to reduce the cognitive complexity of the control problem but also to lower the amount of communication needed to solve it.

Undoubtedly, the divisional as opposed to a functional decomposition maximally reduces interunit communications. A functional structure with its tight horizontal couplings requires massive communication links between components to handle the high-frequency iterative negotiations needed in the joint decision-making process. Thus component decomposability has a "communication saving characteristic to commend it; communication between the parts is reduced by isolating richly-interacting from weakly-interacting parts" (Williamson,

1970:122). And with the nearly decomposable organization, the designers need establish only a limited number of horizontal communication links, since a given component "typically interacts closely with only a few other activities" (Emery, 1969:12).

In building the requisite communication linkages to coordinate the weak and infrequent interactions remaining, designers desire channels that pass much relevant information with little effort. *Standard part numbers*, for instance, permit numerous data to be transmitted with the passage of only a handful of digits. Furthermore, both sender and receiver are likely to encounter little semantic difficulty in the communication of a standard part number inasmuch as each is communicating in a well-understood common language. Thus a single communication of a part number (and price) unambiguously summarizes much information, and no clarifying communication is necessary. Similarly, *acronyms* that make up much of an organization's (or industry's) specialized language aggregate considerable information content in a few symbols.

Besides connecting the firm's components, the planners must ensure that the data formats and processing methods used by the interfacing components are compatible. When they are not, chaos results, as was evidenced after the merger of the Pennsylvania and New York Central railroads in the late 1960s. While both railroads were heavy users of IBM equipment prior to their merger, their information networks could not be patched together easily.

"Coordination between parts [also] can take place through the environment; communication within the nervous system is not always necessary" (Ashby, 1966:222). Kenneth Arrow (1964) alluded to this possibility for the firm. In particular, he stated that many transactions within an organization are similar to those that take place in the market, and, if an entire economy is thought of as a single organization, one is led naturally to think of price "signals" as one of the major devices for coordinating different activities. "Commercial activity, quoting prices for thousands of goods and services, is thus essentially administrative activity for the economy as a whole" (Stinchcombe, 1968:166). Accordingly, large extensively integrated organizations can achieve much-needed coordination by permitting their interacting components to observe each other over the long run through their respective input-output markets. Otherwise, *"coordination of large-scale activities without markets requires a hierarchical authority structure"* (Downs, 1967:52) of considerable proportions to be layered upon the subordinate component stratum.

Stinchcombe (1968) provides valuable insight as to why the market mechanism offers a powerful coordinative device for the economy and, more important here, for the channel-integrated firm:

> We have thousands of engineers, accountants, and market analysts throughout the society trying to figure out the concrete revenue productivity of some new

use of a given quantity of a factor of production. All the concrete grease and grime of this evaluation results in a little nudge on the price of the factor. This little nudge is all the other people in the society [or the other people in the interacting components] want to know about that process. If they knew more, it would only confuse them. In general, then, the information capacity of a channel is increased, from a practical point of view, if the essential information is radically abstracted from all irrelevancy. (p. 166)

Even though various decision units possess much uncommunicated information, total demand and consequently overall price depend on the knowledge of all the market's participants. "In this sense the market price aggregates the various pieces of information" (Grossman and Stiglitz, 1976:249) along the one dimension relevant to all units. Hence price signals summarize many decision variables, reducing the unnecessary high-frequency variety communicated across both firm and divisional boundaries.

Finally, some nonmarket horizontal communications can best be handled via centralized communication channels. According to Emery (1969:11), "hierarchical communication channels—as opposed to direct ones—greatly reduce both the number of total links in the network and the number of links that each separate [component] must maintain." Considerable savings may accrue because fewer communication lines need to be established and these can be more fully used. These routine and repetitive (i.e., high-frequency) information transfers place little load on the central headquarters, for relatively inexpensive communication workers and machines can handle the subordinate-component connections.

Thus far it has been implied that the executive-committee planners could oversee single-handedly the layout of all the firm's lateral communication channels. Such is not the case because many interactions of high frequency but low interdependency are of necessity allowed to cross subordinate component boundaries even when a nearly decomposable structure is adopted. Given the designers' limited rationality, direct design of these less important connections between all components is impossible in a firm of even moderate size, since "there exist $\frac{1}{2}n(n - 1)$ pairs of direct links" (Emery, 1969:11), where n is the number of components. If a firm had 35 product divisions, for instance, there might be an many as 595 horizontal linkage pairs to design, install, and maintain. And the more designers tried to diversify control of the firm's decision variables, the more communication links they would have to forge. There are simply too many wires to connect. Yet if designers cannot expect to provide all the firm's necessary communication channels, how can they ensure that an adequate internal communication network will develop?

The solution lies in the planners' fostering the development of a supportive informal communication network. When operating, this informal grapevine "fills in the information crevices overlooked by the formal system and thus serves the extremely important role of information backstop" (Emery, 1969:35). Since the informal network cannot be blueprinted exactly by designers, it typically "contains too many unreliable and 'noisy' channels for the organization to depend on it as an avowed policy." So the informal communication mechanism cannot replace the firm's formal information network; it can only supplement it.

Several policy avenues are open to the planners as they attempt to encourage lower-level managers to fill out the communication design requisite to the firm's amalgamation. First, by creating an atmosphere where individuals and groups make their own contacts with members of adjoining components, the planners supplement the formally designed communication channels. Provision of ample telephone and travel budgets also encourages managers to synchronize their decisions with those of neighboring components.

The informal construction of communication channels can be stimulated even further by rotating key personnel among components so they understand the information needs of the many units, as well as know the personnel who are likely to possess the needed information. The underlying hypothesis behind this policy of personnel rotation is that transferred managers "have larger communication networks than those who have not" (Edström and Galbraith, 1977:258). Indeed it has been found that "managers having interdepartmental experience communicate laterally to a larger number of colleague managers than managers not having interdepartmental experience" (Galbraith, 1973:49). Decision makers, however, must be kept moving to foster connections among units, for "people transferred ten years ago behave the same way as individuals who have had no experience."

Still another thing designers might do to stimulate informal communication would be to hold meetings or conventions of a broad spectrum of decision makers, who, when together in a single arena, could contact individuals possessing needed information. Once made, the contacts could be maintained at relatively low cost even though the decision makers have returned to their separated components.

A way in which designers can reduce the number of direct communication lines needed within the firm is to create a series of central storage centers through which each component can access "a common information pool, or *data base*" (Emery, 1969:12). Decision makers, whenever they need to, can then quickly query those intelligence centers for data rather than having to search for knowledgeable managers working in the many adjacent components. Intercomponent subunits can serve as such common information pools. In a divisionalized firm, for example, an interdivisional engineering committee, along with its support staff, can function as a repository for the firm's engineering knowledge. Libraries, of course, also provide a permanent *organizational memory* accessible by all decision makers.

Finally, some communication channels need to be *blocked*. To foster product differentiation among divisions in a firm producing several similar products, for instance, design departments should be restricted to their own facilities and forbidden to communicate with similar units in other divisions.

CONNECTING THE SUBORDINATE COMPONENTS TO THE SUPERIOR COMPONENT

Vertically, the planners must fashion communication links directly between the superior-component decision makers and the various subordinate-component decision makers. The vertical connective structure includes: (a) lateral communications for dissemination of nonroutine coordinative or performance-improvement information among the subordinate components via the superior component; (b) downward communications for instruction from the superior unit to the subordinate units; and (c) upward communication for review of the particular causes behind and overall (long-term) results of the subordinate units. In addition, simultaneous downward and upward communications are established through the firm's budget processes. And simultaneous lateral, downward, and upward connections are formed via the firm's committee latticework. Through these budgetary and committee linkages flows the requisite low-frequency coordinative information. That information knits the superior and subordinate components into an integrated whole capable of unified decision making and (ultimately) environmental response.

Lateral Communications

In firms with tightly coupled subordinate components, the central headquarters will have to transmit much information laterally among the subordinate units. The purpose of this lateral information transfer is "avoiding or adjusting incompatible demands, and balancing gains in efficiency which may arise out of a new policy for one department against possible decrease in the efficiency of other departments" (Herbst, 1969:218). Tightly coupled subordinate components cannot be expected to coordinate highly competitive demands themselves.

With loosely coupled factorizations, on the other hand, the headquarters unit can avoid most involvement in the subordinate component's high-frequency dynamics (Simon, 1969:109) because such day-by-day coordination activities are imbedded mostly within the components and do not operate across their outermost boundaries. Here, then, the central headquarters involvement is limited to mediating those infrequent negotiations among subordinate components over such overlapped long-term issues as standardized parts specification or transfer-pricing policies.

If the subordinate units are highly comparable as well as nearly decomposable, the designers will want the headquarters to concern itself with subordinate-component performance-improvement efforts. That is, the designers must provide for the dissemination of the high-performance variable settings discovered in particular units. The intercomponent decision subunits, introduced in chapter 4, present a natural vehicle for bringing together the decision makers who need to communicate, whether for coordination or improvement purposes. Since performance improvements are discovered only over the long-run or *relatively infrequently*, the lateral passage of such information should impose no great load on the decision makers involved.

The cooperative/competitive tensions among the various subordinate components may make units developing performance-improvement techniques reluctant to divulge their means of attaining high performances, particularly when the improvements are transferred without an intercomponent payment or discovery reward. Moreover, the receivers of the performance-improvement information may not want to acknowledge their shortcomings or incur the costs of change; status quo performance is sufficient. Only the presence of headquarters representatives will encourage discoverers to divulge, by ensuring recognition of them, their valuable firm-wide contributions, and it will motivate users to implement them by implying follow-up reviews. To enhance lateral dissemination further, decisions "assigning people to groups, rewarding performance, and budgeting resources must support the group processes. These formal organization practices 'communicate' to individuals how important these groups are and influence their willingness to incur the psychological costs of confrontation" (Galbraith, 1973:65) plus the economic expense of change.

Lateral communication processes involving the headquarters unit encompass strong upward and downward dimensions. The latter are generally vital because control "can be exercised over the behavior of another person only if that person can find out what the power-holder wants and only if the power-holder can find out what the person is doing. The amount of control by the power-holder can be only as great as the capacity of the two-way communication channels between him and the person" (Stinchcombe, 1968:9).

The more nearly decomposable the subordinate components become, the more vertical is the firm's communication orientation. At one extreme, the corporate headquarters of the highly diversified conglomerate need mediate few, if any, lateral linkages. Hence, diversified firms generally have "a vertical organization, through which top management directs the activities of the various business units" (Porter, 1985:384).

Downward Communications

Thus the superior component, from its central firm-wide perspective, must instruct the subordinate components regarding desired variable states. Long-term policy directives exemplify such specific downward communications. So while the central headquarters does not regulate the variables directly, it still controls the desired (input) variable settings; the subordinate components simply contribute the regulatory capacity to assure that the actual (output) variables are maintained at the centrally desired states.

Besides setting specific desired variable states for the subordinate units to seek, the central headquarters must specify their overall long-term perform-ance objectives. Each subordinate unit then attempts to regulate its actual performance to achieve its particular performance goal. (This total performance regulation, of course, takes place within constraints imposed from policy parameters and variables controlled by the superior component, by other subordinate components, and by the firm's environmental decision units, which must also be communicated to the subordinate components.)

Upward Communications

Undoubtedly, the most important design efforts in vertical recomposition cre-ate the upward communication channels needed to provide the superior unit's decision makers with information on each subordinate component's past, current, or expected performances, whether specific or general. This information is used periodically to adjust the long-term variables that the superior unit controls, to issue updated policy guidelines or revised instructions to the subordinate components (regarding the variables they regulate), and most important, to ensure that these lower-level units act as the most perfect regulators possible over many short-run decision periods.

Designers desire perfect regulation from the subordinate components because "the fact that R [the subordinate regulator] is a perfect regulator gives C [the superior controller] complete control over the output, in spite of the entrance of disturbing effects. . . . Thus, *perfect regulation of the outcome by R makes possible a complete control over the outcome by C*" (Ashby, 1956:213-14). Review improves regulation, in turn, since it influences subsequent decisions. That is, when decision makers come to anticipate reviews of their actions and the invocation of sanctions against them should their decisions fail to conform to instructions, then they may be expected to avoid transgressions (Simon, 1965:234).

Securing near-perfect regulation from the subordinate components can be enhanced by multiple factors that increase the observational power of the headquarters without swamping its information-handling capacity. This power of review must be strengthened yet not overloaded, quite simply because a small group of top-level line officers are forced periodically to appraise and redirect the efforts of a very much larger group of lower-level managers (Downs, 1967:144). Seven observation-heightening methods are now considered in detail.

Reliable Local Data Sources

First, in developing adequate upward communication the planners must grant the superior unit access to *reliable* local data sources (Stinchcombe, 1968:167) in the subordinate units. A corporate headquarters, for instance, is greatly handicapped when divisional comptrollers report to the division manager rather than to the corporate comptroller. "If officials know that performance reports are never verified through independent information channels, the temptation to falsify these reports will become irresistible" (Downs, 1967:146).

In general, then, since information is to cement organizations together, it must be reliable. Credible information flows are especially important in the vertical direction, since these channels establish the firm's main internal communication linkages. On the other hand, inaccurate data from lower levels initially misdirect top management's scarce attention and eventually necessitate additional information gathering plus decision making. That is, *the variety of internal variable states increases erroneously.*

To make information credible, the planners must remove as much *bias* as is feasible from the observational process. The firm's financial and other functional staffs should serve the corporate line officers as unbiased divisional observers. These staff investigators provide the general officers "with important informational inputs . . . that are less subject to the data distortion that occurs when information is processed up through the organizational hierarchy" (Williamson, 1970:124). Such staff observers also permit the corporate line executives "to audit divisional performance in a way which, left to [their] own resources, would be impracticable" (pp. 124-25).

Focusing on the particularly critical financial-control area, a study of 129 firms from *Fortune*'s "1000" list indeed found more and more companies granting the corporate controller greater authority over the divisional controllers (Sathe, 1978:99). Improved trustworthiness in divisional reports typically results from this strengthening of the firm's vertical feedback mechanisms. In fact, because the financial staff's overall performance reviews are so vital to the board of directors and its finance subcommittee, this group's ultimate direction must be located even beyond the corporate headquarters. (Separating the financial staff from the entire line management is discussed more fully in chapter 8.) In contrast, the less critical functional staffs (e.g., those in engineering, purchasing, manufacturing, and marketing) can safely remain under the corporate-headquarters jurisdiction, though well beyond the division spheres of influence.

To maintain information objectivity and reliability, the corporate functional staffs reviewing the divisional variable settings should be: (a) trained and promoted by the corporate headquarters, (b) guided by the corporate-headquarters measurement policies when operating in the division, (c) rotated across units (costs permitting) to reduce bias resulting from personal relationships, and (d) returned to the corporate headquarters for periodic reorientation and re-education. Consider, for example, Geneen's use of his corporate staff at ITT:

> There was a staff man always looking over your shoulder, and he was outside your jurisdiction and the control of your operating management. In fact, sometimes the staff man was outside of any authority or jurisdiction except the Office of the President. The staff men were routinely rotated in assignments to avoid any rapport being achieved between division management and the staff. (Burns, 1974:62–63)

Access to Information

A second way in which the headquarters' observational powers can be increased is to have the designers eliminate any "institutions of privacy" surrounding the subordinate units and denying access to information to the holders of sanctions (Stinchcombe, 1968:167). A firm with a history of decentralized operations might have to break down divisional privacy by instituting plant visits, staff audits and inspections, intercomponent committees, and the like. As the barriers of privacy diminish in strength, the headquarters can gain access to the subordinate components' operations and examine them more thoroughly whenever their long-term performances warrant it, thereby eliminating the possibility of overloading the headquarters with erroneous information.

Taken together, the establishment of reliable local data sources and the elimination of privacy institutions create a series of *undistorted* and *unimpeded* feedback channels connecting the divisional components to the corporate headquarters. These unbiased and free-flowing channels heighten the central office's observational power while they conserve its information-processing ability.

Differential Review

Third, since the corporate headquarters possesses a limited channel capacity for observation, the subordinate units have to be reviewed, or observed, differentially. That is, *exceptionally important* subordinate components require added scrutiny and attention. Thorough observation becomes especially important where designers have coupled the critical subordinate components to the superior unit, for the headquarters needs considerable information from these lower units to set the centrally controlled variables affecting their performances. Closer proximity can be achieved if the decision makers of important components serve on the intercomponent committees with corporate executives; then critically important lower-level executives can be monitored without overloading the central office's observation capacity. Thus designers can enhance the headquarters' power of review by varying it situationally (Stinchcombe, 1968:169-71) to match the subordinate unit's importance.

Cross-Monitoring

Fourth, subordinate components also can monitor each other and report unfavorable variable settings to headquarters. In channel-integrated firms, for instance, supplying units should have their price, quality, and delivery performances inspected periodically by receiving components. The recipients, in turn, will have their design changes, order lead times, and the like scrutinized by the input components. Such cross-checking is a *peer review* process with a call for hierarchical intervention whenever significant and persistent (i.e., long-term), intercomponent disruptions arise. It offers two important advantages: (1) the superior unit's channel capacity is husbanded for performance-improvement communications rather than being expended on detection, and (2) relatively few (i.e., infrequent) corrective instructions will be needed since each subordinate component will want to avoid having parallel units report its failings to headquarters. Cross-monitoring, however, must be used cautiously, for it can stimulate competitive tensions that undermine cooperative contributions toward the overall goal.

Periodic Inspections

Fifth, the corporate line officers—the group executives and the president— need to employ more direct means of divisional observation, in particular, "personal inspections, preferably without prior warning" (Downs, 1967:147). Such personal visits to the scene of the action provide considerable information about long-term problems and opportunities not found in highly formalized staff reports and divisional complaints. Moreover, the threat of periodic inspections increases the subordinate components' self-regulating efforts over the many periods without taxing the channel capacity of the headquarters executives. Selecting the division-level decisions to sample, however, presents a significant problem. Choosing only particularly critical items to monitor, on the one hand, quickly leads subordinate decision makers into permanently ignoring less important issues (Downs, 1967:146). On the other hand, picking review items randomly forces subordinates to tend to all variables in their responsibility zones regardless of priority ranking. In balancing these conflicting inspection procedures, the designers should instruct the corporate-level decision makers to lean toward the priority approach, since it focuses attention throughout the organization on the high-impact decisions.

Management-by-Exception

Attending to long-term performance variables only when they transgress acceptable limits presents a sixth technique for the planners' attention-conserving repertoire. By ignoring information unless it triggers some *exceptionally bad* or *exceptionally good* threshold, the corporate officers do not squander their efforts reviewing satisfactory results; instead, they concentrate them on improving the long-run performances of those units needing correction.

Summarizing Performance Measures

A seventh, and final, method presented here for increasing the observational power of the superior unit is to use long-term *summarizing* performance measures to gauge overall subordinate-component contributions. For example, the divisions' quarterly rates of return and their transfer prices capture huge sets of repetitive decisions in a few numbers; thus they provide the headquarters with most of the information it needs to gain a firm-wide perspective yet do not overload its information capacity with short-run unaveraged details. That is the reason the Sloan-Brown design team at GM "converted the broad principle of return on investment into one of the important working instruments for measuring the operations of the divisions" (Sloan, 1964:140). Such aggregated performance indicators conserve top management's extremely scarce attention by condensing information and absorbing detail (Simon, 1971:42–43). Ideally, this "data compression" reduces "the volume of data communicated throughout the organization without reducing too severely their information content" (Emery, 1969:41).

While review processes improve regulation, they usually reduce subordinate-component innovation and autonomy: "review influences decisions by evaluating them, and thereby subjecting the subordinate to discipline and control" (Simon, 1965:235). At ITT, Burns (1974:65) observed, "The system of a staff man overseeing each major line function did not encourage an entrepreneurial business climate."

Review processes, as has been mentioned, can be separated into two categories: specific-cause and overall-performance reviews. Specific-cause review processes check whether or not certain variables, such as those related to purchasing, are set by the subordinate components according to the superior component's long-term policy guidelines. As can be expected, such focused reviews especially tend to stifle innovation (Rosner, 1968), for the subordinate units attempt to comply—perhaps even blindly—with central headquarters directives rather than trying new procedures or adopting techniques from the environment. "Even where, as is usually the case, the inspectional unit has no power but that of reporting its findings to the top executive, the line organization will become responsive to its viewpoints" (Simon, 1965:168). General-performance reviews, instead of checking on the causes of performance outcomes, simply measure the subordinate components' overall results and inhibit innovation less than do specific reviews (Rosner, 1968). In either case, however, review procedures can be expected to diminish subordinate autonomy.

Upward and Downward Communication: The Budget Process

The firm's long-range *operating* budget supplies the principal means for reviewing each unit's overall performance as well as for integrating the entire firm into a coordinated whole. "As each participant acts on the budget he receives information on the preferences [i.e., priorities] of others and communicates his own desires through the choices he makes. [Therefore,] the budget emerges as a network of communications in which information is continuously being generated and fed back to the participants" (Wildavsky, 1964:3). Since the divisional components possess only the weakest lateral connections, the central office—quite naturally—operates as the main clearinghouse in the budgeting process. And the vertical communication channels linking the superior component to its subordinate units serve as the key conduits of budgetary information.

Given that the headquarters is attempting to coordinate the firm into an integrated whole, operating budgets of necessity must be prepared in highly aggregated or summarized dollar terms for all the firm's segments. Only a universal measure such as money can establish a basis of commonality among the enterprise's units at this high level of integration.

Ideally, the budgeting framework follows the organization's decomposition scheme. Hence in a product-divisionalized firm each division has its own budget, which separates into various supporting functional schedules for such activities as purchasing, engineering, production, and sales. These subsidiary budgets, like the functional subunits of the product division, are tightly interrelated. For instance, material purchases cannot be budgeted without knowing production quotas, and manufacturing activity cannot be planned without a sales forecast. Since sales usually limit overall activity, the sales department's budget is set first and then all the other subunits' budgets are generated from it. When combined and summed over all the division's subunits, these schedules yield a composite divisional budget.

Looking upward, the various divisional budgets are summarized and integrated into the company's master budget by the financial staff. So once the budgets have been developed for each product line, they are passed to the corporate line executives for approval and alterations. Changes, of course, will be needed whenever the master budget exceeds the firm's resource availability. When this excess occurs, as it usually does, another iteration of budgeting process is needed, for which the corporate executives must specify reduced resource allocations for each division.

In formulating the corporate and divisional budgets, upper-level and lower-level managers obviously must work together. Corporate executives, for instance, cannot and *need not* be aware of the short-run operating details (see the component-decomposability discussion in chapter 4), but must rely heavily on lower-level decision makers to assess their units' individual long-term performances given particular budget allocations. Moreover, the divisional managements' involvement in the budgeting process enhances the designers' motivational and educational efforts. Lower-level managers, for instance, tend to feel recognized as valuable members of the team. Furthermore, budget involvement makes the document's goals somewhat self-imposing, and therefore more readily accepted as valid and reasonable subunit objectives (Dunbar, 1971:90). Finally, budgeting participation gives a lower-level manager a better perspective on how his or her segment fits into the whole firm and perhaps why it receives less than everything desired.

Participation in the budgeting process by top-level managers is essential for several reasons. First, their presence minimizes the possibility of budget padding by lower-level managers bent on boosting the slack resources under their control. Most important, top management possesses the firm-wide view needed to ensure a coordinated budget, i.e., a balanced resource allocation over the long-run. Here, it is essential to avoid involvement in the short-run concerns and problems of the subordinate components and to concentrate on their long-term interdependencies—as is feasible with a nearly decomposable controlled set of variables (see chapter 4). This high level of operating budget review, then, "forces a simultaneous consideration of all competing claims for support.... [And] the budget transports upward in the administrative hierarchy the decisions as to fund allocations to a point where competing values must be weighed, and where functional identifications will not lead to a faulty weighing of values" (Simon, 1965:214).

Besides being segmented hierarchically, the budgeting process can also be separated over time into three phases: precontrol, current control, and postcontrol (Litterer, 1965:234). Precontrol budgeting, which takes place prior to the act being controlled, centers on preventing undesired behavior and/or on fostering desired activities. Current control, on the other hand, seeks to adjust performance still taking place in order to achieve an objective or standard (p. 234); hence it is more likely to involve lower-level executives adjusting their own short-run performance than to involve direct upper-level management, as does precontrol. Finally, postcontrol involves a longer-run effort to determine whether events came out as desired (p. 234). A firm balances its books at the end of the month or quarter, for example, to see if it made the desired return on invested capital. Such checking after the fact means that information is gathered regarding results, but current-control corrective action in the just-completed budget period is foreclosed (p. 234). However, changes to improve current operations of the next budgeting cycle, as well as future operations of even later planning cycles, still can be implemented. Consequently, postcontrol evaluations for the last operating period merge with current and precontrol decisions of the present and future budgeting cycles.

This relationship among multiple budgeting cycles is shown graphically in figure 6-1. From figure 6-1 it can be seen, then, that a given firm proceeds through an endless string of budget cycles, each of which yields at some point a current budgetary period.

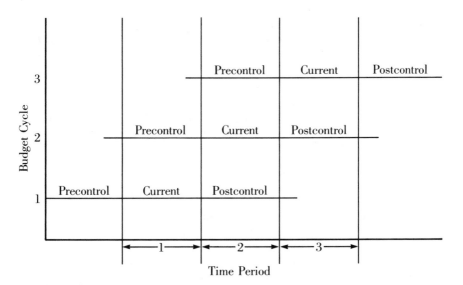

Figure 6-1. A firm's multiple budgeting cycles.

The question now arises as to how long the basic budget period is to be. If it is too long, the corporate and division managers will not receive timely or sufficient feedback from prior periods necessary to control current performance adequately. Too short a period, in contrast, may generate an information overload. "For example, reduction of the planning cycle from one month to two weeks doubles the amount of information processed" (Galbraith, 1973:32). It appears that most major enterprises have settled on monthly, quarterly, and yearly cycles for their operating budgets, as Sloan and Brown did at GM many years ago. More specifically, GM's planners adopted a rolling budget in which each cycle's report summarized the past month's performance, specified the current month's goal, and projected the three future months' (the next quarter's) targets. The quarterly targets, in turn, were set in relationship to the yearly goals or Divisional Indices established by the corporate headquarters in conjunction with the divisions.

Lateral, Downward, and Upward Communications: The Committee Latticework

Finally, the planners must develop a latticework committee structure "with each work group linked to the rest of the organization by . . . persons who are members of more than one group. These individuals who hold overlapping group memberships are called 'linking pins' " (Likert, 1967:50).

GM's Sloan mastered the technique of arranging the requisite informal group meetings and formal committee structure; moreover, Sloan excelled at using the linking-pin concept to coordinate the formalized committees into a unified team. In the 1920s Sloan's extensive committee structure for GM's joint decision making included: (a) a series of Interdivisional Committees in functional areas like engineering, purchasing, sales, advertising, manufacturing, and maintenance, (b) an Operations Committee, (c) an Executive Committee, and (d) a Finance Committee. The Interdivisional committees brought together corporate staff officers and their divisional counterparts along with corporate line executives. Moving upward, the Operations Committee linked the divisions' general managers with the Executive Committee members— the principal line and staff decision makers of the corporate headquarters. While GM's Interdivisional Committees focused on reviewing functional specifics, the Operations Committee concentrated on judging the divisions' monthly and quarterly financial performances. The Executive Committee, in turn, set corporate-wide policy, reviewed long-run capital-allocation needs, and made investment recommendations to the Finance Committee—which controlled the firm's strategy via its capital-budgeting purse strings.

When interlocking these committees for coordinated, simultaneous decision making, Sloan himself filled the major linking-pin role. Accordingly, in 1927 Sloan chaired two Interdivisional Committees and was a member of the other two. Furthermore, he chaired the Operations and Executive Committees and occupied a seat on the pinnacle Finance Committee. Sloan's close colleague, Donaldson Brown, chaired the Interdivisional Committee on sales and joined Sloan on the Operations, Executive, and Finance committees. Still another prominent member of the corporate headquarters, C. S. Mott, sat on each of the Interdivisional Committees as well as on the Operations and Executive committees. Other notable client representatives or corporate executives—in particular Pierre duPont, John Raskob, John Pratt, Fred Fisher, Charles Fisher, and Lawrence Fisher—also served on multiple committees and thereby helped knit GM into a well-coordinated decision-making body. Here, then, was a thoroughly recomposed—i.e., unified—firm, much akin to contemporary Japanese enterprises emphasizing consensus management.

The committee latticework thus offers an ideal means for fusing the firm's decision makers into an integrated team. By the very nature of their multiple memberships, committees make decisions less frequently and deliberate more slowly than do individuals. Fortunately, infrequent and extended deliberations are ideally suited to handling the longer-term interunit dependencies addressed in the recomposition phase of the SDPC model. Whereas fast-acting individual decision makers—the president, group executives, corporate staff officers, divisional managers, and functional department heads—make the higher-frequency decisions for the separated components, they meet together only infrequently to deliberate the few dependencies that affect all their operations. When the committee is convened, its relatively slow pace allows various viewpoints and perspectives to be aired and a corporate consensus reached. Between meetings, then, the group's decision helps guide the individual committee members in their faster and narrower decision making.

Moving down the firm's hierarchy of committees, the pace of repetition quickens and the focus of decision narrows—exactly as happens when descending the ladder of executive positions; for example, from president to divisional production head. Thus an interdivisional committee on production should meet more frequently, deliberate more quickly, and focus on tighter and narrower dependency relationships than the pinnacle Executive Committee, which is charged with overseeing the recomposition of the entire firm's controlled set of variables. In other words, much time must pass before performance feedback becomes available to gauge the efficacy of the executive committee's coordinative decisions.

Compared to the Executive Committee, the even loftier Finance Committee—consisting of a minority of insiders (drawn from the executive committee) plus a majority of outside members—meets even less frequently. The finance committee need not convene as often, since its unification responsibility is to design the connective links and information flows necessary to coordinate the firm's less variable exogenous dependency relationships. So by no means are the planners' communication-design tasks finished, for they still must link the unified firm to its immediate external surroundings. Just as the designers coordinate the firm's internal decision centers with one another, they also need to synchronize the whole enterprise with those environmental variable setters that also affect its performance.

7

Monitoring the Environment: Synchronizing the Controlled and Uncontrolled Variables

The designers cannot rest content until they establish communication channels across the firm's external boundary—from the uncontrollable environment to the controlled set of variables and back again—to ensure that the enterprise is synchronized, or in step, with its variable surroundings and capable of adequate performance regulation. Of course, the more an organization conflicts with its environment "or depends on it for the achievement of its central goals, the more resources it will allocate to the [environmental] intelligence function" (Wilensky, 1968:320). Similarly, the more uncertain an organization's surroundings grow—that is, the more exogenous variety it confronts— the greater its need for external information (Leifer and Huber, 1977:238). "Firms facing competitive uncertainty," for instance, often recruit executives who have spent considerable "time in other organizations within the *same* industry" (Pfeffer, 1982:200). In this case, intelligence information is literally imported through the minds of the new decision makers.

The environmental-synchronization discussion covers four topics: (1) the need for incoming and outgoing information, (2) the difference between feedback (past) and feedforward (predicted) information, (3) the sources of environmental intelligence, and (4) the centralization of the firm's environmental communication network.

SUPPLYING INCOMING AND OUTGOING INFORMATION

Incoming information supplies the firm's *second* line of defense against the uncontrolled environment. The first environmental barrier is erected during the composition design phase, when the finance committee planners position the controlled-set perimeter to avoid, or at least cushion, exogenous disturbances. The second defense depends on importing knowledge across the controlled set's outermost boundary to cope with the remaining environmental shocks. (Eventually, this information will be used to reformulate the firm's composition strategy.)

Thus, as part of synchronization, the designers seek to help the decision makers learn the states, or values, of variables they cannot control so as to adjust their controllable variables accordingly. Ideally, the unknown becomes known, and internal decision making adjusts to this external intelligence.

Unfortunately, many institutions commit serious intelligence blunders by not securing or using available environmental information. Catastrophic intelligence failures like Pearl Harbor, the Bay of Pigs, and Vietnam are well-known and thoroughly documented. (See, for example, Wilensky's *Organizational Intelligence.*) Less dramatic lapses, though still quite dangerous for the organizations involved, occur constantly. American universities and colleges, for instance, were among the first organizations to feel the brunt of the population's diminishing youth cohort. Almost without exception they failed to monitor the size of this group that had generated their all-important applications pools. And because of their delayed reactions to an increasingly unsupportive environment, many educational institutions have been hard put to survive. Those less prestigious schools without assured incoming classes that have adapted, if only sluggishly, have done so by diversifying into the older age groups, where the United States population bulge is now settling.

Gaining valid environmental intelligence destroys variety beyond the firm's boundaries. No longer do *all* disturbances appear equally probable. Without knowledge about environmental variables, designers and decision makers must assume that the environment harbors an unlimited variety of disturbance possibilities. But once they discover how the environment typically behaves or is constrained to behave, they can safely narrow their contingency plans and concentrate their efforts accordingly. What were thought to be uncontrolled variables turn into parameters and the problematic environment shrinks. The "complicated" observer, as Weick (1979) explains, "safely (that is, insightfully) ignores that which will not change" and "concentrates on that which will" (p. 193).

Since *"only variety can destroy variety"* (Ashby, 1956:207), "sufficient diversity" must be kept "inside the organization to sense accurately the variety present in ecological changes outside it" (Weick, 1979:188). Still, the retention of sufficient executive talent to sense key environmental shifts is usually better than retaining the decision variety to handle all contingencies and better than catching up after the fact.

At some point, however, compensation for the environment's actual or expected variable settings is a technique that has limits. Too much environmental data may overload the decision makers' information-handling capacity. The need to know about the environment must therefore be balanced against management's most scarce resource: its attention (Simon, 1978:13).

Just as the components within the firm must both import and export information, the firm too—"as a functionally differentiated subsystem of a larger social system" (Parsons, 1956:66)—must present environmental decision makers with information on its actual or expected decisions. "The organization and the environment are parts of a complex interactive system. The actions taken by the organization can have important effects on the environment, and, conversely, the outcomes of the actions of the organization are partially determined by events in the environment" (Cohen and Cyert, 1973:352). Consequently, a two-way communication flow needs to be established by the firm's planning team.

Why must external decision makers receive information on an organization's internal-variable settings? At least three reasons exist. First, environmental suppliers of materials or services must know what is expected of them. Second, decision makers in the environment, considering the organization's products or services, need to know what it is offering currently before transmitting their requests to the favored providers. A failure to advertise in the output market, not surprisingly, can seriously impair performance. For instance, along with ignoring readily available intelligence on the population's changing age-mix, institutions of higher education have also neglected the transmission of outgoing information to environmental decision makers. The third reason for exporting information arises from the fact that decision makers holding authority over the firm require knowledge of its decisions to keep its course aligned with their latest objectives.

As with incoming data flows, excessive outgoing information demands will overload the firm's dissemination units, and the environmental decision makers will not receive the requisite data. Or, to fill the gap, key decision makers within the firm will be unwillingly drawn into the information-distribution process. Small businessmen operating without extensive staff support, for example, complain bitterly of the debilitating diversions they endure to submit the numerous forms required by various government agencies. These consequences, of course, endanger the firm's survival.

Compressing the data passing through the incoming or outgoing channels helps the firm's decision makers cope with the heavy information load. So negotiations with suppliers should focus on aggregate variables such as the prices of standardized commodities or parts. Similarly, advertising copy should stress broad images and eschew unnecessary detail. Besides reducing the dissemination load, shorter ads lower costs and appeal to a broader market. More important, abridged copy lightens the public's load—a particularly vital concern, since most decision makers are deluged with messages. Thus a brief advertisement offers the greatest likelihood of piercing the potential customer's information-overload defenses. Undoubtedly, the penetrating quality of brevity explains why so many corporations carefully publicize their logo, which "serves as [a] visual shorthand for the company's formal name" (Sandage and Fryburger, 1975:354). Through such compendious symbols as logos, brand names, trademarks, and slogans, the firm hopes to impart a positive image of its activities and thereby elicit favorable responses from environmental decision makers.

To prevent another form of potential performance damage, the enterprise will wish not to broadcast potentially damaging intelligence. Obviously, there is always some information that environmental decision makers should not receive, since such knowledge leads to antagonistic external responses.

It can be seen, then, that synchronizing the firm with its environment entails a circular communication-decision process. Throughout the remainder of this chapter, however, attention centers on incoming communications; outgoing flows receive only a cursory glance because they play a less critical role in the enterprise's success.

Inward information flows assume their prominent position, first, because the environment's vastness in comparison with the firm's decision set means there are likely to be more data to import than to export. Second, instructions descending from environmental units holding authority over the firm must take priority in gaining the decision makers' attention; otherwise serious environmental sanctions are likely to be imposed from above. Third, incoming reactions from environmental decision makers *verify* the quality of the firm's decisions. Outward information flows, on the other hand, convey only the decisions the enterprise has reached, not what it has truly achieved in the eyes of less biased external evaluators. Thus, when Henry Ford ceased advertising in the mid-1920s to rely solely on his products' "showroom appeal" and the customers' word-of-mouth dissemination, he might be excused. When he ignored incoming data on plummeting sales figures, however, his conduct must be dismissed as foolhardy. It should be added that incoming information that anticipates upcoming environmental demands not only helps the less successful organization to improve its future performance but also aids the more prosperous enterprise to maintain its position.

SUPPLYING FEEDBACK (PAST) AND
FEEDFORWARD (PREDICTED) INFORMATION

Looking toward the time dimension, there are two ways in which the synchronization process proceeds. One depends on feedback information, another on feedforward information.

If system control is defined as an operation (performed by the firm's decision makers) directed toward reducing the difference between the desired value of the performance measure and its actual or expected state, *feedback control* can be defined as an operation using past-performance information to guide the error-reducing efforts of the decision makers. Thus, "small errors are allowed to occur; then, by giving their information to R [the regulator], they make possible a regulation against great errors" (Ashby, 1956:224). The above definition implies that the error must be sensed and measured, and that it must trigger appropriate corrective action. In turn, *feedback* can be defined as information on past performance through which present or future behavior is adjusted.

Feedback-control processes exhibit the property of "constant watchfulness" over the components' and firm's performance measures. Operating constantly, without specific knowledge of the error-producing variables or their states, such feedback regulators inexpensively guard against a wide variety of internal and environmental disturbances. They correct for unidentified disturbances simply by sensing the deviations these cause in the system's error function $E = M_c - M_s$ and by adjusting the controlled variables to compensate so that the system's actual state M_s approaches the client's desired state M_c.

In this synchronization loop "the feedback path exists through the [controllable/uncontrollable] boundary, passes through the environment (with attendant modification of the information) and re-enters at the ... boundary, the rest of the loop being completed within the [firm]" (Powers, Clark, and MacFarland, 1960:65). The firm's decision makers control their variables at states they hope are appropriate to the environment; the environmental decision makers observe these variable settings (perhaps through advertisements, price quotations, salesmen's visits, or the like) and set their variables accordingly. Finally, the organization's decision makers observe how the environment's variable settings influence their divisional and corporate performances and reset, or adjust, the controlled variable settings as necessary. More specifically, the management of a poorly performing division might raise quality, improve delivery, or lower prices. Should such corrective responses fail and should the corporate executives also be unable to correct the laggardly division's performance, they can then trim its budget and shift the released resources to higher performing units, thereby still helping keep M_s close to M_c. Either way, performance information (i.e., environmental variety) feeds back into the firm and enables it to synchronize itself with the immediate economic environment. This circular process becomes so routine and repetitive as to go almost unnoticed. Yet performance feedback provides the firm with one of its primary sources of vital synchronization information.

The performance-control potential of this feedback process, unfortunately, is strictly limited. The controlled variables never have adequate variety to compensate for the measurement and communication lags; so M_s hunts after M_c, at some finite distance, with the firm unable to close the error gap. The planning team, for instance, cannot let its decision makers rely solely on delayed market-clearing operations to synchronize quantities produced and prices charged with current demand levels. Lowering prices drastically to move overproduction reduces profit margins, and holding excess inventory until demand revives lowers capital turnover. Neither approach, then, solves the environmental-coordination problem satisfactorily, for investment return diminishes needlessly. "Thus any lag in the system will impose a limitation on performance which cannot be overcome unless some way is found of reducing the lag or of predicting future feedback" (Annett, 1969:20).

Feedforward control uses such predicted information to guide the error-reducing efforts of the decision makers. Here, the potential error must be forecast (from a model of past system responses), and it must trigger appropriate anticipatory action. Accordingly, *feedforward* can be defined as the information on expected future performance through which present behavior is adjusted. Ashby (1956:201) aptly termed feedforward regulation "defence by skilled counter-action."

To minimize the system's error, then, the designers will want to construct information channels to monitor critical uncontrollable variables such as consumers' desires, demand levels, and market prices so that the decision makers anticipate their future states and hence correct for performance deviations before they actually occur. In terms of the system control model $M = F(C_i, U_j)$,

> values of the control variables are found which maximize (or minimize) the measure of the system's performance:

$$C_i = g(U_j).$$

> The solution, therefore, consists of a set of rules, one for each control variable, which establishes the value at which that variable should be set for any possible set of values of the uncontrolled variables. In order to employ these rules it is

necessary to set up procedures for determining or forecasting the values of the uncontrolled variables. (Ackoff, 1969:125)

Such forecasting, of course, is possible only for those environmental variables the designers can identify and assign decision makers to predict. Hence, in contrast to feedback control, which is plagued by lags but independent of specific environmental information, feedforward control corrects for lags but requires particular environmental knowledge.

Since predicting exogenous conditions can add considerable variety to management's information-processing load, the designers should reserve feedforward control for *critical* decisions requiring *appreciable* lead times. "Prediction for its own sake is a costly and pointless game" (Simon, 1977:130). In the production-control example cited above, feedforward control would be warranted because months of planning are needed to keep stocks synchronized with current demand. In many less critical areas, however, delayed feedback data are sufficient, for the decision makers can adjust the controlled variables quickly enough to ensure proper environmental correspondence and minimal performance errors. So whenever the controlled variables possess sufficient flexibility (i.e., variety), additional information (again variety) does not need to be imported from the environment in the form of feedforward data. Under such circumstances, it becomes less taxing (and costly) to feed information back.

Before concluding that feedforward control is something quite different from feedback regulation, one should realize that all rational *predictions* are based on *past* experiences with the uncontrolled environment. If history did not repeat itself, prediction—not to mention planning—would be totally impossible. The prognosticator simply assumes that exogenous constraints hold steady at or cycle back to previous states, thereby reproducing earlier environmental behavior patterns. Hence the basis of feedforward control lies in the organization's collective memory of the performance impacts of prior exogenous fluctuations. And the better its recall, the better its chances for avoiding past mistakes, as well as repeating earlier successes.

Numerous sequences can be found recurring in the environment. The most commonly observed time-series patterns include: (a) secular trends, (b) business cycles, and (c) seasonal variations. Secular trends point toward extended movements of a variable, either higher and higher or lower and lower year after year. Besides being much shorter than secular trends, business cycles (averaging about four years per cycle) exhibit sequences containing both up and down movements—the well-known boom-and-bust phenomenon. Seasonal variations show the same form of repetitive periodic movement, but the period contracts to something approximately a year in length. The automobile industry's recurring spring sales peak after its winter-quarter slump presents a classic example of the seasonal time-series pattern.

Such predictive information, of course, affords tremendous planning advantages to the aware management. For instance, once GM's Financial Staff had plotted the seasonal and yearly fluctuations in automobile demand in the early 1920s, the firm's control of production rates and inventory levels improved immensely. Knowledge that automobile demand cycled through a pattern of recession, normalcy, and boom every three years, moreover, aided capital-budgeting and model-introduction decisions. These improvements, in turn, raised GM's investment return significantly.

Much additional experience with the economy's rhythmic cycles, teamed with considerable development in macroeconomic theory, now makes possible the building of quite large predictive models. Nevertheless, econometric forecasting models exemplify two disadvantages of *all* feedforward information generators: expense and unreliability. Even though the economic-prediction problem is tractable, its solution remains extremely expensive, for models with hundreds of equations and huge data bases are not cheap. Thus one observes major corporations and government units contracting with boundary-layer firms—like Data Resources, Inc., Chase Econometric Associates, and Wharton Econometric Forecasting Associates—for the information rather than generating it themselves. Expense must be shared in spite of the size of each of the purchasers. Furthermore, expensive though they are, these macroeconomic models still suffer from a reliability problem, particularly severe in the middle and late 1970s, when the economy exhibited unique (i.e., as yet unrepetitive) conditions of high unemployment coupled with high inflation. Unreliable predictors, of course, provide no information (i.e., variety) with which to prepare for upcoming environmental conditions.

So whenever the environment diverges from old predictable behavior patterns, the firm must temporarily rely on slow feedback correction rather than on predictive models to achieve the requisite synchronization. Should the environment's altered mode persist, however, the firm can use the new feedback information (i.e., experience) to build other anticipatory models for future operating periods. Finally, some feedback data are always needed to supplement feedforward intelligence, given the latter's inherent unreliability. With completely accurate prediction unattainable, feedback still allows the firm to align its plans with the environmental conditions that actually materialize. Sloan and Brown, for instance, constantly updated GM's (predicted) production schedules with biweekly sales data fed back directly from the firm's dealers.

When combined with the feedback (or postcontrol) responses of the decision makers, therefore, their feedforward (or precontrol) efforts should ensure a close correspondence between the enterprise and its environment. Either way, the information imported across the controllable/uncontrollable boundary enables the firm to remove variety from the performance measure's fluctuations.

LOCATING THE REQUISITE
ENVIRONMENTAL INTELLIGENCE SOURCES

One of the designers' first synchronization tasks is to determine how many environmental connections they must construct and, in turn, the decision makers need monitor. Briefly, the number of communication channels required between the controlled set and its environment depends on the interface, or surface, area exposed during the firm's composition. In that strategy-formulation phase the designers on the finance committee try to broaden the base of operation so a diversity of input and output opportunities always exists. Ashby's law of Requisite Variety, however, cautions against excessive expansion and against strained decision-making capacity.

Overloaded information-processing capacity also limits growth. Extensive channel integration and product diversification may require too many communication linkages with the outside world. For example, merely contracting with multiple vendors to diversify the risk of a supply shortage increases the interface area, since coordinative information must flow between each supplier and the planners' firm. The environmental surface grows still larger with channel integration, for multiple supply sources plus market transfer-pricing information become needed to connect every pair of the integrated units. Product diversification with its multifarious outlet possibilities adds still more environmental contact points, as the firm's decision makers must convey data to all their diversified customers and in addition must predict future conditions in *each* of the relevant industries and markets besides the level of general economic activity. Multinational corporations, inhabiting the economies of many different countries, experience even greater information floods. Not only do they need considerable data on each of their host countries, but they also require knowledge of international economic variables like currency-exchange rates. Given the case in which a firm's surface area mushrooms, thereby exposing numerous communication problems, one can safely conclude that environmental-information overloads pose a decided threat to performance control.

However, one should immediately note that while increasing a firm's surface area indeed requires the building and monitoring of more communication channels, the very number of these linkages makes each one relatively unimportant. The highly diversified multinational firm maintains numerous noncritical information linkages with its diverse surroundings. Still, in the final analysis, the extremely broad-based enterprise suffers from a fractured or unintegrated response to the environment; but more on this later.

Beyond its contacts with the immediate environment, at what other points must the planners attach the firm's environmental sensors? Certainly, the economy's vastness negates complete surveillance. Fortunately, the broader industrial order allows most noncontiguous environmental variables to be ignored with reasonable safety. Leontief's pioneering studies (see, for example, *The Structure of the American Economy, 1919-1939*) on the input-output relationships among the economy's sectors uncovered a loosely coupled network, exhibiting few ripple effects or domino reactions. Or, as Simon (1969) explains:

> In economic dynamics, the main variables are the prices and quantities of commodities. It is empirically true that the price of any given commodity and the rate at which it is exchanged depend to a significant extent only on the prices and quantities of a few other commodities, together with a few other aggregate magnitudes, like the average price level or some over-all measure of economic activity.... An input-output matrix of the economy ... reveals the nearly decomposable structure of the system—with one qualification. There is a consumption subsystem of the economy that is linked strongly to variables in most of the other subsystems. (p. 107)

Hence, the exterior environment closely resembles the well-designed firm's own simply constructed interior. And only the economy's consumption function—which operates much like the firm's own budgetary mechanisms, since it distributes resources among the various industrial sectors—diminishes the environment's decoupled nature. A firm's decision makers, then, need to observe only the industries that its divisions actually inhabit, plus the overall consumption function. For synchronization purposes at least, all other industries can be overlooked; their perturbations are isolated by the paucity of interindustry connections.

By no means should it be assumed, though, that the economy's business and industrial sectors are completely decoupled; for, as Leontief (1951a) cautions, a "closer inspection [of the input-output matrix] will lead to the further realization that every single figure in the chart is dependent upon every other" (p. 19). These relationships describe "the fabric of our economy, woven together by the flow of trade which ultimately links each branch and industry to all others" (p. 18). Ultimately, they reflect the structure of the country's production technology and distribution channels, as "determined by relatively inflexible engineering considerations or by equally inflexible customs and institutional arrangements" (p. 19). Still, such technological and organizational dependencies are strongest within, not between, industry sectors.

After all, if the economy did not operate through a nearly decomposable structure, it would require a massive central-planning apparatus to mediate the iterative contacts needed among all sectors. But since disturbances in one sector do not reverberate endlessly throughout the remainder of the economic environment, an inexpensive (and informal) communication network performs efficiently. Indeed, the undirected market mechanism adequately synchronizes the economy's various sectors with each other only because comparatively little coordination is demanded. Every firm can pretty much conduct its own business while worrying only about its closest neighbors in the production-distribution chain.

The only strong economic linkages beyond the firm's boundaries that the planners need focus on, then, exist between its respective industries and the economy's total productive activity, most commonly indexed by the gross national product (GNP) variable. Given the firm's tight coupling to the general consumption function, monitoring overall economic activity via *summarizing* variables such as the GNP, the index of leading economic indicators, and the disposable-income measure assumes paramount importance.

In light of the significance that gauging the buying public's consumption level holds for the firm, it is indeed fortunate that aggregated measures are available to the prognosticators. These overall indicators of economic activity not only capture the behavior of many, many households in a single number, but they also allow the environmental sensors to ignore the volatile behavior of individual households. Lumping all these minuscule decision units into a single aggregated group dampens the high-frequency fluctuations in the buying behavior of individual households and leaves only the low-frequency variations of a massive aggregation. It is to these latter fluxes that the firm must synchronize its current and future operations.

The essentialness of aggregate economic activity to the firm's performance control plus the unpredictability of its fluctuations largely explains why so many large corporations go outside and pay econometrics firms for their detailed prognostications. Such anticipative information is so vital, in fact, that some businesses purchase the forecasts of several prediction services because they know full well that feedforward intelligence lacks reliability.

Having the firm's own prediction, plus perhaps one or more external predictions of possible aggregate economic fluctuations in hand, the decision makers next must gauge how the expected disturbances will affect the particular industries in which their divisions reside. As early as 1923, for instance, GM's Financial Staff had discovered a correspondence between disposable income and automobile demand. "As additional statistical material on the over-all economy became available, [they] were able to refine [their] techniques and demonstrate the remarkably close correlation between car sales and personal income, a correlation that still exists today for car sales and disposable income after taxes" (Sloan, 1964:137). By knowing that personal-income variations preceded demand fluctuations and that demand amplitudes moved beyond the income fluxes by a fixed amount, GM's decision makers could synchronize the firm's controllable variables—most noteworthy, inventory levels—with the *forthcoming* environmental shifts.

In general, industries supplying products or services like consumer and capital durables, where sales are tightly coupled to general economic activity, endure the greatest performance perturbations. In contrast, sectors of the economy somewhat insulated from general economic undulations, such as food processors and drug producers, undergo less dramatic sales swings. To help the staff economists and statisticians of affected enterprises estimate such economy/ industry correlations, several of the econometric-data firms now operate micromodels for certain major industrial sectors. In addition to connecting specific industries with the macromodels of the entire economy, the industry models also aid the firm's environmental sensors in anticipating high-frequency (e.g., quarterly) oscillations in sales volume caused by such disturbances as seasonal buying patterns. With or without the aid of these industry micromodels, the firm's prognosticators must update past economy/industry correlations to arrive at specific expected sales figures for the industries relevant to their firm.

Looking past the prediction of short-run business-cycle oscillations and seasonal variations, disruptions further out on the firm's planning horizon need to be foreseen. For instance, how will shifting age-income demographic patterns influence the firm's sales performance? Even if the age mix of the consuming public were to hold perfectly constant, designers still would need to fashion communication channels to sense the consumers' future demands, for tastes change with time. As Charles Kettering, GM's early research chief, noted over a half century ago: "So long as we have younger generations, so long as we have 25,000,000 new people every 10 years, we will have changes. Their views are new, their tastes are new, their likes are new—and emphatic" (O'Shea, 1928:359). For example, when it introduced a new line of so-called natural baby foods in the middle 1970s, the Baker/Beech Nut Corporation hoped to synchronize its products with the emerging tastes of American mothers, who were coming to prefer foods without added sugar, salt, and preservatives.

When taking such extended outlooks, firms hope to foresee how government units, businesses, and consumers will allocate the economy's total purchasing power. That is, they want to know in advance how the economy's purchasers, whether public or private, are likely to spend their money on the then-available products and services.

But now the planners face a new problem: how to study efficiently the wants, desires, attitudes, beliefs, and buying behavior of the vast industrial and consumer markets (Sandage and Fryburger, 1975:163). Fortunately, by sampling just a small cross section of the population, one can estimate the characteristics of the entire market with reasonable (and measurable) accuracy. "In fact, a sample may have more information in it than a complete census. If in order to take a complete census one has to use less skilled measurement (e.g., less skilled [or more overloaded] interviewers), then one may gain more by accurate measurement in a sample than one loses by sampling variations" (Stinchcombe, 1968:168). Thus a carefully drawn sample can yield population estimates of the required accuracy while still conserving the scarce channel capacity of the firm's information gatherers.

Attempting to satisfy future wants does not mean that potential purchasers will be questioned about detailed product specifications. Typically, the customer possesses neither the inclination nor the capability to participate this fully in the decision process. "The consumer is not an engineer," for instance, and "cannot . . . tell the manufacturer the length of the stroke or the cubic displacement of an automobile engine" (Sandage and Fryburger, 1975:158). Rather, he or she can specify economy of operation as more desirable than excessive speed, and then the engineers can develop the product accordingly. So while the enterprise's internally focused decision makers deal with the product or service in minutia, the organization's environment sensors will shun detail to direct their information-gathering efforts toward the consumer's global concerns instead.

To develop the products for tomorrow's institutional and individual purchasers, the finance committee must authorize the creation of market-research groups as well as research and development staffs. The market researchers, charged with determining exactly what new products will be demanded, endeavor in particular to locate and monitor *leading* markets—supposedly like California— where consumers tend to anticipate the consumption behavior of the rest of the nation. Research and development staffs, in turn, must discover the scientific knowledge and production technology needed for the new products.

All this research and development activity can be viewed as a form of applied scientific, or controlled, inquiry. Its purpose is simply to convert an indeterminate situation into one that is better understood; and since science generates knowledge, it can be loosely equated with information gathering on the firm's uncontrolled environment.

The organization, however, does not simply want to know more about its surroundings; for masses of raw empirical observations, though potentially helpful in countering disturbances, quickly overwhelm the firm's managers. Rather, "in a knowledge-rich world," scientific "progress lies in . . . extracting and exploiting the patterns of the world so that far less information needs to be read, written, or stored" (Simon, 1971:47). Thus, science is "the process of replacing unordered masses of brute fact with tidy statements of orderly relations from which these facts can be inferred" (p. 45). Discovering the constraints—or systematic relationships—among the environment's many variables, then, promises the greatest chance for improving the enterprise's performance regulation (Ashby, 1956:247). The quest of the firm's research-oriented decision makers to uncover such environmental connections is applied theory building. And, as with all good theory, the critical test of its usefulness lies in the ability to predict future events with accuracy and parsimony.

Besides anticipating consumer behavior and product technology, the planners must also keep their decision makers in touch with competitors' activities and plans. For example, constantly testing competitive products and ranking them against the firm's own offerings (i.e., conducting product comparisons) yields valuable, even if delayed, feedback on market-share potential. In general, "answering . . . questions about competitors creates enormous needs for data" (Porter, 1980:71).

When compared with analyzing the competitions' past decisions, attempts to generate insights about their future intentions run into more formidable information barriers. Some managers try to circumvent their competitors' security safeguards and obtain vital feedforward data by resorting to industrial espionage. Such a questionable legal and moral practice cannot be condoned by the larger society. If it were, innovation would suffer. Scrupulous executives should suffer little serious disadvantage anyway by avoiding the engagement of industrial spies; Wilensky (1967:66-74), a leading authority on organizational intelligence, asserts that little is gained by such covert activity. The personnel employed and the secrecy involved in undercover endeavors simply do not encourage a thorough consideration of competitors' intentions. Consequently, "modern intelligence agencies spend far more time on overt sources with far better results" (p. 69). After all, much "relevant information on competitors can be obtained from public sources such as financial statements, from information gathered from the firm's salesmen, and from executives who meet rival executives at professional meetings" (Cohen and Cyert, 1973:354-55). Moreover, trade journals can be scrutinized, new patents checked, and new construction and acquisition activity observed. "All of these sources can be utilized to build up a data base on each of the firm's major competitors."

The finance committee will need to authorize still other additions to the corporate intelligence apparatus. Specifically, some of the units and personnel needed to receive incoming data and to transmit outgoing information are: (a) consumer-complaint teams, (b) corporate-advertising specialists, (c) labor-relations negotiators, (d) company purchasing agents, (e) public-relations experts, (f) trade-association representatives, (g) legal officers, and (h) lobbyists.

In addition, on especially sensitive environmental fronts, outside firms— specialized in operating at the periphery between the enterprise and its environment—can be engaged to aid the firm's decision makers. Advertising agencies, law firms, and public-relations consultants exemplify such boundary-layer organizations.

Top corporate executives should not be satisfied even with such extensive lists of environmentally focused communications teams, for "intelligence failures are built into complex organizations" (Wilensky, 1967:179). One of the problems is that staff units insulate line officers from direct environmental contact. Thus, "the alert executive is everywhere forced to bypass [or diversify] the regular machinery and seek firsthand exposure to intelligence sources in and out of the organization" (p. 179).

Indeed, research—namely, Keegan's (1974) study of the information sources used by headquarters executives in multinational companies—confirms that top corporate officers depend heavily on informal environmental contacts. These personal connections include associations with executives and professionals in advertising agencies, law and accounting firms, consulting establishments, insurance companies, banking institutions, and governmental offices, plus the usual acquaintances with managers in supplying, purchasing, and competing firms. In addition to this so-called old-boy network, top executives cull considerable general environmental knowledge from such publications as the *Wall Street Journal* and the *New York Times*.

So one can hypothesize that the relative freedom and ease of communication within the United States society enables top decision makers to build an extensive informal communication network and procure environmental intelligence directly wherever needed. This informal synchronization net, coupled with the country's extensive market mechanism, accounts for much of the interfirm coordination occurring within the American economy.

CENTRALIZING THE FIRM'S ENVIRONMENTAL COMMUNICATION NETWORK

At this point, it is important to question exactly where all the various synchronization linkages should be connected within the firm. In general, most of the environmental-information channels should emanate from the corporate headquarters. The enterprise's central unit presents the best place to attach most of the incoming (and outgoing) data junctions for four reasons: (1) proper orientation as to time and breadth; (2) evaluation by an evaluator outside any single division; (3) stable operation at low cost; and (4) coordinated response to the environment.

The broad long-run view taken by the corporate headquarters is most appropriate for synchronizing the firm with its surroundings. The divisions typically assume too short a time horizon, given the naturally faster decision pace of these smaller units; a narrow emphasis on day-to-day activities blinds one to the longer-run environmental movements. Moreover, divisional managements, especially those of conservatively diversified and highly integrated firms, should focus primarily on synchronizing themselves with neighboring units within the firm and only secondarily with the whole firm's broader and more slowly changing environs.

Furthermore, it is necessary to provide feedforward environmental intelligence directly to the central unit so it can set realistic performance standards for the divisions and firm as a whole. In addition, attaching most of the incoming channels to the central headquarters ensures that vital evaluative feedback reaches the firm's top administrators, who bear ultimate responsibility for comparing and improving the divisions' performances. If instead this corrective feedback were to go directly to the divisions, the corporate office might discover only belatedly, if ever, that certain units failed to meet external demands. As with all types of audit information, routing environmental feedback through the headquarters maximizes the chances for uncovering and correcting the subordinate components' shortcomings.

Centralized accumulation of environmental data, fortunately, also minimizes synchronization costs and stabilizes operations. The firm avoids "collecting the same information more than once. It is an oft-cited maxim of systems design that a given item of data should be collected at only one point in the system and then communicated . . . to other parts that need it" (Emery, 1969:38-39).

A more costly design possibility the planners should reject combines decentralized acquisition with lateral dissemination in an attempt to avoid the expense of duplicate intelligence-gathering. With this option, instead of having each unit repeat the others' collection efforts, only one division would acquire a particular bit of data and transmit it to neighboring units. But since the subordinate components are linked only sparsely, they possess far too few horizontal connections to disperse adequately any environmental intelligence they unearth. To build and operate such linkages solely for this purpose, furthermore, would be extremely costly given the number of connections necessary.

Worse yet, connecting the components laterally in this way could degrade the organization's internal stability. The more numerous these linkages are, the greater is the chance that disturbances will continuously ricochet throughout the organization, creating a perpetual state of turbulence (Ashby, 1966:192-204).

The corporate headquarters, in contrast, is ideally situated to collect, filter, and distribute most of the firm's incoming information, inasmuch as it already occupies the focal point of the internal communication network. From this one central node, *all* other decision centers can be contacted through the firm's free-flowing vertical channels. In fact, the budgeting channels strung during the recomposition phase were intended exactly for the downward transmittal of such environmental predictions as sales forecasts (see chapter 6).

To reduce dissemination costs and to increase internal stability, corporate executives should compress the data communicated downward by absorbing uncertainty from it (Emery, 1969:43). The greatest data compression results where a random variable shrinks to a single parameter; for example, the mean of a probability distribution. Other summary statistics, of course, may be used: "an 'optimistic' sales forecast 10 per cent over the mean of past sales, for instance." Since uncertainty absorption occurs when inferences drawn from a body of evidence substitute for the complete data mass (March and Simon, 1958:165), only top headquarters officers—with their broad overview of the organization and its environs—can safely summarize the information for all the divisions.

The unified synchronization responses that result present the strongest argument for centralized data collection and dissemination. So just as the designers earlier recomposed the firm to act as a concerted whole whenever necessary, they will not want it to disintegrate on contacting its environs. An army division, for instance, cannot unilaterally alter a coordinated battle plan merely because it advances without resistance on a particular front. Such an unharmonious deviation from the planned assault on the enemy might jeopardize the success and perhaps even the survival of the entire army. Similarly, the divisions of a firm see only their small portion of the environmental front, and therefore their response is likely to be only locally optimal. In general, then, where the performances of all units within an organization depend on common or connected exogenous variables, each component's synchronization efforts must be coordinated with its neighbors' responses. Hence environmental connectedness, wherever present, requires the central headquarters to modulate the environmental reactions of all the subordinate components. A coordinated environmental response is then more likely because the central unit's elevated position gives it a better view of the total environmental landscape.

Surprisingly, "a strong case can be made for consistent action, even if it is based on [mistaken] inferences. If the organization has a mechanism for attaining consistent behavior, it is likely to be able to respond adequately to errors in prediction. This is not the case if every fragment of the organization follows its own bent—even if many of the units are 'correct' in their predictions" (Emery, 1969:43).

Finally, concerted environmental adaptation is necessary inasmuch as only the whole organization possesses the requisite freedom of action. The individual division cannot match the environment alone; the multiunit firm was created in the first place to overcome the single unit's inadequate variety. Even when included in the firm's supportive internal environment and surrounded by its protective cloak, the division will still be lacking, for it now must satisfy the corporation's constraints. (So with security comes loss of autonomy.)

Accordingly, only the corporate headquarters can decide which will sacrifice so that the others prosper for the enterprise's overall good.

Not all the organization's incoming and outgoing communications, however, can pass through the central office. Even the conservatively diversified enterprise requires that its subordinate divisions synchronize some decisions with the environment. Decentralized synchronization becomes useful to the highly integrated firm whenever the exogenous variables involved fluctuate rapidly and exert only a mild influence on a single division's performance. Besides safely lowering the corporate group's information load, relieving it from involvement in high-frequency, localized environmental responses eliminates the transmission delays associated with passing information between levels and bypasses the slower decision processes associated with the corporate bureaucracy. As the firm's feedback cycles are quickened, its adaptations to the surroundings' less global disturbances are speeded. Moreover, divisional decision makers' frustrations should drop, since they need not cycle through repeated decision periods without receiving answers or instructions from the superior unit in tune with a less repetitive, slower pace. (Of course, if the divisions are to respond quickly to the high-frequency disturbances erupting on their particular environmental fronts, they must retain a modicum of freedom.)

Large conglomerates and multinationals, exposing vast and diverse surface areas, must decentralize their correspondingly vast communications work. So, instead of having the corporate headquarters receiving and transmitting most of the firm's synchronization data, the planners assign much of it to the divisions for processing in their respective spheres. In fact, the divisions' environmental ties may actually be stronger than their ties with their neighboring units within the firm. Therefore it is quite natural for them to adjust to the firm's environment as a series of somewhat separated units only loosely encased within a larger surrounding firm.

But even in the conglomerate enterprise, the corporate headquarters should assume more of an external (i.e., cosmopolitan) role, while the lower-level divisional managements should accept more of an internal (i.e., local) orientation. At a bare minimum, critical aggregate economic variables—such as GNP, price indices, employment levels, and disposable income—must be forecast centrally and transmitted downward to the operating divisions. Then all the firm's resource-allocation planning "is conducted under a uniform set of predictions" (Cohen and Cyert, 1973:354), and the enterprise is most apt to adopt a concerted response to its economic milieu.

Just as all of the vital incoming data should enter the firm via the headquarters unit, the critical outgoing channels should emanate from the central office. The entire organization, for instance, needs a coordinated advertising policy. Given a firm concentrated in a single industry, corporate oversight of publicity checks the divisions' potential for damaging one another directly through their contiguous environmental boundaries. With an enterprise dispersed across diverse economic spheres, the headquarters' control over promotional activities averts diffuse reverberations that diminish the overall corporate image. In either case, then, the organization presents a unified front to the world.

In sum, the planners must connect the firm's most vital environmental linkages to the central headquarters—in particular, to the functional and financial staffs and to the corporate officers directly. In these units and among these executives, the incoming intelligence will be discussed, digested, summarized, and blended with internal information flows.

To formulate the firm's final coordinated response to its economic surroundings, the planners must focus all the information on a particular decision-making body; otherwise, the various possible courses of action cannot be integrated formally into a single plan. Accordingly, a condensed package of reports and recommendations should go to the pivotal strategic-planning group—namely, the finance committee.

As was noted in chapter 2, the finance committee should be outsider-dominated, thus ideally constituted and situated to guide the firm's comprehensive reaction to its immediate economic environment. With a preponderance of outside members, the finance committee will possess the appropriate long-run perspective. It also will be less likely (than the internally focused executive committee) to be blinded to or biased against new investment possibilities. And if the finance committee's outside members come largely from the banking and investment community, they undoubtedly will have the background information needed to evaluate a wide range of investment opportunities. Moreover, if they are knowledgeable money managers, they will be able to judge whether the performances and prospects warrant additional infusions of outside capital or even justify the internal retention of earnings.

To supplement this external expertise, an insider minority will be needed on the finance committee. These individuals should be drawn primarily from the executive and bonus and salary committees. (The firm's president, as a member of all three groups, will play a particularly important integrative role.) These insiders will help the finance committee account for past managerial lapses and, more important, eliminate such failings in the future so that the firm becomes properly synchronized with its immediate economic environment.

The financial staff, which should report directly to the full finance committee, will also play an important role in synchronizing the firm with its environment. As was mentioned in chapter 2, it will need to ensure accuracy and commensurability among the divisions' past-performance figures. Looking toward the future, the financial staff will need to concatenate and summarize (in universal dollar terms) all the feedforward information coming from such corporate intelligence units as market research and product development. Its analysts can use this predictive information in a variety of analytical techniques, ranging in sophistication from average rates of return to payback periods, net present values, benefit-cost ratios, internal rates of return, and so forth.

The information supplied by the financial staff will enable the finance committee to evaluate its initial strategy formulation (see chapter 3) and will guide the committee through successive reformulations (i.e., investment cycles) where liquid cash is invested in fixed assets and these assets are then converted back into cash available for reinvestment. Thus the finance committee will review feedback data on divisional performances and assess feedforward information on their potential. And from the successive cycles of past reviews and future assessments will come the overall synthesis necessary to update the firm's capital-investment or strategic budget. "The most effective strategies of major enterprises," as Quinn (1980) asserts, "tend to emerge step by step from an iterative process in which the organization probes the future, experiments, and learns from a series of partial (incremental) commitments rather than through global formulations of total strategies" (p. 52).

Over the shorter run the finance committee will also give the final approval to the firm's operating budget and authorize any deviations from it to capitalize on current opportunities. When the resources allocated to the divisions can be varied over the comparatively short term, the "allocation process can be made responsive to differential performance" (Williamson, 1970:129). Assuming a fair amount of near-term reallocation flexibility (which of course can be heightened through short-term borrowing from capital suppliers), higher-performing components should have their operating budgets increased to achieve an immediate improvement in the firm's overall performance. Given a temporary oversupply of gasoline, for instance, an automobile manufacturer can trim its small-car inventory allotments and rebudget the released operating funds to its large-car divisions. Such short-run, high-frequency reallocations—i.e., operating-budget adjustments—would not require review by the full finance committee, but only approval by the committee chair in conjunction with the president.

Besides capitalizing on temporary environmental conditions, funds also can be redistributed to dampen the effect that certain poorly managed divisions have on the firm's overall performance. For instance, resources can be diverted over the short run from units unable to meet competitive prices, to sustain their market shares, or, even more important, to earn comparatively high return rates.

The firm's finance committee should take an extended view, however, before it makes drastic resource reallocations that alter the firm's activity composition. Low-performing units should be divested only when their long-range direct contributions to the firm (and their indirect contributions via the other divisions) are expected to remain low. At GM, for example, Sloan, Brown, and their colleagues on the Finance Committee concentrated on each division's long-run economic-return potential, which represented "an average rate of return to be realized over a period including both good and poor years" (Brown, 1924:420).

So even though the current standard of performance will be established by the firm's highest-performing divisions, the finance committee should avoid emphasizing the most prosperous units too much. Other divisions will undoubtedly perform better in subsequent periods, and the preparations for these role reversals should begin early—when sufficient lead time still exists for proper development.

When preparing for the future, the finance committee should focus primarily on assessing whether the conditions facing the firm on various environmental fronts will be declining, stable, or improving. Given this external orientation, the finance committee of necessity will rely on the bonus and ·salary and executive committees to correct any divisional or corporate shortcomings that prevent the firm from capitalizing on its environmental opportunities.

If the finance committee concludes that the long-run potential for a given product or line will be declining, it should begin to liquidate the activity; cash flows should be diverted into more profitable long-term ventures. Even current high performers will be candidates for liquidation, though the pace might then be more gradual. When a division facing an unsupportive environment is already experiencing difficulty, the finance committee should instruct the bonus and salary and executive committees to spend little or no time trying to correct its performance. Attempting to improve the division's decision makers or the firm's organizational structure and communication networks would be wasted over the long run and hence pointless. Here, then, it is time for the finance committee to change the firm's composition strategy by pursuing new environments via product diversification. In short, unsupportive environmental sectors must be abandoned, since the firm can never hope to counter the exogenous variety successfully.

If the finance committee concludes that the potential for an existing product or line will be stable over the long run, it should reinvest some of the available cash flows to maintain the divisional positions into the future. When the divisions are already performing well, little else will need be done. In a narrowly diversified firm, however, the finance committee may well instruct the bonus and salary and executive committees to determine the causes underlying the results achieved by high-performing units so that less capable units can be improved. (There will be little need for such interdivisional comparison in the conglomerate, since the dissimilarity among units greatly reduces the possibility for cross-fertilization.) When a firm's divisions operate in essentially supportive environmental sectors but still perform poorly, the finance committee should instruct the bonus and salary and executive committees to improve the divisions' decision makers and/or the firm's administrative arrangements.

Unfortunately, in such situations it is often unclear whether a poor performance results from a *temporarily* unsupportive environment or from internal deficiencies. After all, activities often have been chosen for their negative covariations in performance (see chapter 3), and some are bound to perform badly at a given point. Under these circumstances the finance committee, with the help of its financial staff, will have to determine the respective contributions of the environment and the firm's own internal operations to a given division's performance.

Two techniques available for separating impact of internal decision making from exogenous factors are standard-volume and market-share analyses. The standard-volume analysis, or base-pricing formula, was developed by Donaldson Brown at GM during the early days of the Sloan-Brown regime. Specifically, Brown wanted "to eliminate from the measurement of productive costs all extraneous and transient factors, particularly those introduced by the fluctuations of the business cycle" (Drucker, 1960:66). Market-share analysis serves the same function. A declining market share, even with an absolute sales increase, means competing firms are outselling the particular division under evaluation. Perhaps a new management team or a revised (e.g., more centralized) organizational structure may be warranted to correct the problem. In contrast, an improving market share with an absolute sales decline points to well-performing divisional and corporate management groups facing a currently unsupportive market.

In addition to tracking a single division's progress or decline over time, the finance committee of a narrowly diversified firm can compare its divisions to one another at the same point(s). Since exogenous factors will have roughly the same impact on all divisional performances (an unlikely possibility for the conglomerate), managerial differences should be easily recognized. However, the many dependencies existing within the narrowly focused firm will have to be discounted before particular units can be identified for improvement. After all, a division may be lagging only because others are diminishing its achievements through high transfer prices, poor quality, late deliveries, excessive price competition, or detrimental ad campaigns.

Finally, if the finance committee concludes that the long-run potential for a given product or line will grow, it should increase the firm's investment in this activity. When the performances of divisions already operating in such supportive sectors are already good, the bonus and salary and executive committees will need to do little other than make sure that progress is steady and no reversals are encountered. If current performance is poor, however, these committees will need to give careful attention to correcting the problems. Since the future of the firm as a whole will depend on taking advantage of the economy's long-run growth sectors, faltering performances here may even induce the finance committee to authorize additional expenditures for market research, product development, introductory advertising, or the like.

Besides establishing the communication channels for evaluating the divisional contributions to the firm as a whole, the firm's planners eventually must provide similar information linkages to evaluate the firm and its immediate environment as an integrated system. Through these conduits flow the aggregated, comparative data for valuing the contributions that the firm and its immediate economic environment generate for the various (dependent) client groups. In contrast to the narrowly focused divisional evaluations conducted during the synchronization phase of the SDPC model, this final evaluation occurs in the larger societal milieu. It eventually results in the firm's adaptation to its very long-term (i.e., parametric) environment.

8

Valuing the Performance: Evaluating the Variables and Parameters

COMPARING PERFORMANCES AND CAUSES

The design issue addressed in the seventh and final phase of the SDPC model is the valuing of the system's past performance as well as its future prospects. To conduct such an evaluation the designers must secure reliable performance data for themselves, the stockholders, and the various other clienteles. Since evaluation implies comparison, various planning groups must cooperate to disseminate the requisite evaluative information. From its perspective, the focal planning group will need to transmit and receive information across the boundary that separates the system variables from the nonsystem parameters.

The Purpose of Evaluation

The first purpose of evaluation is to ensure that the firm's high-frequency design and decision processes are working properly. The firm's financial staff provides the information for this judgment. Should these data show that performance is below standard—i.e., that the firm is not adapting successfully to its variable (economic) environment—the board of directors will need to select new design groups (i.e., board committees) that will guide management's actions. Even if the current performance is acceptable, board changes may still be warranted to anticipate forthcoming shifts in the parametric (societal) environment. Such major environmental shifts require much advance planning to extend management's spectrum of short-term synchronization responses.

The second purpose of the evaluative planning phase focuses on whether the stockholders should alter their resource allocation to the designers' system or perhaps even consider selecting a completely new board of directors. To make these decisions prior to the next planning cycle, the clients must evaluate the system's conversion of their resources into benefits. Again, the data on which this judgment is made must themselves be evaluated (i.e., audited) to ensure their accuracy. The performance information is used not only to value the system's contribution to the stockholders' well-being but also to judge the board of directors' work; therefore, it must be verified by external auditors, independent from the firm's board and top management. Besides being independent from all the firms that engage them to authenticate their accounts, the auditors must also apply the same "generally accepted accounting principles" to ensure performance commensurability across systems.

Third, in the evaluation phase the planners on the board should supply the requisite performance data to the nonstockholding clienteles in the wider society so that they too can assess the system's contribution to their well-being. In turn, the firm's planners will want information on the secondary clienteles' various states of well-being before beginning the next planning cycle. To complete their evaluation, the stockholders too should be supplied feedback from the society's noneconomic evaluators. Socially conscious shareholders concerned with the firm's societal contributions undoubtedly will wish to avoid investing in any enterprise that unnecessarily antagonizes labor, exploits consumers, or pollutes its surroundings. Even the most financially focused investors cannot permanently ignore long-term feedback, for society may no longer tolerate certain antisocial business policies; minimum-wage laws, safety standards, pollution controls, or similar constraints may be legislated. And since such alterations in the parameteric environment often depress the firm's financial performance in upcoming planning cycles, investors need to consider them when selecting a stock portfolio.

The Variable and Parametric Environments

By no means is evaluation a new topic for the designers. They were, after all, concerned with the evaluation of the divisions' departments in the recomposition phase (see chapter 6). And during the synchronization phase they devoted much attention to evaluating the divisions' contributions to the firm (see chapter 7). What is new in this planning phase is the delayed, summarized, and hierarchical nature of evaluation.

Evaluation here is viewed as an overall, slow-paced, high-level accommodation to the system's long-run (parametric) environment. In contrast, environmental synchronization focuses on detailed, fast-paced, low-level adaptation to the firm's short-run (variable) environment. The evaluation phase proceeds at a slower pace because many high-frequency operating cycles must pass before the planners can judge the system's performance definitively. Hence evaluation can be viewed as long-term synchronization or synchronization as short-run evaluation.

In keeping with this distinction, the firm and its short-term or variable environment will be evaluated as a *combined* system, embedded in a relatively stable long-term or parametric environment. Together the firm and immediate environmental actors (such as suppliers, labor, competitors, consumers, government, and the overall economy) generate the total system performance to be judged here. The financial community's decision, for example, to buy a firm's bonds or underwrite its stock issues depends of course on how well management sets the firm's controlled variables. But that decision depends also on how enthusiastically external decision makers support the firm's activities when they set the uncontrolled variables that influence performance. Hence new firms operating on attractive growth fronts of the economy—even though they may be poorly managed—will receive high ratings and financial backing. And mature enterprises existing in less supportive, more competitive environmental sectors must be well managed if they are to retain their financing. Though the total system's performance is being rated here, this final valuation typically will be mapped onto the firm alone. This identification of the whole with the part is appropriate, since the firm was positioned by its planners in the economic environment via their strategy-formulation decisions and the immediate environment's support was elicited via their environmental-synchronization efforts.

The Datum Point

What elements are needed to evaluate the system's overall performance? Scriven (1967:40) provides a partial answer by defining evaluation as a methodological activity that combines performance data with a goal scale. The goal scale used to evaluate performance is none other than the summarizing performance measure M defined in the first design phase. If the primary clients are the stockholders, ROI is the natural performance measure. The actual performance data, in turn, are generated by the system's operation and are found in the state of the performance variable M_s that sums all system states. Besides the performance scale M and the system's actual state M_s on the M scale, the designers and the clients must have a datum point or basis of reckoning to judge the adequacy of M_s. M_c, the clients' desired state, provides that point.

The perfect control situation—where $M_c = M_s$ and the error E equals zero—is a rarely attained ideal, given that clients maintain a fairly rigorous standard. Error can be reduced, of course, by relaxing the standard; that is, accepting a wider variety of M_s outcomes. However, it is assumed here—as by Ashby (1956:246)—that the standard is not changed to solve the control problem.

But what is a reasonable performance goal M_c? That depends on the performances of other systems. To establish a reasonable goal, or datum, of performance M_c, both beneficiaries and planners must communicate with other systems to obtain comparative data: information must be imported across the boundary between the system variables and the nonsystem parameters in order to conduct the final evaluation. In other words, the focal system's performance is evaluated by using one or more systems as a standard for comparison; i.e., as a comparative reference system.

Past performance information may be used to assess temporal progress (comparing a system to itself at an earlier time), but a thorough evaluation necessitates comparison with contemporary systems as well. It is in this multisystem context that the current valuation standard M_c is found; the desired performance level for all systems equals the performance value achieved by the foremost design team(s) operating under prevalent economic conditions. That is, the actual result M_s of the top performer(s) fixes the goal M_c to which all others aspire.

Performance Commensurability

Whether over time or among systems, valid performance comparisons require the use of the same valuation techniques in every case. To achieve performance commensurability, the variables associated with the measurement process must be fixed at parametric values. Should measurement changes occur, their differential effects will have to be discounted. Hence performance measurement methods must be kept in the nonsystem parametric sets of all the systems being compared and cannot be system variables.

Causal Comparability versus System Decomposability

The planners in particular will want to go beyond the final result to assess the causes for their system's good or bad performance. Hence comparisons also are needed to ferret out the many possible causal factors. But since designers and clients deal with real organizations operating in an interdependent environment, definite limits exist as to how much they can determine.

In making their comparisons, designers and clients alike encounter the conflict between decomposability and comparability (see chapter 4). Good comparability is had where systems operate in the same short- and long-term environment, yet when systems occupy the same variable and parameter space, they become coupled more tightly, and it is difficult to separate their interactive influences.

Consider the temporal comparison first. Good comparability is obtained when time periods are juxtaposed, since many environmental conditions remain invariant; i.e., parameters. But the closer time periods are to each other, the higher the probability that previous parameter settings influence present performances. When the compared periods are separated with substantial blocks of time, good temporal decomposability results, yet comparability diminishes since fewer parameters remain fixed over many periods. Take, for example, the case of the board trying to evaluate a new executive committee's effects on performance. If the immediate planning periods before and after the change are contrasted, many environmental factors likely will remain parameters and therefore have no causal connection to any performance changes. However, the effects of the old executive-committee design decisions will still influence performance in the follow-up period. If the planning cycles are separated by a considerable time lapse, on the other hand, the old committee's influence will be dissipated. But the parametric conditions are now likely to be so markedly different that it is they which may be responsible for any performance shifts noted.

Similarly, for interorganizational comparisons, system decomposability grows with the increase of distance between the systems while causal comparability diminishes, and vice versa. To achieve the high comparability usually desired, designers and clients will want to compare firm/environment combinations in the same industry, since they operate under the same parametric conditions. Unfortunately, such systems typically exhibit strong interactive effects, so one cannot serve as a control test system for the other.

For instance, a new finance committee might try to improve performance by altering its diversification strategy. Competitors, in turn, may follow suit exactly or make other policy shifts to counter the first's diversification move. Accordingly, it will be difficult to ascertain the cause of any subsequent performance shifts between the two systems. Firms more removed from the focal organization's industry would be less likely to respond to such policy alterations, but these more distant businesses probably are operating under quite different parametric conditions. Since these conditions are now variables rather than parameters, among the systems being compared, the results of this causal comparison may very well be clouded too.

The conflict between causal comparability and component decomposability, then, leads to an inherent indeterminacy in what the planners or clients can discover about their system's performance variations. Real-world evaluators cannot expect to achieve the successes of investigators using classical experimental designs where parametric conditions between systems are held constant and interactions decoupled completely.

Quasi-experimental Comparisons

Since true experimental design conditions are unattainable in actual organizational settings, the designers must be content to use quasi-experimental designs that only approximate rigorous scientific requirements. However, by being aware of certain common errors made in the comparison process, the planners can reduce the possibility that alternative explanations may account for performance variations.

The previously mentioned temporal and intersystem comparisons supply the two basic forms of quasi-experimental analyses available to designers and their clients. The former, with their deep understanding of their own system but limited perspective on others, will rely somewhat more heavily on temporal comparisons. The clients, on the other hand, with their broad view of many systems yet restricted insight into any specific one, will depend somewhat more heavily on intersystem comparisons.

When the planners are changed, the purpose is usually to correct for policy errors made by prior planning teams. Here, then, the previous system is quite comparable on many dimensions while it simultaneously provides a strong contrast to its successor. The comparison "is a casual version of a very weak quasi-experimental design, the one-group pretest-posttest design" (Campbell, 1969:412).

Given the inherent weakness of the comparison, both clients and designers must proceed cautiously with the evaluation of the new system. Campbell lists five sources of errors that might be encountered: (1) history, (2) maturation, (3) instrumentation, (4) instability, and (5) regression. A sixth results from time lags.

History introduces an error into the temporal evaluation process when environmental parameters shift over time. It is pointless to attribute performance improvements to a policy change instituted by a new planning group when conditions shift appreciably from historical period to period. Similarly, improving or deteriorating performances that result merely from the system's aging or maturation must also be discounted. Regardless of what actions the designers take, the system may improve as it matures, or it may unalterably deteriorate. Neither must the designers' policies be credited or charged with performance improvements or slippages that result from instrumentation changes; i.e., measurement changes that damage temporal performance commensurability.

Instability of time-series data introduces another problem. In Campbell's (1969) words: "All time series are unstable even when no treatments are being applied. The degree of this normal instability [or random variability] is the crucial issue" (p. 413). If the new designers' policy changes do not dramatically and permanently shift the performance curves (either M_s or E), their efforts appear trivial to the clients. To be good performance judges, then, clients and designers must make sure they gain an accurate idea of the natural instability of the system's performance, "and one of the main advantages of the extended time series is that it samples this instability."

Regression (toward the mean) phenomena produce another closely related problem for evaluating system designs. The most likely time for a change in designers is after an extremely high-error year. But, as Campbell says, "if the time series showed instability, the subsequent year would on the average" exhibit less deviation, *"purely as a function of that instability"* (p. 414). That is, "take any time series with variability, including one generated of pure error. Move along it as in a time dimension. Pick a point that is the 'highest so far.' Look then at the next point. On average this next point will be lower, or nearer the general trend." Thus new planning teams should not be credited with minor short-run improvements.

The time lags inherent in major design alternatives present a final problem. As Ashby (1966:219) puts it, "If it takes ten years to observe adequately the effect of a profound re-organization of a Civil Service, then such re-organization ought not to occur more frequently than at eleven-year intervals." Clients and designers must be patient in awaiting the results of design changes.

A refinement of the single-system time-series design adds one or more control systems judged comparable to the system under study. Such comparisons disclose how other systems perform in the environments of the pretest and posttest time periods.

In conducting intersystem comparisons, high comparability is desired on all dimensions except those controlled by the planners so their policy changes may be gauged. Therefore the environment's differential impact on the performances of the various enterprises has to be considered. For instance, inflation greatly affects rate-of-return figures, with current financial statements more accurately reflecting the position of a business with a rapid turnover of assets than the situation of a firm with a slower turnover. Adjusting the accounts of all firms to a single point preserves comparability on an intercompany basis.

In general, two guidelines must be followed when evaluating policy variations. First, where separability is good but comparability poor, the differences among the time periods or systems under comparison must be discounted; that is, the incomparable variables must be made into *artificial* parameters by removing their differential impact from the performance comparison. Adequate comparability is achieved only when all such causal conditions—except for the policy change or difference under analysis—remain invariant.

Second, where decomposability is poor but similarity good, the intertemporal and intersystem effects must be eliminated. In other words, the designers need to estimate the performances "as if" no temporal or system interactions existed. Such allowances transform the interacting variables into simulated constants (theoretical parameters) that separate the time periods or systems for evaluative purposes.

By analytically "converting variables into parameters, most of the potentially operative conditions are made not to vary, so that the influence of one or a few conditions may be isolated and analyzed" (Smelser, 1976:154). In general, "all methods of scientific inquiry and those striving to approximate it, rest on the systematic manipulation of parameters and variables."

THE EVALUATORS

At this point, the focus shifts to a more specific look at the evaluations of a firm that are conducted by several external control groups. Churchman (1968a) draws the distinction between a firm's internal and external control sources: "The central problem of management today is internal control . . . because internal control means instituting procedures to assure a satisfactory performance of the company. But what are the controls of internal control?" (p. 112). Given management's responsibility for the firm's internal control, who exerts external control over the decision makers themselves? In short, "who controls the controller? Who guards the custodian?" Three groups can be identified: the clients' planners on the board of directors, the stockholders themselves, and the secondary or societal clienteles.

The Board of Directors

The board of directors, composed primarily of outside (i.e., nonmanagement) members, occupies the closest external oversight position over the firm's management and its own bonus and salary, executive, finance, audit, and external-relations committees. Thus the full board establishes the clients' final defense against disturbances from the firm's economic environment or from its corporate or divisional decision units. To dampen such performance deviations, the board must supply itself with a reliable source of performance data. The firm's financial staff provides this unbiased information.

The importance of an *independent* financial staff (first mentioned in chapter 2) must be underscored. Just as the corporate headquarters desires a reliable local data source,—i.e., the corporate functional staffs—to generate information on divisional activities and performances (see chapter 6), the outside members of the board of directors need a separate intelligence group. To ensure against having the corporate decision makers distort the reported results, the financial staff should report directly to the board of directors or to its externally oriented finance committee. Moreover, to use the independent financial staff effectively, the board's outside members must break down the institutions of privacy erected by inside directors and corporate presidents around their managements.

Besides providing the board with unbiased information, the financial staff also distills or compresses the performance-review data. Extensively aggregated information, as found in quarterly balance sheets and profit-and-loss statements, will not overload the board's information-handling capacity. Data can be summarized by focusing on larger decision units (e.g., complete divisions or whole firms) and on longer time periods (e.g., full quarters or entire years), appropriate techniques in light of the board's broad-based long-run oversight function.

Since temporal performance comparisons play the dominant role in measuring the impact of the board's policy changes, the financial staff's major role is to provide temporally commensurable performance information. The measurement process must be held constant (either in actuality or analytically). Otherwise, the temporal performance comparisons will be invalid and the effects of the policy changes improperly assessed.

To some extent, the board of directors needs information on the performances of other firms competing for the investors' dollars in order to judge whether policy shifts and committee changes are warranted. Interfirm comparative data also are likely to suggest possible policy improvements. Published material, especially financial reports, on competitors and particularly high-performing enterprises provides the requisite information.

Should such comparisons show that the firm's performance is relatively low at the end of a planning cycle, the board will need to adjust its policies and committees for the next period. More specifically, internally oriented changes might be instituted through a new bonus and salary committee's modification of personnel policies or a new executive committee's alteration of the organizational structure. From its more externally oriented vantage point, a new finance committee might look for ways to improve performance by changing the diversification strategy. A policy change that a new external-relations committee might pursue would be to improve the parameter settings in the long-term environment. To this end, lobbying efforts might be launched to gain more favorable laws or administrative rulings. Similarly, legal action might be taken against secondary client groups in an effort to foster a new parametric environment conducive to high performance.

The Stockholders

The stockholders are not totally dependent on the designers of a given firm. Obviously, they too can hold a variety of investments to diversify their risk at any one point. Furthermore, they can alter their portfolios from time to time. To make investment decisions, investors need reliable performance information on each firm they are considering.

The directors, as the top planning group, are legally responsible for transmitting to the stockholders data on the system's operating results. Though more reliable than the management itself as an evaluative information conduit, even the directors cannot be left without guidelines. In order to gain resource allocations from the clients, the directors could present excessively favorable information on their system's operations as well as hide embarrassing revelations regarding their own policy mistakes.

The Equity Funding Corporation of America scandal presents a classic example of the former. Consider the courtroom testimony of Equity Funding's corporate controller, Jerome Evans: "At the end of a quarter when an interim statement had to be made up I would be in Stanley Goldblum's [former board chairman] office, and a figure of earnings per share would be told to me" ("The Case of the Willing Victims," *Forbes*, November 1, 1974:17). Then to derive the data for the published financial statements, Evans worked "from the bottom up instead of from the top down." He explained the details in this way: "You would take the number of shares outstanding, . . . multiply it by the earnings per share, [and] you would have a bottom-line figure. Your taxes are, roughly, say, 50%, so you would double that figure. You would add to that your actual expenses and arrive at what your income would be to reflect that bottom line." Goldblum and his associates manipulated Equity Funding's financial reports because "naturally the higher the earnings per share, the better the performance would look . . . on the stock market."

To reduce the possibility of such frauds, the Securities and Exchange Commission requires that publicly held firms *open* their books and engage certified public accountants (CPAs) to verify the accuracy of the board's financial statements. Ideally, the auditors, who are accountable directly to the investors, will be more objective and the evaluative statistics they authenticate more reliable than the performance reports generated either by the management itself or even by the board's own financial staff. Hence, "the fact that firms must open their financial records to independent, trained observers leads to a general level of confidence as to the reliability of accounting data" (Buckley and Lightner, 1973:162).

Since the CPA checks to see that the information presented to the clients by their representatives accurately portrays the system's condition, "the auditor's role is essentially that of an evaluator" (Buckley and Lightner, 1973:1173). But rather than assessing the system's overall results, the auditor only appraises the *quality of the information* upon which the clients base their ultimate performance judgment. For the clients' sake, then, the auditor "evaluates [internal] controls in order to determine the degree of testing that is needed. He evaluates evidence as to its validity and reliability. He evaluates the degree and mode of disclosures in terms of the law, the client, and the public interest, and in terms of conformance with accounting standards and principles. He evaluates specific items: the collectibility of receivables, the salability of inventory, the probability of liabilities, and so on" (p. 1173).

If a system's external auditors are to serve as the clients' "reliable local data source," they must be kept at a distance; otherwise, the management or the board might be tempted to co-opt their reviewers. Short of such outright manipulation, close proximity often leads to a sympathetic rather than critical review of the firm's financial statements. Excessively close associations between the audited and auditor can be alleviated via the same techniques employed within the firm; for example, by rotating audit personnel among client firms.

A special problem arises with external auditors in that they, too, compete with other firms to sell their audit and related services. Critics assert that in competing for business—whether the audit engagement or the accompanying tax and administrative consulting services—CPA firms try to please company executives with favorable opinions on the firm's financial reports. To weaken this association between the corporate managers and their external auditors, the board's audit subcommittee, composed exclusively of outside directors (see chapter 2), should engage the CPA firm. Similarly, if too many corporate boards engage oversympathetic auditors to hide their own oversight failures, it may become necessary for an independent government agency, such as the SEC, to assign audit engagements.

Given the discrepancy in size between the audit firm's staff and the audited company, only a sampling of accounts can be taken to establish the soundness of the financial reports. Thus the financial statements are those of the management, affirmed or disaffirmed in the auditor's accompanying authentication. The continued threat of review provided by the sampling process presumably keeps the firm's management and board constantly following generally accepted accounting principles and practices.

Besides establishing a sound information channel to the stockholders from a given firm's management, the external auditing profession also helps to provide commensurable financial data among different periods of time and, more important, across whole sets of firms. The stockholders require this temporal and interfirm commensurability to allocate their capital resources rationally among the economy's various investment opportunities.

Creating a series of uncoordinated "reliable local data sources" (i.e., independent audit units) alone does not result automatically in commensurable performance information because of the *variety* of accounting techniques potentially available to corporate managements. Theoretically, accounting can be viewed as "a set of principles and practices for collecting, collating, and reporting information relating to the activities of an organization, so that they [can] be evaluated in relation to the organization's objectives" (Hauser, 1967:839). And although the use of generally accepted accounting principles and practices is thought by many stockholders to produce unquestionable financial reports, these accounting guidelines are subject to numerous interpretations. Such measurement alternatives allow management a great deal of latitude in representing the financial pictures of their respective enterprises.

The independent accounting profession has been moving as a body to reduce the *variety* of "acceptable" accounting guidelines. In particular, the Financial Accounting Standards Board (FASB), the profession's rule-making body, concentrates on developing guidelines to enhance measurement uniformity. This standardization of accounting rules yields a degree of performance commensurability both across businesses and over time unobtainable from uncoordinated groups of corporate designers or audit teams. Because temporal and interfirm performance commensurability occupies such a priority position for the economy's capital allocations, the government, via agencies like the SEC, has striven to mandate standardized measurement rules, previously accepted only voluntarily by the accounting profession.

As investors seek to value the stocks (and bonds) of the various firms vying for their resource dollars, the overall performances of thousands of enterprises must be judged. At this point, the evaluation effort lacks the precision and early-intervention capabilities of the board of directors' work. The loss of preciseness also arises from the exogenous nature of much of this final performance review. It is principally via the securities market that investors value the designers' and decision makers' contributions. Williamson (1970) characterizes this overall client-conducted evaluation as external control emanating from the larger capital market.

The stockholders' assessment of the firm's performance will influence the long-term availability of capital. If, for instance, investors observe the persistently low prices a firm's shares command in the high-frequency trading occurring on the various stock exchanges, they will shun its new stock issues. Moreover, repeatedly weak ratings from the financial community in general will leave the current board of directors especially vulnerable to potential proxy battles with dissatisfied investor groups intent upon replacing the firm's top planning team.

Recognizing the huge volume and technical complexity of the financial reports and other statistics that firms promulgate, individual investors often employ independent evaluation organizations, such as brokerage houses, to summarize the information into specific portfolio recommendations. Similarly, large institutional investors employ their own in-house evaluators to assimilate and compress the data. Two types of professional financial evaluators are typically found: securities specialists and portfolio analysts. Securities experts concentrate on firms operating within a single industry; in particular, they search for firms occupying the strongest positions. Portfolio analysts, in turn, combine the suggestions of various security specialists into a composite (i.e., multi-industry) portfolio recommendation, tailored to a particular investor's risk/return preferences.

For those relatively few firms attaining maximum performance, their actual system performance M_s exactly equals the clients' desired state M_c, because the top performers' M_s sets the clients' standard. Since no other design teams offer higher performances to attract their investment dollars, the maximally performing firms' current shareholders will be content to maintain or increase their capital allocations. In addition, other investors will now be attracted, offering additional capital to the high-performing design teams should they want to expand into promising, but still manageable, endeavors in subsequent design cycles.

For all other firms besides the handful of top performers, M_c is greater than M_s, and E is positive. Hence the expectations of these firms' investors are not being met. As other firms do better, such shareholders experience positive opportunity costs. Accordingly, they may withdraw funds from corporations performing poorly and place their capital with enterprises generating zero-error performances.

However, since comparatively few high-performing business opportunities exist, not all investors can be accommodated. Consequently, many must tolerate a certain amount of performance deviation, for which they are compensated by lower stock prices, which in effect raise their final return rates.

Another factor moderating the capital flow to high-performance enterprises is the investors' desire to diversify their portfolio risk. Both prudent and speculative investors gladly hold stocks performing at values less than M_c if these investments are likely to displace current top performers in future evaluations.

Note also that the differences between low- and high-performing firms may be less than one might expect. High-performance planners must observe an upper limit in maximizing the stockholders' returns in any particular period. Otherwise, the potential benefit disparities among them and other clienteles may motivate the latter to increase their demands in future periods. In that event, the planners might be unable to satisfy both their primary and secondary clienteles.

Thus maximum results are to be achieved over the very long run, not in any particular planning cycle.

The Secondary or Societal Clients

Financial reports and business statistics are used not only "by the investors for whom they were intended," but also "by others—labor, consumers, competitors—who piggyback upon the published information" (Prakash and Rappaport, 1976:12). What completes the circle of communication across the variable and parameter boundary is the outsiders' response to the aggregated financial data. "The feedback can take several forms. . . . Labor may increase its wage demands. Government regulators may intervene to require something and forbid something else. And the economic policies of the nation . . . may be tailored to conditions indicated by the business statistics."

These more remote performance reviews by the societal clienteles are termed, appropriately enough, "secondary evaluations" (Ball, 1976b:362). Accordingly, "the secondary evaluation occurs when the data and/or the reports of an evaluation are studied and reported upon by another evaluator." The societal evaluation places the designers' contributions in a broader context to determine whether the nonstockholding clients have benefited also. From the negative perspective, the query becomes: To what extent have the planners damaged the societal beneficiaries' well-being through an overaggressive pursuit of narrow economic interests? In other words, what are the secondary effects or, in economists' terms, the externalities of the system's pursuit of its primary, specialized goal (Simon, 1973:269)?

The secondary evaluation seeks "answers to questions not asked [previously] in the primary evaluation," but "the new questions may be unanswerable in terms of the original [performance] measures" (Ball, 1976b:363); the primary evaluation reports do not "provide all the data that might happen to interest a secondary evaluator."

With business enterprises, nonsystem status relegates the secondary clienteles to a veritable information blackout in comparison with the shareholders, for typically it is "*the investors* who are being safeguarded. Only rarely does the law demand that the companies gather and disseminate information in the interest of, say, consumers or neighbors and workers" (Stone, 1976:209). And without government disclosure guidelines, the societal clients usually receive far too little information with which to evaluate the system. The shareholders themselves would also benefit from such a widened perspective.

Some members of the accounting profession have recognized this shortcoming and chided their colleagues to adopt a more encompassing view when generating performance data than has been done to date. While "the profession's microeconomic frame of reference, with its focus on information for [short-run] investor decisions, may have been adequate in the past, . . . its limitations are beginning to show" (Prakash and Rappaport, 1976:12). Accountants must realize that their work entails "not just adding up figures but making social choices as well."

In this regard, some firms have begun to make "social responsibility disclosures" in their financial statements. These disclosures cover such items as environmental protection, energy conservation, community involvement, fair business practices, human resources, and product quality. The Commerce Department considered going further when in the late 1970s it proposed publishing a social performance index for corporations to track how well they meet social needs such as minority hiring, environmental controls, responsiveness to consumer complaints, and product testing.

Such information—which summarizes the system's service to those groups occupying the societal decision space surrounding the principal clients' concerns— would also help planners determine whether, in good conscience, they can continue to optimize the stockholders' benefits while barely satisfying the peripheral beneficiaries' minimum demands. Thus, as the final step of this first design cycle, the planners need to review their original choice of client and objective. If the system's high performance damages nonstockholding clienteles, the planners must consider expanding the system's original boundaries to enfold some of these clients and purposes before embarking on the next design cycle.

Remember that the designers in their first trip through the seven-stage planning process concentrated principally on optimizing the system's performance for the primary client group, given the limits imposed by Ashby's law of Requisite Variety (see chapter 2). But once the planners have solved many of the system's design problems, they will have freed some cognitive capacity. Then, rather than simply fine-tune the existing design for the original primary clients, they can redirect any newly released decision-making and information-handling capacity to improve the secondary clienteles' lots. In subsequent planning cycles, more of the secondary clienteles' concerns may be encompassed (safely) within the designers' primary focal area.

To meet this demanding requirement, planners must review their initial goal choice. But "how can man ever come to be self-reflective about his own goals? This seems to be the very deepest problem of the self-reflective mind" (Churchman, 1968a:112). Worse yet, redefinition of the designers' goal is only part of the redesign problem. The planners also need to reorient their primary clients to perceive the importance of the secondary goals—just as they have to educate the secondary beneficiaries about the importance of the primary goal. The decision makers too must eventually adopt the new goals. But people socialized to accept the old pursuit may be reluctant to change, especially when they identify closely with the original clientele to whom the old objectives are attached (Wildavsky, 1972:510). Thus previous planning work, if overdone, impedes redesign efforts. In sum, the planners may not recognize the need or be able to vary their policy variables fast enough to meet upcoming social and political conditions.

If long-term trends can be foreseen far enough in advance by the external-relations committee, the requisite preparatory design work can be completed before the new conditions arrive. Unless distant parameter shifts are anticipated in this way, the damage to the primary clients' well-being will be severe. American auto makers, for instance, paid dearly for not anticipating that Ralph Nader's objection to the Corvair "was a forerunner of a broad-based consumer movement for safer products and tougher liability standards. Similarly, by ignoring early warnings from environmentalists, hundreds of manufacturers were forced to retrofit plants with pollution-control gear that could have been incorporated more cheaply in the original plant design" ("Capitalizing on Social Change," *Business Week*, October 29, 1979:105).

The external-relations committee's effort to anticipate forthcoming social and political conditions is termed long-run environmental scanning. It relies on the extensive reading of government as well as avant-garde publications to identify various political and social factors that are likely to shape the future business environment. As one top executive believes, "nearly every social trend that will affect business 20 years from now is being 'previewed' today somewhere, and . . . he employs scanners out of 'fear of missing a big opportunity or stepping into a crack' " (p. 106).

Moving beyond the mere anticipation of shifts in societal trends, the planners—via the external-relations committee—may well need to negotiate new long-term agreements with the representatives of the secondary clients. That is, after having tried many decision makers, numerous structures, and several strategies to no avail, businesses may well demand contractual concessions from their workers' unions, request protective tariffs or import quotas against foreign competition, and lobby for weaker safety standards or environmental safeguards. Here, then, workers, importers, consumers, and the public must sacrifice so that investors will be sufficiently rewarded to continue supplying the system with capital.

The firm's financial statements will provide some of the justification for the secondary clienteles' benefit reductions. But, of course, additional public-relations efforts will be necessary to support the appeal for altering the next planning cycle's *parametric preconditions*.

CONCLUSION

To complete the evaluation phase, the feedforward information from the external-relations committee will ultimately need to be blended with the feedback performance data from the cycle just closing, as well as from previous planning periods. These feedforward and feedback data, taken together, will provide the basis for selecting the board's new directors and for altering its committee assignments.

The design team for the next planning cycle will emerge from the deliberations of the full board, with all its constituent committees and planning perspectives. The firm's president, as a member of the bonus and salary, executive, and finance committees, will play a vital integrative role. However, the board chair and nominating committee (mentioned in chapter 2) must serve as the final arbiters, judge the full board's and each committee's past accomplishments, and prepare for the next planning cycle by making the new board selections and committee assignments.

The board chair and nominating committee will rely heavily on the collective evaluation of the financial markets. When the financial community, which judges all available investment opportunities, remains willing to buy the firm's bonds and to underwrite its new stock offerings, few, if any, board changes will need to be considered. (However, a firm's strong financial performance may heighten demands from its noncapital clienteles and require some limited changes in the board's external-relations committee.) If the system's financial prospects appear so poor that investors will not supply its long-term capital needs, extensive board and committee changes will be necessary.

Altering the board and/or committee composition necessitates deciding where the problems lie. More specifically, a new bonus and salary committee might be needed to develop improved personnel policies capable of producing the requisite executive talent, while a new executive committee might be chosen to search for less demanding organizational structures. A new finance committee might be able to devise less expansive strategies or perhaps even more diverse formulations to counter the environment's fluctuations. (In the latter case, concomitant changes would be needed in the bonus and salary and executive committees to handle the added internal variety.) A new audit committee might perfect the performance-measurement apparatus; and an altered external-relations committee might make better long-term prognostications or negotiate more favorable long-term parameter settings with the nonstockholding clienteles.

As usual, intersystem and intertemporal comparisons will help to isolate the source(s) of the problem(s). However, much indeterminacy will obscure the true causes for the firm's past successes or failures, and much uncertainty will cloud the true state of the long-term environment for the forthcoming planning cycle. Unfortunately, then, the nominating committee's decisions must be based more on impressionistic information than on unambiguous, unequivocal data.

If the bonus and salary or the executive committees require new members, different corporate executives will be needed as well; for these board committees are composed largely of such prominent insiders as the president and group executives.

If an overly expansive finance committee seems to be jeopardizing the firm's standing with the financial community, more insiders might be helpful in divesting the unmanageable activities during the next planning cycle. If, on the other hand, the firm seems too narrowly focused, additional outsiders will help to broaden the search for new investment prospects and capital sources. Officers from enterprises with apparently successful strategies will be good candidates for the next cycle's finance committee. New finance committee members might also be drawn from capital suppliers whose executives are aware of many diversification possibilities and the funding sources necessary for their acquisition.

Similar approaches can be taken for changing the audit committee's membership. That is, committee replacements should be sought from the top executives of firms exhibiting exemplary financial-reporting procedures or from the top officers of the financial institutions requiring the audit information.

More capable assessors and negotiators for a new external-relations committee may be found among those who typically deal with nonstocking clienteles or their representatives. Thus labor-relations lawyers, former government regulators, and the like may help improve subsequent performances. Occasionally, when certain secondary constituencies are particularly well organized, they may insist that their views be represented on the board just as the capital interests' perspectives invariably are. In exchange for significant wage and benefit concessions, for example, Chrysler appointed a prominent labor leader to its board.

Changes in the external-relations committee will be needed not only after the system's financial performance has been substandard but also when it has been exceptionally good, for when the disparity in rewards received by the primary and secondary clienteles is large, the firm becomes a target. To cope with any increased demands, new external-relations committee members conversant with the secondary clients' goals will undoubtedly be needed. So consumer advocates, minority representatives, environmentalists, or labor leaders might be considered as candidates for the newly constituted external-relations committee.

Selecting board members acquainted with the secondary clients' interests will expand the system's size in the next planning cycle. That is, variables formerly ignored as nonsystem parameters because they were associated with the secondary beneficiaries will now be system variables. And a broader clientele will be served by simply adding board members knowledgeable about the variables that affect the well-being of these groups.

In conclusion, then, changing the board's membership and committee assignments at the end of a planning cycle will give the system new variety to cope with the demands of the next cycle. When the system's performance has been generally substandard, the board changes will be designed mainly to increase future benefits for the primary beneficiaries. Accordingly, these planning-team alterations will give the system a degree of ultrastability (see chapter 1) and improve its survival prospects in subsequent design cycles. When the system has performed well for the primary clients, the board changes will be made to extend these rewards to the secondary clienteles. Here again, these changes will enhance the system's long-term survivability over many subsequent planning cycles.

The planners now will be ready to begin the next planning cycle—that is, to return to the goal-definition phase. Thus the discussion of the seven-phase SDPC model is complete.

9

Extending the Model to the Department, Division, Economy, and Society Levels

Design activities undertaken at the corporation level, considered in the previous eight chapters, relate to planning phases at the department, division, economy, and society levels. Before looking at the connections across several levels, it is necessary to re-examine the respective positions of the seven planning phases within the basic corporate-planning circuit. Ultimately, the connections to the department's, division's, economy's, and society's planes will emanate from this referent level. Also, by considering all seven design phases in relationship to one another, the corporate planning process can be viewed as a composite whole rather than as a set of distinct design phases, thus far artificially separated for expository purposes.

THE RELATIONSHIPS WITHIN LEVELS

Figure 1-2 presented a graphic representation of the seven phases of a single design cycle, usually assumed to be at the corporation level. As was pointed out in chapter 1, separation and connection are the principal counterpoints of the SDPC model. The *definition, composition,* and *decomposition* planning phases deal with separation, while the *recomposition, synchronization,* and *evaluation* phases focus on connection. The other basic theme of the planning model stems from the amplification-of-control concept. The *amplification* phase obviates the need for additional separation or connection phases at a particular level by treating the remainder as a black box.

In figure 1-2 the *definition* and *evaluation* phases are paired as are the *composition* and *synchronization* phases and the *decomposition* and *recomposition* phases. These depictions emphasize the correspondence between the paired phases. Thus one half of the pair creates a given boundary, and its companion provides for the communication linkages required to span the exact same boundary.

Starting with the upper-left position in figure 1-2, the designers first draw the boundary between the nonsystem parameters and system variables at the *definition* phase. Factors that vary over the planning cycle and influence the primary clients' well-being are considered system variables.

At the *composition* phase, those variables that make the greatest impact on the clients' satisfaction are included within the corporation's controlled-variable domain wherever possible to ensure a proper setting. Variables exerting less influence on performance may be left (safely) to the uncontrolled environment, thereby conserving the firm's specialized decision capacity.

Next, at the *decomposition* phase, the controlled set of variables are factored into more easily managed subsets. As in the previous two design phases, the planners strive to locate the low-frequency/low-dependency cleavages in drawing these boundaries. This end is achieved by separating, to the extent possible, the controlled variables into dependent and independent sets and assigning a given dependent set to a unique decision-making team.

In each separation phase (high- and low-frequency) interactions always continue to span the boundaries that planners draw in spite of their efforts to partition the variables along the weakest interaction cleavages. Thus additional action is required to reduce the boundary interactions and heighten the demarcation lines. To sever as many of the more important (i.e., high-dependency) interactions that remain, the designers attempt to fix critical interacting variables at constant or parametric values for the duration of the relevant decision period. Once they have been fixed as temporary constants, the parameters transmit no variety loads across the boundary.

With the completion of each separation phase, the size of the relevant decision set and its incoming variety load are reduced. Accordingly, the two requirements of Ashby's law of Requisite Variety are likely to be satisfied and performance to be adequate.

Along with separation comes the need for connection. First, at the *recomposition* phase the designers link the decision makers who deal with the independent and dependent controlled variables. Such connections ensure that the firm operates as an integrated whole. But why do a series of decision makers, each controlling a set of supposedly independent variables, need to be kept in contact with one another? These connections are necessary because "independence," as the term is used here, is not absolute but relative. More specifically, independence is a function of the interaction frequency involved. In the short run, the nearly decomposable controlled-variable structure allows each unit to proceed independently; but over the long run, mutual dependencies reassert themselves and communications become necessary. That is, some dependence remains in the long run even between so-called independent decision sets, and communication is required for coordination.

During the *synchronization* phase, similarly, communication lines are strung from the controlled variables to the uncontrolled economic environment and back again to ensure a proper correspondence of variable values. At the final *evaluation* phase, connections are made across the boundary between system variables and nonsystem parameters. This last set of linkages helps make certain that the system's variables are set properly in relationship to the long-term (parametric) environment; i.e. society.

Regardless of the connection phase under consideration, then, communication linkages are needed: (a) to monitor the (high-frequency, low-dependency) interacting variables that could not be fixed at temporarily constant values during the separation phases, and (b) to check the settings of those (low-frequency, high-dependency) variables that were temporarily fixed. This latter check determines whether another setting might improve the connected units' joint performances during the upcoming cycle. The key to providing the necessary postcontrol evaluation and precontrol negotiation information lies in connecting the previously separated segments via aggregate, or summarizing, variables. Not only do such summary statistics convey the requisite information by capturing the overall state of well-being for the various decision sets involved, but they do so while transmitting the minimum variety loads across the partitions. First, with summary measures a mass of unnecessary details are abstracted into a single overall picture. Second, the low fluctuation rates of overall indicators mean that the interacting units proceed throughout their planning cycles without updating their environmental intelligence. Thus the environmental variety communicated across the various boundaries within and around the firm is kept low.

As is shown by the varying oval proportions in figure 1-2, set size (the number of variable and parameter states) decreases with movement from the *definition/evaluation* phases to the *composition/synchronization* phases and on to the *decomposition/recomposition* phases. Correlated with this size reduction is an increase in interaction dependency and an increase in interaction frequency. In turn, as interaction frequency increases, its inverse, the decision period, shortens, as does the related planning horizon.

Such general relationships will hold regardless of the planning level under consideration. The division's *definition/evaluation* phases, like the corporation's, will involve a larger world of variables and parameters than do the division's *composition/synchronization* phases, which in turn will be broader in variable scope than the division's *decomposition/recomposition* phases. Similarly, for any given level the *definition/evaluation* phases will always be associated with the lowest interaction frequencies and dependencies, as is shown on the horizontal axes in figure 1-2. Next come the *composition/synchronization* phases, while the *decomposition/recomposition* phases will exhibit the highest interaction frequencies and dependencies.

These relationships recur at all levels because each boundary that any particular design group draws incorporates within it the most tightly coupled (high-dependency), rapidly fluctuating (high-frequency) variables. At each phase, only the relatively low-dependency, low-frequency interactions are allowed to cross the boundaries. Thus the external variety encountered at each partition is low and easily countered by the internal variety encompassed within the boundary. *Of course, after each successive boundary is drawn the next partition has to be located at a cleavage line of somewhat higher dependency and higher frequency than its predecessor's.*

Finally, it should be noted that the *amplification-of-control* phase appears at the point where the interaction dependencies and frequencies are highest. Here, couplings are so tight and frequencies so high that the upper-level designers can no longer make any further separations or connections, but must turn the design process over to lower-level planners who are more in tune with such intricate interconnections and short time frames.

THE RELATIONSHIPS AMONG LEVELS

Attention now turns to relating the corporate-design cycle described in figure 1-2 to the separation and connection sequences of higher and lower levels. The particular question posed here is: "How does the behavior of a system on one level affect the systems on the adjacent levels?" (Mesarović, Macko, and Takahara, 1970:32). The answer can be found in examining a stacked set of planning sequences, in which each level replicates the others and each design phase connects with several adjoining levels. Thus the complete SDPC model consists of multiple nested levels, each encompassing the seven separate but intertwined planning phases.

Figure 9-1 shows five such levels. To construct figure 9-1, the society's, economy's, division's, and department's planning sequences simply have been added to figure 1-2, the corporation's design circuit. The replication of the planning cycle at the other levels and the nesting relationships are both captured in figure 9-1.

Frames of Reference

A key concept in understanding the interlevel relationships is the context of analysis or the frame of reference for a given level. To convey this concept, three levels will be examined as examples; namely, those of the corporation, division, and department.

At the corporate level, an investigator will start by focusing on the firm as a comparatively small subunit within the society. That perspective prevails in the *definition* and *evaluation* phases. Narrowing the analytical context somewhat, the firm can be treated as a relatively larger unit in the economy, as is done in the *composition* and *synchronization* phases. Next, the firm can be viewed in terms of the divisions that comprise it, as happens in the *decomposition* and *recomposition* phases.

Similarly, a division can be seen as a very small subcomponent in the economy. This view would be taken when an observer is considering the division's *definition* and *evaluation* phases. When the analytical context is narrowed to its more immediate environment, the division would be viewed as a relatively large component within the firm during the division's *composition* and *synchronization* phases. Next, the division can be seen in terms of the departments that make it up, as is done in the division's *decomposition* and *recomposition* phases.

In turn, a department can be viewed as a relatively small subunit in the whole firm. This view would be adopted by an observer concerned with the department's *definition* and *evaluation* phases. When the analytical context is reduced to its more immediate environment, the department becomes a comparatively large component within its parent division during the *composition* and *synchronization* phases. Assuming a still finer view, an observer could perceive the subgroups that make up the department as appropriate for the department's *decomposition* and *recomposition* phases.

In the SDPC model, then, each level has three different (separation and connection) frames of reference relevant to it: the broadest is associated with its *definition* and *evaluation* phases; the intermediate with its *composition* and *synchronization;* and the narrowest with *decomposition* and *recomposition.* Taken together, a level's three frames of reference link it to four other levels. The broadest frame links the level to the two above it, the intermediate to one above and one below, and the narrowest to the two levels below it.

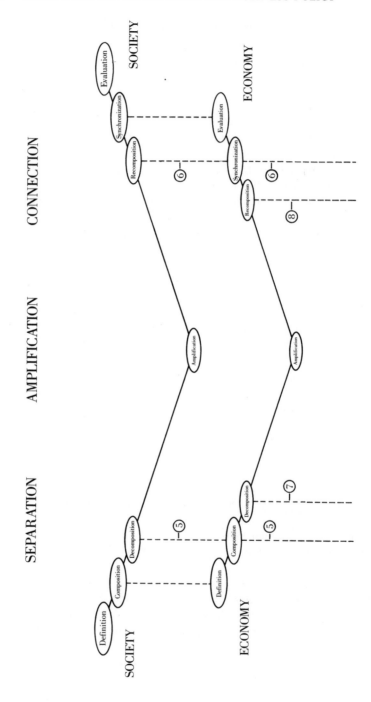

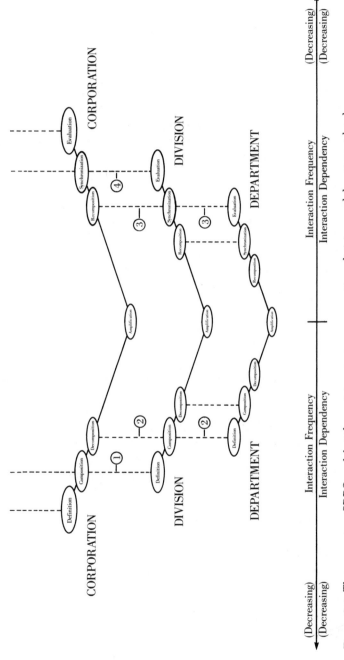

Figure 9-1. The seven-stage SDPC model at the society, economy, corporation, division, and department levels.

Similar Design Phases at Different Levels

It follows that if one focuses on the same design phase at differing levels, then different reference frames, different set sizes, and different interaction frequencies and dependencies will be involved. Observe that in figure 9-1 the same design phase, such as *definition* or *evaluation,* changes in size as the focus shifts across levels. The regular reduction in size, as one moves from one level down to a lower one, occurs because the reference frame in the SDPC model decreases. For instance, the largest frame of reference for the firm will be the society; the largest for the division, the economy; and the largest for the department, the corporation. Thus the lower the level, the smaller the frame of reference and vice versa. Lower levels can be studied (adequately) within smaller frames of reference because they focus on narrower segments of decisions (Mesarović, et al., 1970:54).

Associated with the narrowing frames of reference will be a corresponding increase in interaction frequencies and dependencies. In figure 9-1, comparable planning phases index inward along the horizontal axes when moving from one level to the next lower (or smaller). Thus the higher frequency and dependency dynamics are associated with the lower levels, and the lower frequency and dependency dynamics are associated with the higher levels. "It is generally believed, for example, that the relevant planning horizon of executives is longer the higher their location in the organizational hierarchy" (Simon, 1969:108).

Increased interaction frequency and dependency at the smaller boundaries means that the units within those partitions are both more susceptible and more exposed to shifts in their respective environments. But the fact that the small units, such as the divisions of a firm, exist in a relatively cooperative and stable environment keeps the incoming variety loads low. Within the protective envelope of the firm, then, the divisions are suitably buffered from the full vagaries of the less cooperative external environment. The department, in turn, is insulated from the whole firm by its parent division.

Coincident Design Phases at Different Levels

To develop a more exact picture of the interlevel relationships that exist among the society, economy, corporation, division, and department, the linkages among specific design phases across the various levels must be examined. The nature of the relationships among the five levels is most apparent when one focuses on the coincident phases.

In this regard, note in figure 9-1 that there are several instances in which design phases from different levels are equal in size and are aligned vertically with one another; that is, they occupy the same position along the horizontal axes. For example, note the phases linked by line 2. The corporation's *decomposition/recomposition* phases correspond exactly in size, interaction frequency, and dependency with the division's *composition/synchronization* phases and also with the department's *definition/evaluation* phases: the decision sets, boundary lines, and communication linkages for all three are exactly the same, regardless of the difference in levels.

This parity should not be surprising, for it has already been mentioned that: (a) the corporation's narrowest (*decomposition/recomposition*) reference frame focused on the divisional components making up the firm, (b) the division's intermediate (*composition/synchronization*) reference frame focused on the divisional components operating within the firm, and (c) the department's broadest (*definition/evaluation*) reference frame focused on the divisional components operating within the firm.

So while the phases linked by line 2 in figure 9-1 involve the same frame of reference, they represent different design phases in each of the levels involved. And that is why the same interaction frequencies and dependencies appear different depending on the observational level assumed by the investigators and planners. More specifically, interaction frequencies and dependencies that are high and strong for the corporation's narrowest (*decomposition/recomposition*) reference frame are only moderate for the division's intermediate (*composition/synchronization*) reference frame and decidedly slow and weak for the department's broadest (*definition/evaluation*) reference frame. The relative positions of the coincident phases within their respective levels explain the variations: where corporate planning stops in terms of interaction frequencies and dependencies, divisional planning is still only at midpoint, and departmental planning has just begun.

As noted previously, planners at lower levels are more attuned to dealing with higher interaction frequencies and dependencies than are their counterparts at higher levels. Subordinate planners therefore will quite naturally and almost automatically see interactions as low-frequency/dependency that their superiors would view as high-frequency/dependency. That is, accustomed to fast-paced and tightly connected interdepartmental relationships and the even faster and stronger intradepartmental linkages, the department manager will perceive interdivisional connections as relatively infrequent and fairly inconsequential. From the corporate executive's perspective, on the other hand, interdivisional interactions are relatively frequent and strong compared to the corporation's external bonds. Such shifts occur because time perspectives shorten and interaction sensitivities increase as one descends the corporation's hierarchy.

Comparatively speaking, then, lower-level units will view more variables as temporarily constant or low-dependency—i.e., as parameters. For example, subordinate units make frequent decisions and complete many decision cycles, while the superior units hold their decision variables steady (constant) over relatively long periods. (Many low-level operating cycles are required to accumulate the information necessary for resetting top-level variables.) Hence variables set by the top organizational levels become parameters for the lower-level units, and as one moves down more and more variables are left behind as parameters. Via this progressive changing of variables to parameters, higher-level units absorb uncertainty for the lower-level units, thereby freeing them to proceed with setting their microscopic variables secure in a large (internal) environment of constants. The parametric nature of upper-level variables also explains the frustrations lower-level managers report after repeatedly trying to win policy changes from their slow-acting superiors.

Still, as one moves up the hierarchy more and more parameters become variables; that is, the subordinate's parameter is often the superior's variable. Thus lower-level managers occasionally might be surprised—even shocked—to observe a purported constant or "given" suddenly shifting value after remaining fixed for many periods.

THE INTERLEVEL RELATIONSHIPS OF THE CORPORATION'S DESIGN PHASES

Now, with these general concepts introduced, all the interlevel relationships emanating from the corporate level can be examined. A more concrete analysis will be made of the corporation's planning relationships with lower levels (namely, the division and department) than of the corporation's relationships with higher levels (notably the economy and society) because of the more definitive linkages found within the centrally planned firm. In analyzing the corporation's somewhat amorphous relationships with the surrounding economy and the larger society, the emphasis will be placed more on developing general patterns and less on describing specific relationships.

Relationships of the Corporation's Design Phases with Lower Levels

In this section, the corporation's *composition/synchronization* phases will be linked to the division's *definition/evaluation* phases. The corporation's *decomposition/*

recomposition phases will also be related to the division's *composition/synchronization* phases and the department's *definition/evaluation* phases.

Corporation, Division, and Department

Since it is well understood that the department is embedded within the division and the division within the firm, no effort will be devoted to describing these nesting characteristics. Rather, attention focuses immediately on the coincident separation phases spanning these three levels. Once these phases have been considered, the discussion turns to the corresponding connection phases.

Separation Phases

Beginning with line 1 on the left-hand side of figure 9-1, the first corporate/division relationship to consider runs between the corporation's *composition* of its controlled and uncontrolled variables and the division's *definition* of its variables and parameters. To understand this relationship, the reader should recall that during the corporate composition phase, the firm's board of directors draws the boundary between the uncontrollable and controllable variable sets. This demarcation line, in turn, *defines* the parameter/variable boundary for all the firm's divisions. First, the highest frequency/dependency variables are included within the controlled variable set, while the less active and less critical variables are left to the exogenous environment. To heighten the separation further, temporary walls of constancy are erected between the firm's uncontrolled and controlled variables; for example, via long-term contracts with external suppliers. To the fast-operating divisions housed within the firm, the more slowly changing uncontrolled variables are temporary constants, or divisional parameters.

Second, the corporation's uncontrolled variables are defined as divisional parameters because they are but secondary or low-dependency concerns to the divisions. In contrast, their primary or high-dependency concern is the firm's whole controlled set of variables. Why? Simply because each division's primary client is the firm to which it belongs.

This proposition, then, states one of the central problems of systems theory as presented by theorists such as Churchman: all controllable variables must be set with all other controllable variables in mind. So while a division should be held accountable only for the variables it controls, it must set these variables in a way that helps, not hinders, the other divisions within the parent corporation.

The next interlevel linkage to consider has three tiers. In figure 9-1, reconsider line 2, which runs from the corporation's *decomposition* of its dependent and independent controlled variables through the division's *composition* of its controlled and uncontrolled variables to the department's *definition* of its variables and parameters. Consider the corporate/division relationship first: decomposing the firm's controlled variables into dependent and independent variable sets automatically composes (i.e., draws the boundary between) each division's controlled and uncontrolled decision sets. So a dependent (i.e., tightly coupled) set of variables would be placed in the controlled domain of a single division. And variables independent of the original variable set or loosely coupled to it would be left in the focal division's uncontrolled environment (i.e., in the control of the firm's other divisions).

Accordingly, each division's immediate uncontrolled environment is internal to the firm, and it consists of all the other divisions within the firm's controlled-variable set. At GM, the Pontiac Motor Division occupies a portion of the Buick Division's immediate uncontrolled environment and vice versa. So when an overambitious division manager expands the composition (boundaries) of a particular unit's controlled decision set, all other divisions experience a relative contraction of influence, and, more important, the entire firm's decomposition scheme shifts.

For a slightly different perspective on the connection of the corporate decomposition and the division composition phases, it can be seen that if a multiproduct multifunction firm is decomposed along product lines, a series of multifunction product divisions results. These divisions will be composed of the multiple functions necessary to produce and market each product.

Turning to the division-composition and department-definition relationship, composing the division's controlled variables automatically defines the set of high-dependency variables that its functional departments must consider in serving their primary client, the parent product division. In contrast, those decision variables in the parent division's uncontrolled environment—that is, within the controlled domains of its neighboring components—become the departments' parameters or low-dependency/frequency concerns. So while Pontiac's marketing manager must give all of Pontiac's decision variables primary emphasis, he or she can treat Buick's decision variables as secondary considerations. This relegation to parametric status of concerns outside the immediate parent's controlled set places reasonable bounds on the department manager's job, a necessity given the restricted vantage point of this position. Secondary status does not mean, however, that Pontiac's marketing head can simply neglect Buick's decision problems, for the manager must at a minimum comply with the low-frequency constraints or parameters imposed to decouple temporarily the Buick and Pontiac decision-making efforts.

Before considering the connections across the various boundaries drawn to this point, it is helpful to summarize a bit and look at how the variable and parameter sets shrink as one descends to lower and lower levels. Uppermost, the corporate headquarters, as the firm's superior unit, concerns itself with all the immediate economic variables that influence its financial performance—regardless of the firm's control over these variables. Next, the division's superior subunits (i.e., the respective division managers' offices) focus principally on the firm's controlled variables and treat its environmental (i.e., economic) variables, which are set by surrounding organizations or groups, as parameters. Lowermost, the departmental chiefs within the various divisions concentrate first on their own division's controlled variables but only secondarily on the decisions made by the firm's other divisions.

Connection Phases

Returning to figure 9-1: The next set of relationships to consider is represented by line 3, running from the corporation's *recomposition* of its dependent and independent controlled variables through the division's *synchronization* of its controlled and uncontrolled variables to the department's *evaluation* of its variables and parameters. Considering the corporation's recomposition and the division's synchronization first, one can see that attempting to recompose the firm's controlled variables is synonymous with trying to synchronize every division with its immediate uncontrolled environment; i.e., all the firm's other divisions. Thus, in the multifunction multiproduct firm, establishing communication channels among the product divisions helps to synchronize each with its respective (i.e., the firm's internal) environment as well as to recompose for simultaneous decision making the entire group of product divisions. Now, since the firm's planners (unaided) lack the capacity to design all the requisite internal linkages, lower-level designers—i.e., divisional decision makers—must complete the coordination network. So each divisional staff's efforts to synchronize its controlled subset of decision variables with the other divisions in its immediate environment contributes to the whole firm's coordination, or recomposition. While this so-called voluntary coordination (Litterer, 1965:223) among the divisions is highly useful, it too is limited because the lower-level managers who undertake it lack the necessary vantage point. Hence neither the corporate designers from their heights nor the divisional decision makers from their lower perspective possess the ability alone to coordinate the firm's controlled set of variables completely. But when the supplementary synchronization linkages strung by the divisions are added to the corporate-wide communication channels, a complete recomposition of the firm results.

In the hypothetical case where the corporation is *fully* integrated, each division's synchronization activity would take place solely within the firm itself. Then each division would need to make no external contacts beyond the firm's confines. In reality, a portion of each division's synchronization activity will be directed toward units external to the corporation. The extent to which such (high-frequency) outside contacts are present depends, of course, on the degree of integration within the firm; the greater the integration, the more the division's synchronization efforts will be directed internally—that is, toward its fellow divisions within the firm.

Focusing next on the department's evaluation phase, it can be shown that valuing the contributions of these subunits to the division and corporation merely represents another aspect of each division's synchronization efforts and the whole firm's recomposition work. Consider first the relationship between the division and the department. Here, the department's performance is primarily judged in terms of what it contributes to the successful setting of all the variables included within the parent division's controlled variable domain. So when an overaggressive marketing department generates high sales but causes serious cost problems for the division's engineering, purchasing, and production units, these debits must be deducted from the sales group's overall performance rating. But what constitutes high costs or high sales? Or, for that matter, how can a product-division manager—with only purchasing, engineering, and production units for reference groups—judge a marketing department? Obviously, to make the necessary assessments requires information from other divisions (i.e., from the department's parametric environment); the division manager conducting the evaluation must discover the contributions of other marketing units to the overall performances of their respective divisions. That is, the evaluator's standard for the marketing unit under his or her direction must come from the actual achievements of other divisional sales groups, particularly the best of these performances.

Second, to evaluate the department's positive or negative impact on its parametric environment, the parent division also needs horizontally communicated information from the other divisions plus vertically communicated information from the corporate headquarters. Thus the data flowing into the division as it synchronizes itself with its immediate surroundings within the firm contain the feedback needed to value the department's contributions to the whole firm. Via such synchronizing feedback, for example, the division could determine if its purchasing group was causing supply divisions unnecessary problems with their production scheduling. Similarly, it could tell if its production or sales departments were failing to meet quality standards or shipping commitments and thereby damaging the performance prospects of down-line divisions. In a properly designed firm, the divisional headquarters would seek to correct such situations because its primary concern is the whole firm—just as the department's primary concern is the entire division.

Since a divisional management lacks a complete set of contacts with the firm's other units, one must move to the corporate level for a complete evaluation of the division's functional departments. In this regard, it is usually the corporate staffs that possess the full picture of all the divisions' functional departments. Not only can the headquarters staff provide the divisional management with useful evaluative information on the negative effects of its departments' decisions, but it can also help assess each functional subunit's positive contribution to the remainder of the firm beyond its own division's controlled variables. For instance, the corporate staffs can best judge whether a performance improvement discovered in one divisional department can be adapted to improve the performances of comparable subunits in other divisions. Furthermore, the staffs' corporate-level vantage point (as mentioned in chapter 6) makes it easy for them to disseminate the performance-improvement knowledge gleaned from the departmental evaluation process.

In sum, the corporation's set of variables must be *recomposed* before its many departments can be *evaluated* in terms of their contributions to either their variable or parametric environments. The complete firm-wide picture must be developed before any departmental performance judgments can be finalized. Appropriately, as is shown in figure 9-1, the frequency of the firm's recomposition communications matches the pace of the department's evaluation communications.

The next relationship (line 4 in figure 9-1) to consider involves the corporation's *synchronization* of its controlled and uncontrolled variables and the division's *evaluation* of its variables and parameters. This connection parallels, of course, that of the division's synchronization and the department's evaluation. Briefly, evaluation of the division's contribution to the corporation requires a performance comparison among the firm's various investment possibilities. Since a firm's divisions are considerably more comparable than the departments within a division, much of the evaluative work can be conducted simply by referencing each division's performance to the achievements of neighboring units within the corporation. Still, external comparisons are needed because the evaluators must determine if outside opportunities exist that are capable of generating higher performances. Hence to evaluate divisional achievements fully, performance expectations must be synchronized with the results generated by (present or future) external investment possibilities.

Communication across the corporation's controlled/uncontrolled boundary also is needed when evaluating a component to determine the impact of the firm's environment on divisional performance. Uncontrolled variables (i.e., divisional parameters) buoying or depressing a division's performance cannot rightly be credited to or charged against its decision makers.

Last, the consequences of a division's decisions on the firm's environment must be considered during its evaluation. Since a division within the corporation views its parent's uncontrolled environment as a merely low-dependency or parametric concern, it might be tempted to optimize its own short-run performance at the expense of environmental organizations. Auto divisions at GM, for instance, once forced cars on their dealers to improve divisional market shares and investment returns. This shortsighted practice could not go unchecked by the corporate headquarters, for it jeopardized the dealers' long-run financial health—and a weakened dealer force would eventually damage the entire corporation. Sloan wisely realized the dealers were GM's vital partners, deserving to be treated as part of the corporation's primary field of concern, if not the divisions'. Thus he created communication channels to feed back information on these detrimental divisional practices. Once obtained, this synchronizing feedback information could be used to adjust divisional performance ratings for their environmental damage to the corporation. Moreover, the divisions, knowing the corporate headquarters received this feedback, were less likely to force cars on their retailers.

Relationships of the Corporation's Design Phases with Higher Levels

With the corporation's separation and connection phases now having been related to those of the division's and department's, attention can turn to higher levels; namely, the society and economy. The corporation's *definition/evaluation* phases will first be linked to the economy's *composition/synchronization* activities and the society's *decomposition/recomposition* activities. For this set of relationships, the firm will be viewed as a mere subcomponent and the economy as a component of the larger society. The corporation's *composition/synchronization* phases will next be related to the economy's *decomposition/recomposition* activities. Here, the firm will be treated as a component within the larger economy. Since the relationships between the society, economy, and corporation are more nebulous than the relationships between the corporation, division, and department, the discussion is partitioned. That is, the separation and connection phases that concern the corporation and both of its superior levels (the economy and society) will be examined before looking at the separation and connection phases that concern only the corporation and its immediate environment, the economy. To introduce the relationships involved, a general exposition precedes each pair of separation/connection analyses.

Society, Economy, and Corporation

The first higher level to consider in figure 9-1 is the society in which the corporation's immediate environment—the economy—is embedded. Besides the economy, the society consists of other sectors. More specifically, "economic, religious, political, educational, and other types of activity come to cohere into partially independent systems with units, boundaries, and mechanisms of their own. These systems overlap; and when a relatively broad range of such systems cohere around a common population, we may speak of a society" (Mayhew, 1968:583). Even though a society's component systems form an integrated whole, each contains sets of high-frequency/high-dependency variables that, comparatively, exhibit only very infrequent and weak interactions with other component systems.

In passing it should be noted that the relationships among neighboring societies will be even weaker than the intersystem relationships found operating within societies, for "the boundaries of a [given] society are usually drawn at the outer limits of the interdependencies and commonalities that give it coherence" (Mayhew, 1968:584). Still "there is no reason to suppose, however, that a [particular] society will be self-contained, that it will not overlap with other societies" (p. 583). These intersocietal (i.e., *composition/synchronization*) relationships will not be pursued here, for our concern is with the society level only as it relates to the corporation—that is, with the society's narrowest (i.e., *decomposition/recomposition*) reference frame (as depicted in figure 9-1).

Separation Phases

The first of the two intrasocietal relationships to consider is on the separation side: specifically the corporation's *definition* of its variables and parameters, the economy's *composition* of its controlled and uncontrolled variables, and the society's *decomposition* of its dependent and independent controlled variables (line 5, figure 9-1). With regard to the corporation/economy relationship, the corporation's planners will tend to define all noneconomic variables (i.e., those controlled beyond the economic system) as parameters either because they hold little relevance or change very slowly. Corporate planners can overlook noneconomic variables for long periods because of the economy/society relationship.

In the United States especially, the economy operates quite independently from other systems within the society. The United States has long had a *free*-enterprise economic system much removed from noneconomic domination. Though considerably less independent from societal intervention after the 1930s, the American economic system and its component corporations still operate with a startling amount of freedom. Thus variables controlled within the American economy tend to be influenced minimally by other segments of the society.

In fact, the overall structural decomposition scheme among the various systems controlling variables within the American society is generally marked by a high degree of independence. In the United States, numerous institutions foster intersystem independence: besides the free-enterprise system there are the free press, the separation of church and state, the separation of political party and government, and academic freedom.

Even where noneconomic systems might exert considerable impact on the economy, they rarely disrupt their own equilibrium to alter intersystem behavior patterns. The economic and political systems, for instance, go for long periods without disturbing each others' equilibrium, and periods of heavy interaction such as that seen in the 1930s and during World War II are comparatively infrequent. Similarly, the judicial system, founded on a vast body of slowly evolving common-law precedents, changes almost imperceptibly compared to the interaction frequencies occurring within the economy. Similarly, the larger society—as represented by the legislative and executive branches of the federal government—moved very slowly to impose pollution standards on the American economy. And once set, these standards have tended to become inviolate precedents (i.e., long-term parameters) because powerful countervailing forces within the society have fought to maintain them. So while businessmen have lobbied against the tightening of pollution controls, environmentalists have worked to uphold them. In light of these opposing forces, even dramatic changes in administration achieve only slight shifts in policy standards.

In sum, then, noneconomic variables can be treated as parameters by corporate planners. The economy's independence and the society's stability enable this treatment.

While the United States economy remains markedly independent, its once-sharp boundaries are now somewhat blurred because of increased governmental intervention in its activities. Probably the first notable incursion of the government into the economy's operation was the passage of the Sherman Antitrust Act of 1890. This legislation was designed to foster competition by declaring monopolistic activities illegal. The Federal Reserve Act of 1913 created another noteworthy overlap between government and economy. But by far the greatest intertwining of the government with the economy took place in the 1930s.

During that turbulent period a shift occurred in the American society's decomposition scheme (i.e., structural organization), its economy's composition, and its corporations' variable and parametric environments. Massive unemployment along with the collapse of farm prices kindled the popular demand for government to control more of the nation's economic sphere. Given the economy's abject condition, prominent capitalists could not defend the free-enterprise system against the pressures exerted by political leaders and the labor movement.

Businessmen found themselves at a disadvantage in these confrontations not only because of the failure of unfettered capitalism but also because of the unorganized nature of the economic system. While leaders from prominent corporations—men like GM's Sloan and Brown—tried to maintain the economy's exclusive control of its variables, they did so disparately; their efforts were disjointed, piecemeal, and thus to no avail.

Hence, President Roosevelt's administration made significant inroads onto the economy's controlled-variable space with a broad series of New Deal measures. Though still a *very* long way from a government-dominated planned economy, the American free-enterprise system was modified substantially. Thereafter, the economy's large corporations have shared control with various government agencies, and America has had the rudimentary beginnings of a mixed economic system.

Losses to organized labor also made a significant impact on the economy and its corporations. The widespread labor unrest of the 1930s led to another major reorganization (i.e., new decomposition) of the society. In essence, labor did much to remove itself from the economic system's vagaries. No longer would wages, hours, and conditions be decided solely by the supply-and-demand forces operating within the economy—forces controlled almost exclusively by the large corporations. Given that the corporations had lost their monopsonist control over these vital performance-related variables, it became paramount for them to stabilize the situation. The wildcat strikes, work slowdowns, industrial sabotage and espionage, and adverse publicity had to stop.

For the corporations to be able to resume normal planning and operations, the labor-related variables that had slipped from the industrialists' grasps had to be converted into unvarying parameters. The answer proved to be the *long-term* labor contract negotiated with stable unions capable of securing and delivering a cooperative work force to the corporations. Slowly, Sloan and other business-men incorporated this solution into their policy frameworks and the vicious battles with workers subsided. Thereafter, wage rates and related variables have been fixed at parametric values negotiated between the large corporations and big labor unions. Wage rates, in particular, are no longer responsive to the high-frequency variations within the economic system. They are now far less variable because the labor movement, with society's support, mobilized its political power to withdraw from the economic system and to create a separate system designed to further workers' aims—just as the free-enterprise economic system pursued the capitalists' goals.

By no means were all labor-related variables removed from the control of the capitalists' economic system. Most notably, employment levels still fluctuate in response to the economy's variations. American workers have yet to attain guaranteed lifetime employment, though some progress has been made to assure yearly minimums in hours worked. Less critical issues like local griev-ances also continue to be worked out within the confines of the economic system.

Generally, the gains made by labor during and after the 1930s have been paid for by the consumers who, because they are unorganized, have remained within the economic system. The corporations and unions have protected their respec-tive clienteles' well-being by passing on increased costs in the form of higher prices and/or lower quality. To some degree, the larger society through its legislators has attempted to ameliorate this situation. Product-standard legislation has been imposed in an attempt to guarantee that items purchased by consumers are, at a minimum, safe, energy-efficient, and the like.

Besides the apparently permanent shift in the economy's composition that occurred in the 1930s, there have been temporary or transient changes. During World War II most notably, the government allocated scarce resources and administered prices. It even became involved in internal corporate affairs on occasion. But with the return to peacetime, the economy regained its prewar independence.

In sum, the American economy even into the 1980s continues to enjoy a high degree of independence. While the society—via the government—has come to set more parameters, such as pollution standards, that the corporations must satisfy, decision makers within the economy largely decide how most resources get allocated, which groups manage these resources, and what prices are charged. Thus, the separation of economic and political powers remains basically unaltered.

Connection Phases

The next series of intrasocietal relationships to examine in figure 9-1 is depicted by line 6, which runs from the corporation's *evaluation* of its variables and parameters through the economy's *synchronization* of its controlled and uncontrolled variables to the society's *recomposition* of its dependent and independent controlled variables. Consider first the corporation/economy relationship. To evaluate the corporation's positive or negative impact on its parametric environment, the economy needs information communicated from the other societal sectors beyond its boundaries. Accordingly, the data flowing into the economy as it synchronizes itself with its immediate surroundings within the society contains the feedback needed to value the corporation's contribution to the whole society. Via such synchronizing feedback, for example, the resource allocators within the economy learn if a given corporation is causing problems for the society's other systems. The economy's investors will want to avoid such "antisocial" firms, knowing full well that if these practices continue over the long run the larger society is likely to impose more stringent parameters on all firms.

Consider next the corporation/society relationship: the society's entire controlled set of variables must be recomposed before its many corporations can be evaluated in terms of their contributions to either their variable (economic) or parametric (noneconomic) environments. The complete society-wide picture must be developed before any corporate-performance judgments can be finalized. And as has been shown before in figure 9-1 for other cases, the frequency of the society's recomposition communications matches the pace of the corporation's evaluation communications.

One can also see that attempting to synchronize the economy with its immediate uncontrolled environment (i.e., all the society's other sectors) is synonymous with attempting to recompose the dependent and independent variables within the society's controlled set. Establishing communication channels among the societal sectors helps to synchronize each with its immediate (i.e., the society's internal) environment as well as to recompose for simultaneous decision making the entire group of societal components—including the economic system and the labor movement. Compared to the rather specific information flows found within the firm, the intrasocietal linkages are somewhat more amorphous and the mass media provide a significant conduit for coordinating society's components. Therefore, when the economy booms, labor will know and increase its demand for a larger share of the benefits. Labor's generalized demand, in turn, will be translated into more lucrative long-term labor contracts at the firm level. And when the economy slumps, government may ease its constraints and requirements. At the corporate level again, this relaxation may well be felt in terms of less stringent pollution standards, safety requirements, and similar parameters that individual firms must satisfy.

Economy and Corporation

In addition to the linkages among the corporation and its two higher levels (the economy and the society), there are linkages between the firm and the economy that have no counterpart at the society level. These intraeconomy relationships are depicted in figure 9-1 by lines 7 and 8; namely, between the economy's *decomposition* and the corporation's *composition* activity and between the economy's *recomposition* and the corporation's *synchronization* activity.

Only a limited analysis will be made of the corporation's design relationships with the economy because the designers of United States corporations function in an economic environment that still possesses a strong ateleological aspect.

There appear to be two system-theory explanations behind the unplanned nature of the firm's immediate environment. First, connections that link firms are considerably weaker than a given firm's internal linkages. These weak interorganizational relationships are to be expected, given the decreasing interaction dependency that occurs as the level being considered is heightened. Simon (1969:109) notes that in "nearly decomposable" hierarchies "intracomponent linkages are generally stronger than intercomponent linkages." Thus interdivisional connections are stronger than interfirm relationships, and the firm's immediate environment of necessity remains more amorphous than the divisions'. This environmental shapelessness, in turn, both inhibits higher-level planning and requires less of it.

Second, the economy still lacks a fully developed central planning unit because much of its evolutionary development remains incomplete. In exploring the evolutionary progress of the American economy, one can envision three advancing structural configurations: (a) an unplanned field of laterally linked organizations, (b) a developing pattern with mediated interorganizational relations, and (c) a planned economy with guided organizational components (Lehman, 1975). Given an unplanned field of laterally linked organizations, "the state is expected to refrain from interfering in the relationships among organizations unless absolutely necessary, and mainly to avoid major public injury" (Etzioni, 1964:110). For many years the country's many small firms could be left to coordinate their own business relations within such a laissez-faire environment. But once modern communication and transportation techniques enabled these small firms to coalesce into large corporations, the threat of public harm increased substantially. This development forced the government to begin regulating "a much larger variety of organizational interaction, including that between financial and productive organizations (e.g., in the stock exchange), . . . and so on." Consequently, the American economy has evolved into the very early states of hierarchical development.

Still the American economic system has yet to develop to the extent of Japan's economy, for there the economy's planners (particularly officials from the Ministry of International Trade and Industry) and executives from the principal business establishments routinely coordinate their decision-making efforts through numerous informal meetings. And because a handful of giant enterprises produce more than half of the total Japanese GNP as well as influence many of Japan's smaller firms, synchronizing them with the economic planners and each other harmonizes much of the economy's activity. In fact, Japan's economic system appears so thoroughly integrated that it has been dubbed "Japan Incorporated."

Since the American economy has not attained the degree of coordination found in Japan, it indeed falls far short of being a formally coordinated system whose planners centrally direct the subordinate corporate components—as the corporate headquarters does for its divisions. Thus American firms are rarely subordinated to state planners. Furthermore, their executives are unlikely to receive either formal or informal directives from superior state organizations regarding national economic goals, capital and material allocations, or the like. And because of the essentially unplanned nature of the American corporation's economic environment, the corporation/economy interlevel relationships of necessity are somewhat nebulous.

Separation Phases

To visualize the first of the corporation/economy relationships to be considered, refer to figure 9-1, where line 7 runs from the corporation's *composition* of its controlled and uncontrolled variables to the economy's *decomposition* of its dependent and independent controlled variables. Whether noncentrally created by the firms themselves or centrally planned, the structure of the economy should consist of a cluster of relatively independent decision centers. Thus each firm attempts to control those variables upon which its performance is highly dependent, leaving to other businesses the control of variables from which its performance is relatively independent. In this way, the individual enterprise faces the minimum variety load and the economy as a whole functions (without complexity) as a series of loosely coupled decision clusters.

Given the laissez-faire atmosphere underlying the American economy's development, designers of industrial firms have been given extremely wide latitude in composing their controlled variable sets. Over the years the government has, via its antitrust laws, declared certain corporate compositions illegal, but such antimonopoly rules remain relatively sparse. Thus the ways firms compose their vectors of controllable variables essentially creates the economy's decomposition scheme. Stated differently, permitting corporations to circumscribe their own controlled variable peripheries, with only minimal intervention, allows their designers to lay out the economy's internal boundaries. In short, *the strategies of firms when taken together create an economic structure.*

A planned economy, in contrast to the above laissez-faire economic development, would exhibit more of a top-down approach to structural design. Under these conditions individual firms would be fitted within an overall structure instead of creating its decomposition scheme themselves via their separate strategy decisions. Such a downward design of the economy would parallel, then, the way in which most corporations create their own internal structures.

Connection Phases

The next corporation/economy relationship to consider in figure 9-1 runs along line 8 from the corporation's *synchronization* of its controlled and uncontrolled variables to the economy's *recomposition* of its dependent and independent controlled variables. Synchronizing each corporation's tightly coupled controlled-variable set with its uncontrolled economic environment (to which it is comparatively loosely coupled), when summed over all firms, recomposes or coordinates the economic system's many (relatively) independent decision centers. The methods used to connect these internally dependent but externally (relatively) independent decision-making bodies range from market mechanisms to planning directives, depending on the degree of central direction in the economy.

To a large extent, recomposing the American economy has been left to individual firms communicating via the market mechanism. Hence all firms' individual efforts to synchronize their individual decisions with those of parallel organizations and higher agencies, when aggregated over all enterprises, generate a coordinated decision solution of truly mammoth proportions for the whole economy.

As the United States economy evolves toward a more planned pattern, however, the central direction of the economy's recomposition can be expected to grow. Logically, one of the first steps in national economic planning would be to coordinate and quicken the flow of information between various sectors of the economy so firms could draw on more accurate information when synchronizing their activities with the economic environment.

Leontief's input-output techniques provide the logical basis for generating these improved forecasts on the economy's expected condition. Yet, as it now stands:

> Simultaneously, but separately from each other, big, small, and medium-sized businesses in all sectors of the national economy are engaged in [a] frustrating and costly guessing game. If all these forecasts were brought together, it is most unlikely that they would prove to be compatible with each other. This means, of course, that many of them turn out to be very wrong. It is not surprising that internal company production plans and investment decisions based on such disconnected forecasts may prove to be either entirely abortive or much less profitable than originally expected. (Leontief, 1964:172, 176)

To correct this situation, Leontief "calls for market research efforts which are coordinated, designed to get consistent sales forecasts, and combined with short- and long-run output projections for all branches of manufacturing, mining, transportation, and the service industries" (p. 176).

Only a combined business and government planning consortium could hope to design and operate such a vast, integrated information network, and the decision makers of such an agency would have to reconcile planning disparities among the economy's numerous corporate enterprises. At that point, the United States economy would be very close to being run as a centrally directed system in which business firms were decidedly subordinated to these central economic planners.

THE ANOMALIES AMONG LEVELS

To complete the discussion of the SDPC model, attention must be directed toward its anomalies; namely, those design stages lacking interlevel connection.

The primary theme to be developed here is the trade-off between sense of overall purpose and insight into structural detail. This fundamental dilemma is made explicit via the model's apparent anomalies.

To illustrate this proposition, consider the corporation/division interface, where: (a) the corporation's *definition/evaluation* stages lack division-level connections; and (b) the division's *decomposition/recomposition* phases lack separate corporate-level projections. Man's limited capacity to handle variety explains these omissions.

On the one hand, knowledge about or *"understanding of a system increases by crossing the strata"* (Mesarović, et al., 1970:42). When descending levels, one obtains a more detailed insight into the division's structure; and when ascending, one receives a broader perspective on the corporation's purpose (p. 42). Movement in either direction, however, requires that some previously held knowledge be brushed aside for the newly acquired information. Otherwise, "the complexity of a multilevel system soon gets out of hand" (Emery, 1969:4). Thus no single individual or group can be concerned with more than a few levels.

The SDPC model accounts for this limited interlevel contact by deleting knowledge regarding the corporation's *definition/evaluation* phases when moving toward the division. Similarly, it provides for omitting detailed information on the division's *decomposition/recomposition* phases when moving toward the corporation. So movement toward the division level yields an improved appreciation of organizational detail but a lost sense of purpose about the whole enterprise's overall goals. And movement toward the corporate level produces a heightened appreciation of the firm's objectives at the expense of knowledge about its components' details.

Thus the corporate planners' direct influence will not extend to all the divisional design stages. So when the firm is very large, containing much variety, direct design throughout becomes impossible because of limited rationality. Instead of proceeding through each step of the design process, the corporate planners must skip several lower-level steps, treat the remaining elements as a black box, and leave certain divisional design tasks to subsequent designers (the decision makers), who can continue the corporate planners' work.

Similarly, the divisional decision makers' upward concern is quite restricted. Managers, for instance, with their cognitive limitations, can be expected to look only one or two levels above them for design guidance. "One must in practice settle for a particular level above as the ultimate arbiter of one's own affairs" (Beer, 1972:83). In contrast to the downward black-box approach, this restricted view is termed a *black-umbrella* approach. That is, standing under the umbrella, or inside a large black box, the managers observe relatively little of what goes on above them; the *black umbrella*, like the black boxes they stand on, obscures and restricts their view except for a few small tears and cracks.

Given that the division-level decision makers are out of touch with the corporation's purpose-related *definition/evaluation* design phases, they must be trained to continue the planning process beyond the corporation's *decomposition /recomposition* phases. This training (which substitutes for further corporate-level separation and connection work) is conducted during the corporation's amplification-of-control stage, as is shown in figure 9-1. Thus, at lower levels, training in and selection for value beliefs and factual knowledge replaces detailed planning work, design work well beyond the capacity of the corporate planning group. A similar relationship holds between the division's amplification phase and the department's decomposition/recomposition phases.

Attention now turns to the economy-level amplification, which is particularly illuminating. As noted above, the United States economy is still far from being centrally guided. Thus amplification at the economy level for the United States is not what one would expect to see were the economy fully developed hierarchically. (This situation is probably even more pronounced at the society level.) Instead of a centrally propagated means for orienting, educating, and selecting the many corporate-level planners needed to carry on the central planners' design work, economy-level amplification in the United States is the product of a bottom-up evolution. Interestingly, the resultant effect is very nearly the same now that the decentralized process has continued so long: corporate planners receive *en masse* (in the nation's graduate and professional schools) the highly standardized (accredited) training needed to design and operate their respective large-scale organizations.

Noble (1977) presents an informative account of the development of such an amplification process, which by spreading across organizations and over time has evolved into a unified economy-wide training scheme. At the turn of the century, scientific technology and corporate capitalism fused to form a new and tenaciously self-perpetuating social order. Engineering-oriented executives— men like the duPonts, Sloan, and Brown—started the process rolling. As members of various corporate planning teams, they

> pioneered in formulating rationalized procedures in engineering, manufacturing, finance, and marketing; they quantified and systematized corporate operations, developing methods of cost accounting, statistical controls, forecasting techniques, and the procedures for gathering and processing huge amounts of detailed, accurate data to be used in appraising, planning, and coordinating the operations of extended plant and personnel. Equally important, they created the formal administrative structures for the giant corporations, with carefully defined lines of authority and channels of communication through which to control the process of production. (Noble, 1977:261)

To propagate their work, Noble explains, they proselytized their philosophy throughout "the new institutions of science-based industry, scientific technical education, and professional engineering," all of which "gradually coalesced to form an integrated social matrix . . . composed of the corporations, the schools, [and] the professional societies" (p. 50). "If any single characteristic best defined this group, it was the nature of their education. . . . All received a scientific training, in electrical, mechanical, or chemical engineering, physics, chemistry, or some combination of these. . . . The largest proportion were trained in electrical engineering, and a significant majority received their education . . . at MIT" (p. 51). Given such backgrounds, these corporate planners understood that "education was the critical process through which the human parts of the industrial apparatus could be fashioned to specifications" (p. 168). Thus, "higher education, and especially engineering education, was the means . . . through which the corporate engineers could reproduce themselves" (p. 168) and perpetuate their performance-control methods throughout the corporate economy.

So "by selection, socialization, controlling conditions of incumbency, and hero worship, succeeding generations of power-holders tend to regenerate the same institutions [via] self-replicating causal loops" (Stinchcombe, 1968:111). Accordingly, the amplification stages may be stacked one upon another, as is shown in figure 9-1. And when one ascends the hierarchical ladder the causal loops become more encompassing, as is depicted by the increasing oval sizes for the various amplification phases.

CONCLUSION

In sum, the general explanatory power of the SDPC model lies in: (a) its ability to link logically the design activities of one level to those of neighboring levels and (b) its capacity to guide planning efforts for multiple levels, be they departments housed within divisions, divisions embedded within firms, firms situated within the economy, or the economy encompassed within the society. Moreover, since the model replicates the design phases at each level along with the interlevel relationships, few concepts are employed and considerable conceptual simplicity is achieved. Thus the SDPC model exploits "the world's redundancy" (Simon, 1969:111), or hierarchical repetitiveness, in an attempt to describe and explain business-policy matters parsimoniously.

10

Illustrating the Model with the
Early General Motors/Ford Histories
and Subsequent Problems

GM's Alfred Sloan and FM's Henry Ford embraced different orientations toward
erecting performance-control systems for their firms. Sloan's view on controlling GM's performance paralleled that presented in the SDPC model, while
Ford denigrated and shunned such an approach. Still, when Sloan and his
colleagues assumed command in 1921, GM's prospects for any success appeared
weak: FM dominated the business with its inexpensive Model T. But an epic
reversal had begun. Slowly FM's lead started to shorten. Within a decade the
momentum had shifted and by 1938 GM far outdistanced FM. The following
account is drawn from Kuhn's *GM Passes Ford, 1918-1938*.

FM: AN ANTIDESIGN EXAMPLE

By no means should the impression be left that Henry Ford never valued
systematic planning. In terms of its productive machinery, FM grew in capacity
and efficiency; in the early 1920s the company was becoming the giant of
American industry. Unfortunately, Ford felt that organization in the company
offices should be minimized. Eventually, Ford's strong antidesign attitude

toward systems of performance control made FM a giant ship without a helm.

Identifying the Goal

FM's profitability during the economic crisis of 1920–21 allowed Ford to acquire *all* FM stock, an event that fueled the firm's accelerating decline. Over time, Henry Ford dismissed most of FM's planning-oriented executives; men such as Frank Klingensmith, Norval Hawkins, and Ernest Kanzler. The only designer remaining at FM, Henry Ford's son Edsel, was thwarted by powerful antidesign lieutenants, most notably Charles Sorensen and Harry Bennett. Accordingly, FM was ruled only by Henry's whims. Not only was it impossible to identify a single influential designer at FM, but it was also difficult to discover a single permanent client profiting by the firm. A few temporary client groups such as consumers or labor were dropped abruptly. By the late 1930s no FM client could be pinpointed. Without designers or a group of clients, there was, of course, no goal or any definite measure of performance for FM.

Formulating the Strategy

When formulating FM's capital-investment strategy, Ford again erred. Obsessed with controlling any variable remotely related to the production of FM's cars, he extended his operations into many basic production processes about which FM's decision makers knew comparatively little. Ford's authorization of the ill-fated Brazilian rubber plantation in 1927 carried this policy to the extreme. Not surprisingly, then, the firm's internal variety grew well beyond the decision makers' information-handling and computing capacity. Furthermore, the added internal variety offered little in terms of improved performance control. Numerous outside vendors of standardized products such as iron and glass could have provided better regulation of the variables in question. Ford compounded his backward-channel-integration errors by not using market-referenced transfer prices. Worse yet, the many inefficiencies of FM operations were buried by an overaggregated, "country store" accounting scheme.

Ironically, when it came to more immediate, specialized, and, therefore, critical items such as radiators and automobile bodies, FM often depended on external suppliers. In the forward-integration direction, only belatedly and temporarily did Ford add a consumer-credit unit. Such a component could have played a key role in his low-cost marketing strategy.

Ford also shunned sophisticated product diversification. With a cheap car, first the Model T and later the Model A, and with an expensive low-volume automobile, the Lincoln, the firm lacked the requisite variety of makes that the market demanded. (Even when the Ford-based Mercury and the Lincoln-based Zephyr joined the line in the late 1930s, they were inadequately differentiated from their parents.) Early on, Ford aggravated FM's lack of product diversity further by insisting that his low-priced models be offered in only one color— black—and be stripped of all amenities and options consumers were coming to expect. And when in the late 1920s GM introduced the annual model for an increasingly style-conscious public, Ford refused to upgrade his dated products. When he could no longer resist model changes, his specialized single-purpose machinery impeded the changeover process.

Ford, in sum, concentrated FM's variety along the channel-integration dimension, where it overloaded the firm's decision makers but provided little protection from environmental variations. Conversely, he stripped variety from FM's product-diversification offerings where it would have imposed little added burden upon the firm's decision makers yet would have supplied much needed performance stabilization.

Organizing the Structure

When it came to organizing FM's structure, Henry Ford wanted no part of it. He wanted neither a central headquarters nor delineated divisions or departments. He wanted FM to be one gigantic shop. So rather than build the company's headquarters to provide strong firm-wide direction, Henry Ford dismantled his central units, believing such subunits offered the firm nothing but increased overhead costs. Ford, more generally, failed to fashion a rational internal structure. He delighted in announcing that FM had no formal organization and ridiculed GM's designers for their great interest in administrative structures. Instead, Ford permitted his managers to compose their own jobs; besides causing major competitive tensions within the firm, this practice yielded an ad hoc organizational structure under constant flux, given Ford's continual executive firings. It seems Ford wanted FM's internal boundaries to remain nebulous, so that *all* decisions would funnel to him. He thus refused to recognize his limited abilities or to realize that he might amplify his power of control through a simplified decomposition scheme.

Training the Decision Makers

Moreover, Ford could not amplify his power of control because he wanted nothing to do with a group of well-trained managers. Accordingly, he provided no value orientation for his managers and fostered rather than hindered a

parochial outlook among them. Consequently, instead of making their decisions for the benefit of FM as a whole, FM executives concentrated on their
own concerns and often caused needless problems for their cohorts. Ford also
created no managerial training programs for his decision makers' factual education.
And managers with any formal training were distrusted. Ford's hiring and firing
policies were equally inappropriate. He fired competent executives while retaining
and promoting the incompetent or inexperienced, for he felt that inadequate
managers would be forced to consult with him before reaching any decision.
When, in the late 1920s, Ford's attention was diverted by numerous nonindustry
preoccupations such as the Ford Museum and folk dancing, the firm was left
with its managers deciding matters they were unqualified to consider. Ironically,
Henry Ford's desire to make every decision himself resulted in a loss of control
not only for him but for the firm as a whole.

Coordinating the Firm

Instead of building an information network to coordinate FM's internal activities,
Ford cut many of the internal communication lines that had existed before he
assumed full control of the firm. He disbanded communications units like
accounting and ripped out many of the firm's telephones. Further, he made it
difficult for his decision makers to confer by eliminating their offices and desks
and by forbidding meetings and conferences, which he abhorred. When coupled
with the distrust Ford kindled within his company, such communication prohibi-
tions halted any recomposition contact. Consequently, the firm was left with a
set of decision makers who pursued uncoordinated and suboptimal approaches.

Monitoring the Environment

Henry Ford also dismantled many of the external communication channels
needed to gather environmental intelligence and to export product information
that would improve FM's performance. When external information did manage
to filter into the firm—for example, the pleadings of his dealers to update the
aging Model T—Ford ignored it for as long as possible. Similarly, feedforward
information on forthcoming market or economic conditions did not exist for
him. FM had neither a customer-research component nor an econometric unit.
The firm's research laboratories lacked trained personnel and often pursued
questionable projects. FM also lacked the proving-ground facilities for testing
product innovations and competitive makes. Hence, lengthy delays forced FM
to lag behind consumers' tastes and competitors' products. The Ford V8 first
offered in 1932, for instance, was better synchronized with the expansive 1920s

than the constrictive 1930s, and the car's initial reliability problems only worsened its image with economy-minded consumers.

The firm's market position was undermined too by Ford's antagonism toward product advertising. In addition, his negative public-relations efforts—the anti-Semitic and antilabor campaigns—induced retaliatory actions against the firm and its products.

Valuing the Performance

Finally, Henry Ford did little, if anything, to evaluate or correct the performance of FM. Not only had he no visible client group or any performance measure on which to judge his efforts, but he also ignored his own board of directors. And throughout the turbulent 1930s he refused the government's call for improved labor relations.

If either sales or profits were his concerns, he failed: FM's market share plummeted and its profits plunged. In 1921, for instance, FM boosted its market share to about 59 percent, while GM registered a considerable loss. But after 1924 the Model T lost customers rapidly; and with the extended retooling shutdown for the Model A, FM surrendered its once-solid market footing. (The introduction of the Model A in 1928 allowed FM only a temporary recovery.) So while GM made strong strides in the late 1920s, FM's massive capital investment was underutilized, and its rates of return for both 1927 and 1928 were negative. In 1927 GM's return rate outstripped FM's by almost 70 points and in 1928 by almost 80. During 1929—the Model A's only truly successful year—FM earned its last two-digit return rate. Its performance was to grow still worse in the 1930s.

By World War II FM's deterioration so endangered the war effort in such vital areas as bomber production that the federal government considered placing FM under Studebaker's management. Instead, Henry Ford's grandson, Henry Ford II, was released from military service to revive FM. By the early 1950s he had succeeded largely by hiring a group of GM managers to install at FM the Sloan-Brown control system developed during the 1920s and 1930s.

GM: A DESIGN EXAMPLE

In 1920 few could imagine that GM might one day provide the management model for FM and many other firms. Compared to the FM colossus, GM foundered.

Identifying the Goal

The DuPont Company contributed most of the capital GM needed to survive the 1920 financial crisis at the end of William Durant's presidency. With DuPont's involvement came a host of financially oriented designers: Pierre duPont, John Raskob, John Pratt, and—most notably—Donaldson Brown.

In addition, when Durant left, several home-bred designers emerged from GM's wreckage: among them, Albert Bradley, Charles Kettering, and Charles Mott. Most important, however, was Alfred Sloan, whose organizational skill and financial acumen were critical to the DuPont interests.

Since the Sloan-Brown planners were either large GM stockholders themselves or closely associated with major shareholders, they identified their principal client as the firm's capital investor. During the industry's formative period with its numerous automobile makers, the customer's demands also had to be heard. But when customer and stockholder interests conflicted, the customer's well-being was subordinated.

Given the designers' and clients' financial orientation, return on invested capital became the logical performance measure, or "financial yardstick," on which to build GM's performance-control system. This indicator summarized handily how well the client's resources, or invested capital, were used to generate client benefits, or profits. GM's clients, designers, and decision makers could use ROI to compare the performance of GM with the performance of a competitor, or GM this year with GM last year, of one division with another division, of a big operating unit with a small operating unit. The ROI measure thus provided a unitary, commensurable scale.

From the overall rate-of-return indicator it was a natural step to determine those variables that influenced the client's well-being. Donaldson Brown supplied the principal conceptual tool. Brown's financial model not only identified the system's critical variables but also helped the designers ascertain their relative "essentialness." This priority ranking, in turn, established important guidelines for the GM planners in subsequent design stages.

Formulating the Strategy

GM's Finance Committee, dominated by prominent stockholders, such as Pierre duPont and John Raskob, seized control of the policy decisions related to performance measurement and capital allocation. By stripping headquarters executives and divisional managers of these responsibilities, the planners avoided repeating Durant's earlier strategy-formulation mistakes; in particular, the accumulation of inadequate and overlapped products.

In retrospect, the Finance Committee matched the variety of GM's controlled variables to the variety of its uncontrolled environment. Moreover, the Sloan-Brown planners, in separating the controlled variables and environment, avoided overloading the firm's decision makers.

On the channel-integration front, then, the Finance Committee avoided basic commodity production. Expansion into steel making, rubber production, and glass manufacturing—to name just a few possibilities—offered little in the way of improved performance control yet would have imposed enormous variety loads on the firm's decision makers.

In more vital sectors like input parts production and output credit provision, however, the GM designers were more expansive. For example, the Finance Committee clustered within the firm's operations a wide set of parts units. Even so, the firm did not make all its parts, for capital earned higher returns in auto production. Furthermore, GM needed multiple outside suppliers to diversify the risk of a production stoppage and to generate the transfer prices for divisional evaluation.

To encourage the existence of compatible external suppliers, GM published a book of standard parts (as early as 1923). Numerous GM executives also held key positions in the Society of Automotive Engineers (SAE). Thus a close correspondence existed between GM and SAE standards. The auto industry's prominence, in turn, helped promulgate SAE standards throughout many other industries. Thus much of the environmental variety on GM's input interface came to match its internal variety.

On the output front, the Finance Committee approved the creation of a credit source for its dealers and their customers. The General Motors Acceptance Corporation (GMAC) soon played a key role in the fight against the low-cost Fords.

Not surprisingly, neither the backward integration toward the parts suppliers nor the forward integration toward the dealers and customers overloaded GM's decision makers. The firm already had considerable experience with such production and financial activities.

With respect to product diversification, GM's Finance Committee approved Sloan's plan to offer "a car for every purse and purpose," a strategy that yielded the protection of both brand and price diversification but added little internal variety. At the same time, the Sloan-Brown designers pooled volume and further minimized variety by using many hidden standardized parts among makes; ultimately, the interchangeable-body program of the 1930s raised GM's product standardization to amazing heights.

Sloan's annual-model innovation of the 1920s shielded GM from the burgeoning used-car market as well as imposed huge variety loads on competitors. Product differentiation, as Sloan well knew, had to be achieved since a product that *appeared* standardized year after year soon became just another basic commodity— like the Model T—unable to command a premium price. GM managed the added product variety by using adaptable general-purpose production facilities and by concentrating mostly on styling superficialities that had high customer impact. GM's small competitors could not keep pace, of course, because they lacked the volume to change body dies yearly; and FM hobbled along with its infrequent model changes and specialized plants and machinery.

When the domestic market approached its saturation point in the mid-1920s, Sloan and Brown directed the Finance Committee's attention to foreign markets. In the 1930s they suggested investments in the diesel-locomotive and aviation industries—both potentially damaging auto-industry competitors. But even GM's movement into foreign markets, diesel locomotives, airplanes, and aviation components added little troublesome variety, as all involved mass-producing and marketing large durable-good items. GM, for instance, induced America's idiosyncratic railroads to buy *en masse* the country's first standardized, assembly-line-produced locomotives. These streamlined diesels with their bright and varied finishes soon replaced the nation's bulging, black steam engines, just as GM's stylish automobiles had displaced the Model T a decade earlier. John Pratt had simply extended Sloan's automobile strategy to the railroad industry.

Organizing the Structure

The GM designers excelled in controlled-variable decomposition—i.e., structural organization—as well. Over time, the Executive Committee isolated those variables that exerted the greatest long-term influence on performance and shifted control from the divisions to the corporate headquarters, where such variables could be set from the firm-wide perspective and with the clients' interests closely in view. These critical variables came to include, among others, cash balances, inventory levels, production schedules, capital investments, engineering development, and product styling, as well as personnel, manufacturing, and sales policy.

The designers could centralize so many decisions without overloading the corporate headquarters because they had avoided channel integration and limited product diversification. This strategy left a highly redundant set of divisional components that imposed minimal variety loads on the central office. The corporate executives' long tenures also enabled them to take on more divisional decisions as the once-new and novel became repetitive and routine. And since the centrally controlled variables constrained the remaining divisional decisions through hidden linkages, GM's central headquarters soon exerted an influence far beyond its apparent authority.

The Sloan-Brown designers overtly buttressed their centralization efforts by increasing the corporate headquarters' size. First, the Executive Committee expanded to include more corporate officers. (Only a few division managers retained seats on this important policy-setting unit.) Second, to aid the president, an executive vice-president plus a series of group vice-presidents were employed at various times. Third, Sloan, Mott, and Pratt spent considerable effort in building strong Advisory Staff groups that operated more as decision-making bodies than as advisory units. Pratt and Sloan's Interdivisional Committees of the mid-1920s, designed to handle the functional interconnections often neglected when a firm employs a pure divisional structure, further eroded divisional authority. Extremely powerful and prestigious headquarters executives—Sloan, Brown, Pratt, and Mott—sat next to second-level divisional heads. Later in the 1930s, when Sloan transformed the Interdivisional Committees into Policy Groups, all divisional executives were excluded from membership.

In sum, the firm's subordinate components, the product divisions, were tightly coupled to the leading unit, GM's corporate headquarters. Given their importance to GM's overall performance, the automobile divisions, particularly Buick and Chevrolet, experienced the tightest couplings.

Of necessity, GM's Executive Committee left many less important variables in the control of the subordinate components. To ensure their proper performance, a simplified decision-making scheme was sought.

More than anything else, the designers' retention of Durant's divisional structure and their rejection of the then-popular functional setup helped ease the decision-making problem. GM's organizational arrangement was simplified further via such techniques as unique profit/investment centers, standardized accounting classifications, market-referenced transfer pricing and decoupling schemes, inventory buffers, standardized parts, market segmentation, and geographic separation. A series of components resulted that were relatively small, highly comparable, and loosely coupled. These characteristics facilitated performance improvements through serendipitous discoveries or planned experiments and minimized the variety loads imposed upon both the divisional and corporate decision makers.

Training the Decision Makers

Aware of their limited power to operate their firm directly, GM's designers expended considerable time and effort on training. As a consequence, GM's many decision makers were properly oriented, thoroughly educated, and carefully selected for the decision-making task at hand. The designers' control thereby was amplified.

In orienting the decision makers to the clients' value scheme, the designers instituted a variety of lucrative bonus plans, most notably the 1923 Managers Securities Plan for the firm's top eighty or so decision makers. The bonus took the form of stock options, making the decision makers clients and creating in them the proper decision-making orientation. The recipients' stock awards were based on individual performance contributions to GM as a whole. To ensure that the main body of stockholders remained the prominent clients over the long run, the decision makers' stock allocations were made only after GM earned a minimum return of seven percent, and they were not convertible into a more diversified portfolio. The final safeguard fashioned into the GM orientation schemes was a heavy emphasis on bonuses as opposed to salaries; salaries exhibit less variability and therefore less motivational power than do premiums.

Initially, educational efforts were conducted through ad hoc meetings with individual decision makers in need of aid. Sloan, for example, visited many division managers to teach them improved methods, thereby amplifying his control for many future operating periods. Later, the Sloan-Brown designers achieved even greater amplification by conducting their educational programs with whole groups of decision makers; for example, via the stockholders' meetings of Managers Securities and formal sessions of the Interdivisional Committees. Ultimately, in 1926 GM went so far as to found its own university, General Motors Institute (GMI), to train *en masse* future decision makers; in time GMI graduated many important GM executives.

The designers' careful selection of decision makers went along with their thorough value-orientation and factual-education work. One of their first moves was to remove uncooperative and/or unqualified Durant men from the important auto divisions and replace them with less independent and more financially able executives—a series of changes that signaled GM's shift of emphasis from the production of cars to profits. These replacements helped set the new standard for acceptable managerial behavior.

For the most part, GM's designers selected managers with a strong appreciation for finance or accounting. Initially, the DuPont Company transferred a number of its managers to important GM decision-making positions. Later, GM's parts and accessories divisions served as the training ground from which to select decision makers for key auto divisions and corporate headquarters positions. The small size of the accessory and parts divisions made each a performance-safe training ground and enabled the manager to gain a good understanding of the unit's overall operations. And since all the divisions were configured, or composed, along similar lines, a thorough understanding of a small parts unit yielded strong familiarity with the operation of the biggest auto division. Finally, by refusing, almost without exception, to permit his decision makers to create or compose their own jobs to fit their particular personality quirks, Sloan could always select from a large pool of highly interchangeable decision makers to fill GM's similar executive roles or positions.

In sum, many variables were brought under the influence of the clients and designers via the control of decision-maker orientation, education, and selection. Thus the planners achieved a significant amplification of control by contracting the vector of variables they dealt with directly.

Coordinating the Firm

GM's loosely coupled divisional structure required few horizontal communication links among the divisions. And where lateral contact was necessary—as between the channel-integrated accessories and parts divisions and the auto units—it was facilitated by the firm's standardized parts specifications, which gave the participants a *common language.* Later, GM installed a centrally operated communication network to handle efficiently the routine ordering and shipping information flowing among (and within) its far-flung divisions.

After the mid-1930s GM's tightest lateral couplings existed among Fisher Body and the various auto divisions using the firm's interchangeable bodies. The corporate Styling Staff also entered this iterative decision process, as it developed the divisions' body designs and color schemes. A corporate-dominated Policy Group was created to supply the necessary contact points and communication bridges.

While the divisions' near decomposability reduced the need for intense, high-frequency lateral communication, their high comparability meant that gains could be made in corporate performance if the causes behind high (or low) divisional results were disseminated periodically. To spread the performance-improvement information gleaned from planned experiments or serendipitous findings, GM planners used the various Interdivisional Committees, the Advisory Staffs, the Operations Committee, and the Executive Committee (see chapter 6).

These staffs and committees also linked the corporate headquarters with the various subordinate divisions. Such vertical communication contacts helped ensure that the divisions: (a) received the information needed to regulate their decisions and performances in accordance with headquarters policies and goals and (b) provided the data (feedback) that the headquarters needed to correct and coordinate all divisional decisions.

The planners constructed still other vertical connections, in particular, the monthly budgeting and review process instituted by Sloan and Brown. GM's highly summarized budgetary procedures permitted corporate headquarters to monitor overall divisional operations without communication overload. Furthermore, the simple threat of review kept the divisional decision makers following corporate directives closely.

Since GM had the divisional financial officers report to the corporate office (rather than to the division managers), they acted as reliable local data sources for the central office. Sloan also used his powerful Advisory Staff to break down "institutions of privacy" protecting divisional autonomy; he declared that nonfinancial aspects of divisional decisions should be audited, just as their financial results were. To conserve capacity, Sloan concentrated on the firm's auto divisions and, in turn, had them monitor the parts divisions' price and quality performances.

To supplement these formal communication linkages, Sloan later devised a series of annual conventions, or meetings, where several hundred corporate and divisional decision makers convened to discuss mutual problems. Besides promoting a firm-wide perspective, the resulting informal contacts helped span any remaining communication gaps.

Monitoring the Environment

Extensive contacts were also developed with important environmental groups such as suppliers, labor, competitors, dealers, and, especially, customers. Of all the environmental factors that influenced GM's performance, the consumers' responses to its products were the most important to the stockholders' well-being.

So in the early 1920s, Sloan—often accompanied by Brown and other corporate executives—toured the country visiting with GM dealers and community leaders to gauge product acceptance, consumer demand, and emerging tastes. By the mid-1920s Albert Bradley had established GM's econometric unit, and shortly thereafter a Customer Research Staff was created. Charles Kettering had headed GM's Research Laboratory since 1918, and in 1926 the Proving Ground began testing GM's and competitors' cars. An extensive technical library was maintained, university contacts were fostered, and foreign correspondents were retained to monitor European developments in automotive technology and styling. Moreover, a New Devices Committee reviewed the proposals of independent inventors. All these headquarters units then provided corporate decision makers with feedback and feedforward information so that

GM's production levels and product offerings would be in step with current demand and would anticipate forthcoming trends.

In addition, the GM designers used their environmental sensing units to supplement the firm's advertising efforts. The customer research and advertising units worked together to present customers—i.e., environmental decision makers—with information that induced them to purchase for the ultimate benefit of GM's stockholders.

The designers also provided the pinnacle Finance Committee with performance data on each division and with environmental information. Intelligence on general economic conditions revealed the effect of exogenous or uncontrolled variables on divisional performances and guided the Finance Committee in adjusting internal resource allocations. To ensure accurate and commensurable performance measurement and optimal resource allocation, the Finance Committee retained jurisdiction over GM's Financial Staff, since headquarters executives or divisional managers might otherwise distort the firm's performance reports.

Valuing the Performance

While the divisional evaluations fell to GM's Finance Committee, the overall evaluation of the firm's performance required the full Board of Directors. The Financial Staff prepared the requisite evaluative information. The GM Board, in turn, supplied *reliable* evaluative information regarding their own stewardship to the firm's stockholding clients. As early as 1918 Sloan had engaged the independent auditing firm of Haskins & Sells to certify that the financial-performance data in GM's *Annual Reports* were accurate. Thus the financial reports could be used safely to compare GM's achievements with those of other firms competing for the investors' capital resources.

GM fared well in these comparisons; investors continued to seek the firm's shares and permitted it to retain earnings for expansion. Even customers—though not GM's primary clients—rewarded the designers by doubling GM's market share. Proudly, the designers disseminated their approach and methods through many papers and speeches aimed at other businessmen.

Beyond the narrow confines of the financial and business community, however, GM's success during the late 1930s became all too problematic for Sloan and his colleagues. The social upheavals stemming from the Great Depression meant that maximizing the well-being of GM's primary clients, the stockholders, was no longer sufficient justification for the firm's continued existence in the larger community. Long-stable equity relationships (i.e., societal parameters) among capital, consumers, labor, small business, and the general public were being questioned and realigned.

Under these circumstances, GM's high return rates and market shares drew attention from nonstockholding groups also dependent on the firm for their well-being. Labor and the dealers, especially, became restive about their respective payoffs relative to GM's stockholders. Worse yet, under the Roosevelt Administration's leadership various federal agencies began to scrutinize the conduct of GM and its competitors.

Henry Ford was by far the industry's most vehement opponent of Roosevelt's New Deal, but Sloan and his colleagues also were recalcitrant in accepting the new business relationships defined by the government. They particularly resented government incursions into what had long been their exclusive decision-making domain. Hence, while Sloan adjusted to the new milieu more gracefully than did Ford, he did not do so with inspired leadership. Simply put, *he would not lead GM into the era of broadened corporate responsibilities.*

On the troubled labor front, GM's planners made an important, if reluctant, effort to establish a new long-term accord. Largely inspired by these labor-related experiences, Brown suggested that GM create a policy group to monitor the firm's social and political environment. Although the "Policy Group–Social and Economic Trends" was created and Brown was named its chairman, it operated for only a few years—until the depression receded and the war approached. Nevertheless, major long-term environmental changes continued to buffet the corporation.

In retrospect, the demise of this committee was but part of a trend toward isolation at GM that began with the Board's reorganization in May 1937. Having just lost some independence in the battle with labor while having won increased independence from the capital markets, Sloan, with Brown's support, combined the Board's Finance and Executive committees into an insider-dominated and much smaller group: the Policy Committee. An already far too limited source of outside opinion was further diminished, imprudently, at a time when the corporation most needed a broadened input of views.

SUBSEQUENT PROBLEMS

In 1937, then, Sloan drew GM away from its broader social and political responsibilities. Thereafter, he personally contented himself with fine-tuning his original design and concentrated more and more on GM's internal details. Sloan thereby traded breadth for detail. *GM's success thus would remain limited strictly to the economic arena.*

After the late 1930s GM's economic performances soared ever higher, buoyed by an extended period of prosperity. Here, at last, were the conditions Sloan and his colleagues envisioned from the start: a broadly prosperous America.

In such an environment, throughout the prosperous 1940s, 1950s, and even the mid-1960s, GM assumed the almost unassailable position Ford had held before the middle 1920s. No manufacturer, either domestic or foreign, could hope to challenge GM seriously in the enormously lucrative American market. GM alone set the standard. Consumers accepted the tastes of GM's engineers and stylists as the norm, even when it meant buying a car with a gas-guzzling V-8 engine or with dangerous tailfins inspired by a fighter plane. Gas was cheap, times were good, and GM had the country's pulse. All foreign products, whether from the low-cost Japanese manufacturers or even the high-price European firms, were laughable. Neither GM nor the great mass of American consumers took them seriously.

Until the mid-1980s, then, GM faced little environmental variety that it was not exactly equipped to counter quickly or to exploit advantageously. But political, social, economic, and worldwide competitive conditions began to change, slowly at first, and then with startling swiftness and dramatic proportion. By 1980, GM, along with FM and Chrysler, struggled to adapt to a societal and economic environment that had undergone a complete metamorphosis. The shift had not been sudden except at the climax around 1980, for the various factors that contributed to the changes had started at different times on several fronts and progressed at different rates. In the face of the varied onslaught coming from government, labor, consumers, and foreign competition, the American auto firms staggered into the 1980s. Chrysler requested and received government-guaranteed loans to weather the transition. FM depended on its foreign operations while it (and the United Auto Workers) lobbied for import quotas on foreign competition. Even GM, with its vast economic resources and vaunted performance-control system, shuddered under a variety load it had not prepared itself to counter. Accordingly, GM's market-share and return-rate performances, long held steady at enviable levels, dipped. For instance, in 1980, for the first time since the Sloan-Brown planners assumed control of GM in 1921, the firm failed to earn a profit.

Through some fault of Sloan's, GM had become so narrowly focused, conservatively diversified, overly centralized, and financially dominated that it could not immediately meet the altered conditions of the late 1970s and early 1980s. GM suffered from an old problem: success pursued for too long in a narrow context often begets great problems for surrounding institutions, future generations, and eventually even the successful organization itself.

Specifically, Sloan kept GM's management narrowly focused on stockholders' interest at the expense of labor, consumers, and the general public. Over the years, he placed too much stress on styling, accessories, and large mid-price automobiles. Throughout his tenure, he leaned toward corporate centralization and functional coordination to the extent that the divisions were in constant danger of losing what little latitude they had remaining. Because of Sloan's conservative product strategy and his centralized organizational structure, Chevrolet eventually gravitated toward Cadillac and lost the ability to produce a functionally engineered, low-cost, small-sized car; meanwhile, Cadillac drifted toward Chevrolet and surrendered the ability to build a technologically sophisticated, high-margin, mid-sized vehicle. Last, Sloan's emphasis on rate-of-return performance eventually thrust too many financially oriented executives into GM's top corporate decision-making positions, men increasingly without knowledge of automotive research, design, production, and marketing. Under their cost-cutting and profit-maximizing direction, GM's divisions built a line of cars that lacked technological sophistication, looked startlingly similar, exhibited very poor quality, and cost far too much.

So long as Sloan and his cohorts remained active in GM's affairs, none of these proclivities became serious problems, for they were countered by the early planners' vast knowledge of the business. By the late 1950s and early 1960s, however, the original designers' influence had diminished substantially. Without their constant attention, tendencies quickly grew into irreversible trends. *More important, subsequent GM managements made many alterations that were not in keeping with the early planners' policies.*

Though Sloan cannot be credited with expanding GM's horizons as he might have, his complacent successors deserve more blame. Unlike Sloan, they did not even attempt to keep pace with the long-term shifts in the surrounding society. While Sloan abhorred Roosevelt's New Deal, for instance, he still accommodated to it quickly enough so that GM's public reputation suffered little serious damage. Moreover, he bequeathed to his successors a superbly functioning business enterprise with few, if any, immediate economic problems. Hence those succeeding Sloan (particularly Harlow Curtice and Frederic Donner) had at their disposal the financial resources and managerial time to encompass, if not embrace, the concerns of dealers, consumers, labor, and the general public. But, instead, they focused on the stockholders' short-term interests. Because of this myopia, they squandered Sloan's legacy.

In the early 1950s, for example, the then GM president, Harlow Curtice, adopted a Durant-style management based on dynamic personal leadership. He ignored Sloan's carefully constructed network of oversight committees; instead, he instantly dispensed millions of dollars for expansion. More significant, Curtice disregarded the 45 percent upper limit Sloan had placed on GM's market share to avoid government antitrust actions. Whether from the need to make his own mark or from the lure to compete, the salesman Curtice escalated a sales battle between FM and GM, in particular between the Chevrolet and Ford makes.

The sales competition soon degenerated into Detroit's now-infamous horse-power race. Car size and accessory loads kept pace with the power increases. Throughout the 1950s and 1960s GM added high-profit items like automatic transmissions, power steering, power brakes, power windows, air conditioners, and numerous less notable gadgets. Mileage declined, pollution increased, and safety suffered.

During this period GM's stylists resorted to superfluous gimmicks such as Cadillac's tail fins. What had begun under GM's Harley Earl twenty-five or thirty years earlier as a noteworthy effort to streamline and beautify motor vehicles was now compromised. Clean lines gave way to distracting novelties and chrome expanses; tired designs kept breathing only with the help of sales stimulants like the portholes, or "ventiports," Curtice had stamped in the Buick front fenders when he managed that division.

With Curtice pressing GM's divisions for increased sales, the firm's dealers found themselves under severe pressure. The "factory forcing" that Sloan had done so much to minimize in the 1920s and 1930s again ran rampant. Unresponsive dealers had their franchise agreements canceled. By the mid-1950s Sloan's carefully nurtured dealer network was decimated.

The meaningless battles over market shares during the 1950s also eroded the dealer-consumer relationship. Since the early 1930s, the GM planners had known that consumers' satisfaction with dealers' sales and service efforts played a far bigger role in selling cars than did advertising. But when GM's divisions pressured their franchises for increased volume, the dealers in turn used high-pressure sales pitches on their customers. An era of shoddy and short-sighted selling tactics followed. At the same time, the industry's push for sales volume began to diminish product quality. Moreover, high-volume dealers who skimped on customer service were not admonished by the factories to correct their ways. Consumers felt abused, but as yet they had nowhere to turn.

Not surprisingly, the federal government again focused its attention on the automobile industry. Repeating the 1930s scenario, the dealer lobby petitioned the federal government for protection against the manufacturers. The government also became concerned about consumer treatment—both by the dealers and by the manufacturers.

In response to GM's growing market strength and the weakening of the few remaining independent manufacturers, the government's administrative branch launched a series of antitrust actions, most notably the Justice Department's divestiture suit against DuPont. When the Supreme Court finally directed DuPont to sell its GM holdings, the effect was ironic, hastening the time when GM, instead of being guided by long-held proprietary interests, became dominated by professional managers. Unfortunately for all involved, both the Board's and management's time perspectives shortened from long-term well-being to near-term profit performance. GM's horizons, rather than expanding as they should have, further narrowed and constricted.

Meanwhile, the federal government had begun to criticize GM for not building a small car such as the Volkswagen. Since the sales strength of the imports did not subside, Curtice relented and planned to offer an American car to counter the Volkswagen. This Chevrolet car would be called the Corvair, and like the Beetle, it would be driven by an air-cooled rear engine.

Shortly after authorizing the Corvair's development, Curtice retired as GM's president and chief executive officer. Simultaneously, Albert Bradley, who had assumed the board chairmanship from Sloan, retired. Frederic Donner ascended to fill both roles. Not since Sloan had become both chairman and chief executive officer in 1937 had one person held GM's top two positions. But in contrast to Sloan, Donner arrived at GM's pinnacle via finance, with relatively little experience in domestic operations.

Shortly thereafter, GM's first domestic small-car venture turned into a debacle. As part of a short-sighted cost-cutting program, Chevrolet's division manager and chassis engineers proposed a cheap but unsafe design for the Corvair's rear suspension. Several prominent GM engineers found the design lacking, and subsequently critics like Ralph Nader charged it was clearly unsafe. Before the corporate headquarters finally allowed Chevrolet's new division manager to correct the 1964 models, accidents involving the Corvair killed and maimed a large number of people.

The reverberations, however, would soon break a legislative logjam. Safety requirements came first, then pollution constraints, and finally mileage limitations. Not since the mid-1930s, with their spate of labor legislation, had GM seen such inroads made into its once-exclusive decision-making domain. Worse yet, GM's once-proud research and engineering staffs were unprepared, for they had long concentrated on developing convenience items such as automatic transmissions and air conditioners.

Much of the blame for the quality decline, design defects, and diminished differentiation in GM's products also is attributable to the Donner administration. Donner's creation of the General Motors Assembly Division (GMAD) over divisional objections, for instance, stripped the automobile assembly function from the product divisions. (There was always a predisposition for this essentially one-product firm to gravitate toward a functional structure where one unit focused exclusively on assembling finished automobiles.) But such a unit could be judged only in terms of costs. And while short-run costs indeed decreased, labor relations and product quality plummeted under the GMAD lash. All too soon, an increasingly alienated work force refused to cooperate in raising productivity or maintaining quality, yet it demanded wage increases that gave foreign competitors a decided cost advantage.

Besides creating GMAD, Donner insisted that all preliminary engineering designs be done at the corporate level and that the divisions share as many parts as possible. Design defects now permeated the entire corporation because GM's decision-making was dominated by a single entity: the corporate headquarters. The attempt, then, to extend Sloan's interchangeability philosophy at this time was questionable, for interchangeability only yields acceptable results where cars are quite similar in size and weight. Furthermore, it is risky during periods of rapid technological change. Strong foreign competitors like the Japanese, for example, prefer to engineer completely new vehicles rather than accept the compromises and hidden costs of fitting old parts.

Worse yet, under constant pressure from Donner's handpicked successors to cut costs, the divisions' cars looked more and more alike. While Sloan had started this trend in the 1930s with his common-body program, he always worked hard to maintain GM's product diversity. By 1980, ironically, GM had a product line more muddled, overlapped, and defective than the one Pierre duPont and Sloan had inherited from Durant.

By this time also, a series of fuel shortages caused consumers to question long-held enthusiasms for GM's overlarge, grossly inefficient products. And a long inflationary spiral, fueled first by the Vietnam War and then by skyrocketing energy prices, forced "sticker-shocked" purchasers to be even more cautious. The protracted recession and high interest rates of the early 1980s further accentuated the trend. Gone were the days when demand could be stimulated by styling changes and new accessories. Consumers now wanted functional value that GM—along with FM and Chrysler—could not deliver immediately. A long history of technological stagnation stood in their way.

Unfortunately for the domestic auto industry, progressive firms in Europe and Japan offered a varied array of desirable products. Moreover, because Detroit had avoided the low-cost small-car and the high-cost luxury-car markets for so long, foreign manufacturers had finally established the extensive dealer networks so necessary to compete in the American marketplace. In retrospect, the Japanese and European manufacturers had welcomed the altered economic environment because change to them presented an otherwise unavailable opportunity to crack the high-volume American market wide open.

GM, along with FM and Chrysler, in contrast, had little to gain from such altered circumstances. To those on top, change offered mostly discontinuity, uncertainty, and risk.

At GM another factor perhaps blinded the corporate executives to the forthcoming competitive challenge: they were too secure! The men in power in the 1960s, 1970s, and 1980s had never known their firm as anything but the top automobile company. To them, success was natural, and they were always right—consumers did not want reasonably sized, technologically sophisticated, high-quality, fuel-efficient cars. Unlike Sloan and his cohorts, they had not seen

GM when it survived on the market's leavings that the then-dominant FM organization neglected to gather.

Perhaps such a limited sense of history even explains why GM's supposedly sophisticated corporate managers failed to monitor the market's shifts just as the once-successful Henry Ford had failed to do fifty years earlier. But whatever the cause, GM's modern managements overlooked the possibility that the developing foreign manufacturers could profit from the strategy Sloan had used to pass Ford back in the 1920s when FM was supposedly unchallengeable. In those days, FM alone set the standard. Even Ford's strongest competitor, GM, could only hope for a shift in consumer preferences from basic function to stylized form and be ready to exploit the flux at Ford's expense. In essence, here was Sloan's strategy. So whereas Ford resisted the shift by clinging to his standardized, outmoded Model T, Sloan and his colleagues embraced the metamorphosis by offering a varied array of updated makes and models. But fifty years later, the tables had turned. In 1980 it was GM that was caught with the stagnant, standardized product line.

Bibliography

Periodical articles without author credit are not included in the Bibliography, except in the case of *Fortune* articles. Full citations are included in the text.

Ackoff, R. L. "Systems, Organizations, and Interdisciplinary Research." In J. A. Litterer (Ed.), *Organizations: Systems, Control and Adaptation.* New York: John Wiley and Sons, 1969, 120-26.

————. *A Concept of Corporate Planning.* New York: Wiley-Interscience, 1970.

————. "Towards a System of Systems Concepts." *Management Science,* 1971, *17,* 661-71.

Alexander, S. S. "The Effect of Size of Manufacturing Corporation on the Distribution of the Rate of Return." *Review of Economics and Statistics,* 1949, *31,* 229-35.

"Alfred P. Sloan, Jr.: Chairman." *Fortune,* 1938 (April), *17,* 72-77+.

Andrews, K. R. *The Concept of Corporate Strategy,* rev. ed. Homewood, Ill.: Richard D. Irwin, 1980.

Annett, J. *Feedback and Human Behavior.* Baltimore: Penguin Books, 1969.

Ansoff, I. *Corporate Strategy: An Analytical Approach to Business Policy for Growth and Expansion.* New York: McGraw-Hill, 1965.

Arrow, K. "Control in Large Organizations." *Management Science,* 1964, *10,* 397-408.

————. *The Limits of Organization.* New York: W. W. Norton, 1974.

Ashby, W. Ross. *An Introduction to Cybernetics.* London: Chapman and Hall, 1956.

————. *Design for a Brain: The Origin of Adaptive Behavior,* 2nd ed., rev. London: Science Paperbacks, 1966.

————. "Analysis of the System to Be Modeled." In R. M. Stogdill (Ed.), *The Process of Model-Building in the Behavioral Sciences.* Columbus: Ohio State University Press, 1970, 94-114.

Ball, S. "Audit of Evaluation." In S. B. Anderson, S. Ball, and R. T. Murphy (Eds.), *Encyclopedia of Educational Evaluation.* San Francisco: Jossey-Bass, 1976, 40-42(a).

————. "Secondary Evaluation." In S. B. Anderson, S. Ball, and R. T. Murphy (Eds.), *Encyclopedia of Educational Evaluation.* San Francisco: Jossey-Bass, 1976, 362-64(b).

Barnard, C. I. *The Functions of the Executive.* Cambridge, Mass.: Harvard University Press, 1966.

Beer, S. *Cybernetics and Management.* New York: John Wiley and Sons, 1964.

―――. *The Brain of the Firm: A Development in Management Cybernetics.* New York: Herder and Herder, 1972.

Boulding, K. E. *The Organizational Revolution.* Chicago: Quadrangle Books, 1968.

―――. Intersects: The Peculiar Organizations. In E. C. Bursk (Ed.), *Challenge to Leadership: Managing in a Changing World.* New York: Free Press, 1973, 179-201.

Bradley, A. H. "Financial Control Policies of General Motors Corporation and Their Relationship to Cost Accounting." *N.A.C.A. Bulletin,* 1927, 7, 412-33.

Brown, D. "Pricing Policy Applies to Financial Control." *Management and Administration,* 1924, 7, 417-22.

―――. *Some Reminiscences of an Industrialist.* Port Deposit, Md.: Author, 1957. Reprint: Ann Arbor, Michigan: University Microfilms, 1981.

Brown, P., and R. Ball. "Some Preliminary Findings on the Association between the Earnings of a Firm, Its Industry, and the Economy." *Empirical Research in Accounting: Selected Studies,* 1967; Supplement to *Journal of Accounting Research,* 1967, 5, 55-77.

Buckley, J. W., and K. M. Lightner. *Accounting: An Information Systems Approach.* Encino, Calif.: Dickenson Publishing, 1973.

Burns, T. S. *Tales of ITT: An Insider's Report.* Boston: Houghton Mifflin, 1974.

Campbell, D. T. "Reforms as Experiments." *American Psychologist,* 1969, 24, 409-29.

Chandler, A. D., Jr. *Strategy and Structure.* New York: Anchor Books, 1966.

Churchman, C. West. "Why Measure?" In P. P. Schoderbek (Ed.), *Management Systems,* 2nd ed. New York: John Wiley and Sons, 1967, 122-28.

―――. *Challenge to Reason.* New York: McGraw-Hill, 1968 (a).

―――. *The Systems Approach.* New York: Dell Publishing, 1968 (b).

―――. *The Design of Inquiring Systems: Basic Concepts of Systems and Organization.* New York: Basic Books, 1971.

―――. "The New Rationalism and Its Implications for Understanding Corporations." In E. M. Epstein and D. Votaw (Eds.), *Rationality, Legitimacy, Responsibility: Search for New Directions in Business and Society.* Santa Monica, Calif.: Goodyear Publishing Co., 1978, 52-68.

Cohen, K. J., and R. M. Cyert. "Strategy: Formulation, Implementation, and Monitoring." *Journal of Business,* 1973, 46, 349-67.

Cordiner, R. "Problems of Management in a Large Decentralized Organization." *General Management Series,* No. 159. New York: American Management Association, 1952.

Cotter, A. *The Authentic History of the United States Steel Corporation.* New York: Moody Magazine and Book Company, 1916.

Cyert, R. M., and J. G. March. *Behavioral Theory of the Firm.* Englewood Cliffs, N.J.: Prentice-Hall, 1963.

Dale, E. "DuPont: Pioneer in Systematic Management." *Administrative Science Quarterly,* 1957, 2, 25-59.

_____, and C. Meloy. "Hamilton MacFarland Barksdale and the DuPont Contributions to Systematic Management." *Business History Review*, 1962, *36*, 127-52.

Davis, G. B. *Management Information Systems: Conceptual Foundations, Structure, and Development*. New York: McGraw-Hill, 1974.

Dean, J. "Decentralization and Intra-Company Pricing." *Harvard Business Review*, 1955 (July-August), *33*, 65-74.

Deutsch, K. W. *The Nerves of Government: Models of Political Communication and Control*. New York: The Free Press, 1966.

Downs, A. *Inside Bureaucracy*. New York: Little, Brown, 1967.

Drucker, P. F. *Concept of the Corporation*. Boston: Beacon Press, 1960.

Dunbar, R. L. M. "Budgeting for Control." *Administrative Science Quarterly*, 1971, *16*, 88-96.

Edström, A., and J. R. Galbraith. "Transfer of Managers as a Coordination and Control Strategy in Multinational Organizations." *Administrative Science Quarterly*, 1977, *22*, 248-63.

Emery, J. C. *Organization Planning and Control Systems*. London: Macmillan, 1969.

Etzioni, A. *Modern Organizations*. Englewood Cliffs, N.J.: Prentice-Hall, 1964.

Fama, E. F., and M. H. Miller. *The Theory of Finance*. New York: Holt, Rinehart and Winston, 1972.

Galbraith, Jay. *Designing Complex Organizations*. Reading, Mass.: Addison-Wesley, 1973.

_____. *Organization Design*. Reading, Mass.: Addison-Wesley, 1977.

Galbraith, John K. *The New Industrial State*. Boston: Houghton Mifflin, 1967.

Grossman, S. J., and J. E. Stiglitz. "Information and Price Systems." *American Economic Review* (Papers and Proceedings), 1976, *66*, 246-53.

Hamermesh, R. G. "Responding to Divisional Profit Crises." *Harvard Business Review*, 1977 (March-April), *55*, 124-30.

Hauser, P. M. "Social Accounting." In P. F. Lazarsfeld, W. H. Sewell, and H. L. Wilensky (Eds.), *The Uses of Sociology*. New York: Basic Books, 1967, 839-75.

Herbst, P. G. "The Analysis of Social Flow Systems." In J. A. Litterer (Ed.), *Organizations: Systems, Control, and Adaptation*. New York: John Wiley and Sons, 1969, 214-19.

Hrebiniak, L. G., and W. F. Joyce. *Implementing Strategy*. New York: Macmillan, 1984.

Kaufman, H. *The Forest Ranger: A Study in Administrative Behavior*. Baltimore: Johns Hopkins University Press, 1960.

Keegan, W. J. "Multinational Scanning: A Study of the Information Sources Utilized by Headquarters Executives in Multinational Companies." *Administrative Science Quarterly*, 1974, *19*, 411-21.

Klir, J. "The General System as a Methodological Tool." *General Systems Yearbook*, 1965, *10*, 29-42.

Kuhn, A. J. "An Application of a System Control Model to Business History: The General Motors Corporation under Alfred P. Sloan, 1920 to 1935." Ph.D. diss., University of California, Berkeley, 1971.

_____. *GM Passes Ford, 1918-1938: Designing the General Motors Performance-Control System*. University Park, Pa.: Pennsylvania State University Press, 1986.

Lehman, E. W. *Coordinating Health Care: Explorations in Interorganizational Relations*. Beverly Hills: Sage Publications, 1975.

Leifer, R., and G. P. Huber. "Relations among Perceived Environmental Uncertainty, Organizational Structure, and Boundary-Spanning Behavior." *Administrative Science Quarterly,* 1977, *22,* 235-47.

Leontief, W. W. "Input-Output Economics." *Scientific American,* 1951, *185*(4), 15-21 (a).

———. *The Structure of American Economy, 1918-1939,* 2nd ed. New York: Oxford University Press, 1951 (b).

———. "Proposal for Better Business Forecasting." *Harvard Business Review,* 1964 (November-December), *42,* 166-67+.

Likert, R. *The Human Organization: Its Management and Value.* New York: McGraw-Hill, 1967.

Lindblom, C. E. *Politics and Markets.* New York: Basic Books, 1977.

Litterer, J. A. "Systematic Management: Design for Organizational Recoupling in American Manufacturing Firms." *Business History Review,* 1963, *37,* 369-91.

———. *The Analysis of Organizations.* New York: John Wiley and Sons, 1965.

March, J., and H. A. Simon. *Organizations.* New York: John Wiley and Sons, 1958.

Markowitz, H. "Portfolio Selection." In E. J. Elton and M. J. Gruber (Eds.), *Security Evaluation and Portfolio Analysis.* Englewood Cliffs, N.J.: Prentice-Hall, 1972, 407-19.

Mayhew, L. H. "Society." In *International Encyclopedia of the Social Sciences,* vol. 14. New York: Macmillan, 1968, 577-86.

Mesarović, M. D., D. Macko, and Y. Takahara. *Theory of Hierarchical, Multilevel Systems.* New York: Academic Press, 1970.

Miles, R. E., and C. Snow. *Organizational Strategy, Structure, and Process.* New York: McGraw-Hill, 1978.

Miller, J. C. "Adjusting to Overloads of Information." In J. A. Litterer (Ed.), *Organizations: Systems, Control, and Adaptation.* New York: John Wiley and Sons, 1969, 313-22.

Noble, D. F. *America by Design.* New York: Alfred A. Knopf, 1977.

O'Shea, P. F. "General Motors Budgets for Change: An Interview with Charles F. Kettering." *Magazine of Business,* 1928, *54,* 359-61+.

Parsons, T. "Suggestions for a Sociological Approach to the Theory of Organizations—I." *Administrative Science Quarterly,* 1956, *1,* 63-85.

———, and N. J. Smelser. *Economy and Society.* Glencoe, Ill.: The Free Press, 1956.

Penrose, E. T. *The Theory of the Growth of the Firm.* New York: John Wiley and Sons, 1959.

Pfeffer, J. *Organizations and Organization Theory.* Boston: Pitman, 1982.

Porter, M. E. *Competitive Strategy.* New York: The Free Press, 1980.

———. *Competitive Advantage: Creating and Sustaining Superior Performance.* New York: The Free Press, 1985.

Powers, W. T., R. K. Clark, and R. L. McFarland. "A General Feedback Theory of Human Behavior." *General Systems Yearbook,* 1960, *5,* 63-83.

Prakash, P., and A. Rappaport. "The Feedback Effects of Accounting." *Business Week,* 1976 (January 12), 12.

Quinn, J. B. *Strategies for Change: Logical Incrementalism.* Homewood, Ill.: Richard D. Irwin, 1980.

Raskob, J. J. "Management the Major Factor in All Industry." *Industrial Management,* 1927, *74,* 129-35.

Rosner, M. "Administrative Controls and Innovation." *Behavioral Science,* 1968, *13,* 36-43.

Rumelt, R. P. *Strategy, Structure, and Economic Performance.* Cambridge, Mass: Harvard University Press, 1974.

Samuels, J. M., and D. J. Smyth. "Profits, Variability of Profits, and Firm Size." *Economica,* 1968, *35,* 127-39.

Sandage, C. H., and V. Fryburger. *Advertising Theory and Practice.* Homewood, Ill.: Richard D. Irwin, 1975.

Sathe, V. "Who Should Control Division Controllers?" *Harvard Business Review,* 1978 (September-October), *56,* 99-104.

Scriven, M. "The Methodology of Evaluation." In Ralph M. Winter, Robert M. Gagné, and Michael Scriven (Eds.), *Perspectives of Curriculum Evaluation.* American Educational Research Association Monograph Series on Curriculum Evaluation. Chicago: Rand McNally, 1967, 39-83.

Shannon, C., and W. Weaver. *The Mathematical Theory of Communication.* Urbana, Ill.: University of Illinois Press, 1949.

Simon, H. A. "On the Concept of Organizational Goal." *Administrative Science Quarterly,* 1964, *9,* 1-22.

_____. *Administrative Behavior,* 2nd ed. New York: The Free Press, 1965.

_____. "The Architecture of Complexity." In J. A. Litterer (Ed.), *Organizations: Systems, Control, and Adaptation.* New York: John Wiley and Sons, 1969, 98-114.

_____. "Designing Organizations for an Information-Rich World." In M. Greenberger (Ed.), *Computers, Communications, and Public Interest.* Baltimore: Johns Hopkins University Press, 1971, 37-72.

_____. "Applying Information Technology to Organization Design." *Public Administration Review,* 1973, *33,* 268-78.

_____. *The New Science of Management Decision.* Englewood Cliffs, N.J.: Prentice-Hall, 1977.

_____. "Rationality as Process and as Product of Thought." *American Economic Review,* 1978, *68,* 1-16.

_____, and A. Ando. "Aggregation of Variables in Dynamic Systems." *Econometrica,* 1961, *29,* 111-38.

_____, D. W. Smithburg, and V. A. Thompson. *Public Administration.* New York: Alfred A. Knopf, 1950.

Sloan, A. P. "The Most Important Thing I Ever Learned about Management." *System,* 1924, *46,* 137-41+.

_____, in collaboration with B. Sparks. *Adventures of a White Collar Man.* New York: Doubleday, Doran and Company, 1941.

_____. *My Years with General Motors.* Garden City, N.Y.: Doubleday and Company, 1964.

Smelser, N. J. "Economy and Society." In *International Encyclopedia of the Social Sciences,* vol. 4. New York: Macmillan, 1968, 500-506 (a).

_____. *Essays in Sociological Explanation.* Englewood Cliffs, N.J.: Prentice-Hall, 1968(b).

———. *Comparative Methods in the Social Sciences.* Englewood Cliffs, N.J.: Prentice-Hall, 1976.

Stinchcombe, A. L. *Constructing Social Theories.* New York: Harcourt, Brace and World, 1968.

Stone, C. D. *Where the Law Ends: The Social Control of Corporate Behavior.* New York: Harper and Row, 1976.

Thompson, J. D. *Organizations in Action.* New York: McGraw-Hill, 1967.

Toda, M., and E. H. Shuford, Jr. "The Logic of Systems: An Introduction to a Formal Theory of Structure." *General Systems Yearbook,* 1965, *10,* 3–27.

von Bertalanffy, L. *General System Theory.* New York: George Braziller, 1968.

Weick, K. E. *The Social Psychology of Organizing.* Reading, Mass.: Addison-Wesley, 1979.

Weston, J. F., and E. F. Brigham. *Managerial Finance,* 3rd ed. New York: Holt, Rinehart and Winston, 1969.

Wiener, N. *The Human Use of Human Beings.* Garden City, N.Y.: Doubleday and Company, 1954.

———. *Cybernetics: Or Control and Communication in the Animal and the Machine.* New York: John Wiley and Sons, 1961.

Wildavsky, A. *The Politics of the Budgetary Process.* Boston: Little, Brown, 1964.

Wilensky, H. L. *Organization Intelligence: Knowledge and Policy in Government and Industry.* New York: Basic Books, 1967.

———. "Organizations: Organizational Intelligence." In *International Encyclopedia of the Social Sciences,* vol. 11. New York: Macmillan, 1968, 319–34.

Williamson, O. E. *Corporate Control and Business Behavior.* Englewood Cliffs, N.J.: Prentice-Hall, 1970.

Index